TERRORISM AND COMMUNISM

Terrorism
and
Communism

A Reply to Karl Kautsky

by LEON TROTSKY

FOREWORD BY MAX SHACHTMAN

With FRANCE AT A TURNING POINT
and INTRODUCTION TO THE SECOND ENGLISH EDITION
BY LEON TROTSKY

Ann Arbor Paperbacks for the Study of Communism and Marxism
The University of Michigan Press

Fourth printing 1972
First edition as an Ann Arbor Paperback 1961
Foreword and translation of Trotsky Preface to French edition by Max
    Shachtman copyright © by The University of Michigan 1961
All rights reserved
ISBN 0–472–06056–2 (paperback)
ISBN 0–472–09056–9 (clothbound)
Published in the United States of America by
The University of Michigan Press and
in Don Mills, Canada, by Longman Canada Limited
Manufactured in the United States of America

Terrorism and Communism was originally published in this country
as *Dictatorship vs. Democracy* and in Great Britain as
The Defence of Terrorism.

Foreword to the New Edition

By MAX SHACHTMAN

Trotsky's work should be paired with a somewhat earlier work by Lenin which had much the same theme and purpose. The two were probably the most important and, in the Communist movement of the time, the most influential polemical defenses of the Bolshevik course in the Russian Revolution of 1917, and both were aimed at the severe critique of Bolshevism by its best-known socialist adversary, Karl Kautsky.

The first shot fired at the Bolsheviks by Kautsky in the summer of 1918, *The Dictatorship of the Proletariat,* drew a reply from Lenin at the end of the same year. The temper of the rebuttal may be judged from its title, *The Proletarian Revolution and Renegade Kautsky.* Despite urgings by some of his friends to desist, Kautsky resumed the attack the next summer in his *Terrorism and Communism.* Trotsky used the same title for his answer— the present work—written a year later, then translated into several languages and widely distributed, above all in Communist ranks.* To this Kautsky replied in turn in 1921 in his *From Democracy to State-Slavery,* and in similar writings for years thereafter.

The choice of main target for the Bolshevik barrage was not accidental. The leaders of the Russian socialist opposition to the Bolsheviks—the Mensheviks and the Social Revolutionists—were very little known to the mass of the socialist movement outside of Russia; their writings were even less well known. The position of Kautsky was altogether different.

Karl Kautsky had known both Karl Marx and Friedrich Engels in his youth. After their death, he became the principal literary executor of the two founders of modern socialism. His writings on

---

* The American edition, published in New York in 1922 by the American Communists (Workers Party), bore the inaccurate title, *Dictatorship vs. Democracy,* a misnomer which considerably annoyed Trotsky.

v

a wide variety of subjects were regarded everywhere as classical statements of the socialist view. He virtually founded and for thirty-five years edited the theoretical organ of the German Social Democracy, *Die Neue Zeit,* and it is no exaggeration to say that no other periodical had so profound an influence upon the whole generation of Marxists before World War I, not in Germany alone but throughout the world. In his own party and in the Socialist (the Second) International for most of its quarter of a century before the war brought about its collapse, he was unique in the prestige and authority in the sphere of Marxian theory that he enjoyed among socialists of all schools. His renown was scarcely diminished, at least up to the outbreak of the war, by occasional questioning of his Marxian orthodoxy by the small but more radical wing of socialism or by the fact that the actual political leadership of his party shifted steadily away from him. It is worth noting, too, that except for the Poles and of course the Russians, no one in the international socialist movement showed a greater interest, knowledge, and understanding of Russian problems under Tsarism and of the Russian socialist movement than Kautsky. The Russian Marxists of all tendencies held Kautsky in almost awesome esteem. Up to August 1914, the writings of Lenin in particular are studded with the most respectful and even laudatory references to Kautsky, with whose views he sought to associate himself as much as possible and whose approval he, Lenin, adduced whenever he could as a most authoritative contribution to Russian socialist controversies.

The International foundered in the war. Most of the socialist parties of the belligerent countries supported their respective governments, among them the majority of the leaders and members of the German Social Democracy. This position Lenin denounced furiously as a betrayal of socialist principle and of earlier decisions of the Socialist International. A socialist minority opposed support of the war. In Germany the minority ranged from the extreme left, represented by Karl Liebknecht and Rosa Luxemburg, to a more moderate, more-or-less pacifist wing represented by Hugo Haase and supported by Kautsky. This wing (and Kautsky in particular) was no less furiously assailed by Lenin for its "Centrism," its heterogeneity of thought and action, its conciliatory attitude toward the majority, its failure to orient toward uncompromising revolutionary struggle, and especially for its refusal to organize a new, clear-cut revolutionary party of its own and a new socialist International, the Third International toward which Lenin strove from the beginning of 1915. By 1917 the antagonism between majority and minority in the German Social Democracy reached the splitting point. The latter, with Kautsky's support, organized a new party, the Independent Social-Democratic Party of Germany (USPD) in protest against the war policy of the majority and against its arbitrary actions toward the minority inside the party (Kautsky, for example, was in effect ousted from the editorship of *Die Neue Zeit* and replaced by a partisan of the majority, Heinrich Cunow).

The schism did not moderate Lenin's attacks upon Kautsky. They were, if anything, intensified. When the Bolsheviks took power in Russia later the same year and Kautsky, not unexpectedly, promptly came forward as their opponent on an international scale, so to say, the breach between them became wide and deep and irreparable.

From the very beginning of the revolution, the Bolsheviks sought the active support of socialists outside of Russia, not only as sympathizers of the revolution they had already carried out but for the world revolution which was to be led by the Communist (the Third) International which they proposed to establish as quickly as possible. The opposition of a socialist of Kautsky's standing was therefore a matter of exceptional concern. Hence the vehemence, the intensity, and extensiveness, of Lenin's and Trotsky's polemics, of which the present work is an outstanding example.

Trotsky's defense of Bolshevism is devoted to two basic questions. One is the question of the revolutionary seizure of power to establish and maintain the dictatorship of the proletariat in the Soviet form, the kind of party required for this purpose and the role it must play in achieving it. The other is the question of the methods to be pursued by a socialist revolution in realizing socialism, that is, in reorganizing the economic foundation of society. Although the questions are distinctive, they were intimately related in Trotsky's mind. They proved to be not less closely related in the reality of the following years.

On the first question, Trotsky did not waver in any essential aspect of his views from the day he set them down to the day his life was brought so cruelly to an end. He reaffirmed them in 1936 when he wrote a new preface to the French edition and on more than one occasion before then and afterward. In the period in which he wrote his work, the position of the Bolsheviks in the international socialist movement, particularly in Europe where it had its predominant strength, was gaining influence at a rate which was all the more extraordinary when compared with the nearly complete isolation of Lenin's group even among the European left wing during the war. Trotsky, like Lenin, of course, aimed at advancing and consolidating this position.

In pursuing this aim, the Bolsheviks were impelled by the most urgent considerations. Primary and basic was this one: while they believed that special circumstances had made Russia ripe for a socialist revolution—the seizure of power—the same Russia was not at all ripe for the establishment of a socialist society. That achievement was excluded in general by the principle that socialism requires the collaborative efforts of the economically most advanced countries and in particular by the fact that Russia was not even one of the advanced countries but rather one of the most backward. The European revolution was therefore regarded by all Bolsheviks as the only salvation of the Russian revolution. The success of this wider revolution was, in turn, dependent upon the quickest possible formation of parties in the West cast in the mold of the Bolshevik party, which meant above all other things parties sharply divided from the then dominant right and center wings and from their theoretical, political, and organizational positions.

The other urgent consideration was this: the prewar socialist international had not yet been reconstituted, whereas the Communist International had already been formally founded at its first world congress in Moscow in March 1919. But the new International was still more a prospect than a reality, for its first congress represented little more than the Bolshevik party. The decision on where to cast their lot was still to be made by most of the European socialist parties. In some of them, the position of the right wing was fairly solid: the German Social Democracy, the British Labour Party, the Belgian, Dutch, and Danish parties. But in virtually all the others in Europe, the leadership and membership were divided in different proportions between middle-of-the-road radicals and elements much closer to the Bolsheviks if not already identified with them. Among the former, a movement was growing for the "reconstruction of the International," which would exclude

the right-wing socialists, especially those heavily compromised by
their support of the war and the war governments, and include the
Communist and other left-wing parties without, however, risking
domination by the Bolsheviks or the adoption by all parties of the
uniformity of program and practices on which Moscow insisted.
This movement, originally sponsored, it seems, by the Swiss socialist leader Robert Grimm, then by his party, and soon after by
such important organizations as the German Independents, the
French socialist party, the British Independent Labour Party, the
Austrian party, even won sympathy among some of the elements
of parties, like the Italian and Swedish socialists, that had already
formally acknowledged the Third International.

The Bolsheviks had cause for alarm. It was this movement, regarded as the political embodiment of Kautskyism, that became
the central target of the Bolsheviks. They wanted an International
and national parties completely free not only of the right wing but
of the centrists as well. And they wanted them right away. Time
was of the essence, and both necessity and opportunity were
pressing for drastic decision. To the extent that Trotsky's work
contributed, as indeed it did, to the decision favored by the
Bolsheviks, it must be reckoned as one of the most outstanding
literary and polemical successes in modern politics.

It was finished on the eve of the second congress of the Communist International, held in July–August, 1920. In attendance,
the second congress was far more representative and impressive
than the first. The Bolshevik power now appeared to be firmly
consolidated in Russia; it had as good as mastered the armed
opposition to it in the civil war; its policies were gaining in confidence and prestige among socialists abroad whose hearts and
hopes lifted at the thought that the first socialist revolution was
now an established success. The Russians felt strong enough to
propose at the congress a detailed ultimatum to all parties as conditions for affiliation. On their initiative the congress adopted the
famous Twenty-One Conditions (in actuality, there were twenty-
two, a prohibition against Freemasonry having been added to the
original Russian list). Affiliated parties had to be highly centralized—both nationally and internationally—with the main empha-
sis on the latter; they had to be Communist in every respect—in
theory, in policy, in perspective, in structure, in leadership; and
above all they had to exclude from their ranks both the right wing

and the centrists, particularly their leaders who were even specified by name.

The conditions could hardly have been more deliberately stringent. The Bolsheviks simply reasoned that parties not wholly Communist would be prevented by vacillators from utilizing the revolutionary opportunities to seize power as the Bolsheviks had done in 1917, and to establish a Soviet dictatorship of the proletariat. The persuasive force of this reasoning, in the light of what appeared in 1920 to be the confirmation of Bolshevik views in Russia and the failure of their adversaries in the socialist movement abroad, quickly showed remarkable, even spectacular results.

The struggle to align the Western socialist parties with the new International seemed to go immediately from victory to victory. Two months after the second world congress, in October 1920, the Halle congress of the German Independents endorsed the Twenty-One Conditions and voted affiliation with the Communist International. Shortly afterward it merged with the then small official German section of the International to form the United Communist Party of Germany. The Independents, with their 800,000 members, were then the largest socialist party in the world based on individual membership (as distinct from parties like the British Labour Party made up in large part of block affiliation from trade unions and other groups). The anti-affiliationist minority retained the old party name; another minority despairingly withdrew from membership; but the fact that a majority of the delegates at Halle voted for the Communist International and the uncompromising fight for the dictatorship of the proletariat, made a tremendous impression in European politics. Another two months later, in December 1920, the French Socialist Party congress met at Tours and this time too a majority voted for affiliation with the Communist International and acceptance of its conditions. Again the inevitable split, with the majority renaming itself Communist and the minority retaining the old name. At the Italian socialist congress in Livorno (Leghorn), February 1921, the result was less favorable. The party had voted affiliation before the second world congress, but now it was confronted with the new conditions. The Livorno majority, still favoring affiliation, nevertheless balked at excluding the right-wing minority. The extreme left wing, with about a third of the delegates, then split away to form the Italian Communist Party. The victory here was dubious; in any case it was shattered a short while later by Mussolini's march on Rome. One more important congress deserves note: in May 1921 the Czechoslovakian socialists, with an imposing 450,000 members, voted affiliation with Moscow almost unanimously (562 delegates for, only 7 against). This marked the last of the important socialist parties, or any substantial segment of them, to come over to the Communist side. There was never again to be another.

Less than a year after Trotsky finished his polemic, the principles he defended in it were subscribed to in wide and decisive areas of the European working class. The confidence of the Bolsheviks which exudes from every page of Trotsky rose to its highest peak. The strength of the Communist International appeared tremendous, almost irresistible. It proved to be more appearance than reality.

The Russian Bolsheviks, and following them their partisans abroad, overestimated the power of the postwar revolutionary wave and in part misjudged its character; and it could be but thin consolation to them that the same error dominated the thoughts and fears of many of their opponents in liberal and conservative circles on the Continent. They underrated the resistive and recuperative strength of capitalism, which they subjected to so many perspicacious and telling criticisms. They miscalculated the extent to which the bulk of the socialist mass in Europe was determined to attain its goal by democratic parliamentary means. Above all else, perhaps, they were mistaken about the ease with which insurrectionary Bolshevik parties could be hurriedly created outside of Russia, with their revolutionary purity assured by statutory and other mechanical devices. Caricatures and simulacrums of the Bolshevik Party were forced into existence abroad. But a living image of the party as it was when it took power in Russia in 1917, as it was after an organic development under the unique conditions of Tsarism, has yet to be found anywhere in the world.

This soon became evident. The Russian Bolshevik revolution was not reproduced anywhere else. The Finnish revolution of 1918 was swiftly and brutally suppressed. The so-called Spartacist uprising in Berlin in January 1919 was a *Putsch*,* in so far as it was

---

* This term, impossible to translate in a word, may be defined as an armed conspiratorial attempt at state power by a minority not only of the population as a whole but of the working class as well, without the support of the working class or even against its opposition. It is so defined that this term has entered the vocabulary of radical politics.

an attempt by an armed minority to seize state power. So was the eighteen-day attempt to set up and maintain a "Soviet Republic" in Bavaria in April of the same year. The so-called "March Action" which the German Communist Party launched in 1921 was a *Putsch*, even if on a larger scale, and the ensuing disaster broke the back of German Communism. Two years later, during the deep social crisis of 1923 when a real bid for power seemed warranted and, indeed, an uprising had been extensively planned in Berlin and Moscow, the German Communists withdrew from battle at the last moment and whatever opportunity there was for a revolutionary success slipped by completely and beyond their recall. In Hungary the Soviet regime lasted less than four months, after its leadership had committed, by Bolshevik standards, every political mistake that could be compressed into so brief a time; years later, when discretion was no longer imperative, the chairman of the Communist International characterized the Hungarian revolution of Bela Kun as a *Putsch*. An emissary of the beleaguered Kun prompted the Austrian Communists to launch an uprising in Vienna in June 1919, but the Austrian Communists, then and ever since, were a perfectly negligible political force and the *Putsch* ended with its birth. A strange and obscure "Croatian Soviet Republic" was set up for a fleeting moment by troops from Kun's Hungary, but it is hard to trace even in Communist records. The Bulgarian Communists, among the very first to join the Communist International, a first magnitude power in their homeland, stood by as disdainful and passive observers on the two occasions, 1918 and 1923, when there was a truly revolutionary situation in the country; then in 1925 some of their leaders tried to compensate for the un-Bolshevik conduct of the past by blowing up the cathedral of Sofia. The hopes for a Polish Soviet Republic were dashed during the Russo-Polish war of 1920, when the Red Army had to retreat from Warsaw and take back with them the three Polish Communist leaders who were to be established in power if the military assault were supplemented successfully by an uprising of the Polish proletariat. But it did not rise, and Pilsudski remained in power—the same Pilsudski who was supported for a brief and tragic moment by the Communists six years later when he set up a military dictatorship! The last attempt at a Communist seizure of power in Europe was made in Reval on December 1, 1924. A group of exactly 227 modestly armed Estonian Communists began the seizure of key points in the capital at 5:15 A.M.; four hours later it was all over. The Estonian working class knew nothing about the uprising and showed no interest in it. Some 500 Communists, including the leader of the party, were shot by firing squads; about as many were given prison terms. In informed Moscow circles, Zinoviev, then chairman of the International, was said to have connived at this grisly *Putsch* and even to have instigated it for reasons of personal prestige, a charge for which some evidence has survived.

But from this series of events, followed by the fierce struggle for power in the Bolshevik party after 1923, the Communist International did not survive, at least not as an organization of revolutionary parties such as Lenin, and Trotsky in the present volume, sought to promote outside of Russia. What remained of them after the ensuing years of devastating internal wars, expulsions, purges, and reorganizations, was metamorphosed into obliging instruments at the disposal of the Russian Foreign Office. Such a role was nowhere in the minds of the founders of the Communist International. This helps to explain why so very few of its still-living founders are in the ranks of Communism today.

This is not the place to enlarge upon the "other question" dealt with by Trotsky: the socialist reorganization of the Russian economy. Yet, it would not be appropriate to pass over it without comment.

Trotsky was writing at the height of the period of "War Communism." This regime was imposed upon the country by the exigencies of a bitter civil war and foreign military intervention, coupled with a suffocating blockade enforced by the European war victors. The revolution had to fight the civil war in a land already exhausted by the unparalleled losses, in human and economic terms, suffered by Russia in three years of World War. The Bolsheviks tried to subordinate everything that was left of industry and civilian manpower to sustain the efforts of a newly created Red Army. In the cities, a rough equality for all was maintained by ration cards—the *payok*—with evenly divided national poverty determining a universally pitiful living standard. In the countryside the peasants' surplus, as fixed by decree and often without decree, was simply requisitioned by the government in exchange for little more than promises of goods, for there was by then little more than promises available. By 1920, industrial production was down to a level that almost defied credulity; the transportation system, never very elaborate, was at the point of total breakdown. Even though the civil war was nearing its end and military attention was concentrated mainly on the war with Poland, the Bolshevik leaders rejected a tentative proposal by Trotsky to modify the regime of "War Communism" and saw no way out of the economic difficulties except to maintain the quasi-military rule over industry and agriculture, to hold to that line of conduct until the siege was lifted by the European revolution on which they laid their main stake.

Trotsky thereupon generalized for the whole of the economy from two specific experiences: the "labor armies" into which some militarily inactive detachments of the Red Army had been converted, and the notable success in improving railroad service achieved by a special transportation committee which Trotsky directed by essentially military, dictatorial measures. The generalization amounted to the militarization of the national working force, so ardently urged in this work.

Labor would be commanded like soldiers in an army at war and the trade unions would play no autonomous role. Since the state is the worker's state, there is no need or room for the worker to be in conflict with it, as he pointed out in his debate with the Mensheviks, which is included in this volume. This standpoint, and the practice that followed from it, encountered rising resistance not only outside the Bolshevik party but within its ranks. The dispute was a fierce one. It came to a head at the Bolshevik caucus meeting for the Soviet Congress at the end of 1920. Trotsky's view was repudiated and, what was decisive, repudiated by Lenin.

To call our regime a workers' state, argued Lenin, is an abstraction, because it is, in the first place, a workers' and peasants' state, and in the second, it is a deformed workers' state because it is shot through with bureaucratism. "Our present state is such that the entire organized proletariat must defend itself; we must use these workers' organizations for the defense of the workers from their state and for the defense by the workers of our state."

It would be difficult to overstate the significance of this thought and of what it clearly implied. If the unions of the workers are to defend themselves from the state of the workers, they must have the means wherewith to conduct this defense. In essence, this cannot signify anything less than the right to discuss freely different views on the problems which the state-as-employer presents to them, to decide freely on their position toward these problems and to select freely the leaders who are to voice and work for the position adopted. If, however, the unions are not allowed to have leaders outside the ranks of the only party that leads the government, all of whom are rigorously subject to decisions and discipline not adopted by the unions, the "defense of the workers from their state" is at best dependent on the good will of the party that heads the state from which "the entire proletariat must defend itself." In other words, the "defense of the workers from their state" required, for it to be meaningful, the same political rights for non-Communist workers as for the Communists. It required full democratic rights.

This was precisely what the Bolsheviks, converting the expediencies and necessities of the civil war period into virtues and principles which had never been part of their original program, were determined not to permit. Lenin made particular note of this at the Tenth Party Congress in March 1921. The crisis had just reached an explosive point. The discontent of the peasants was clear throughout the country, manifested even by armed risings. Numerous strikes had just broken out in Petrograd. Then, a week before the Congress opened, the Kronstadt sailors rose in arms against the regime. By arms they were finally suppressed.

But the events had their effect. The Bolsheviks could not ignore the fact that Kronstadt was the first uprising against their rule that demanded the revival of the Soviets and the Soviet power, shorn of the Communist political monopoly, of bureaucratism, of military rule of the economy. All talk of militarization of labor, of incorporating the unions into the machinery of the state, came to an abrupt end. Lenin was obliged to acknowledge that the Bolsheviks had become isolated not only from the peasants but from most of the workers. He confronted the Congress with the first outlines of what became known as the "Nep," the New Economic Policy, which soon replaced the military requisitioning of peasant stocks with extensive freedom for the peasant to trade, and relaxed the rigid, supercentralized administration of industry; small private enterprises and private trading were to be allowed within limits; and plans were even made to grant mining, timber, and other concessions to foreign capital. The Congress endorsed the Nep almost without discussion. But on one score Lenin became more adamant than ever. Precisely because we are making these economic concessions to capitalist modes of production and exchange, he insisted, the repression of all other parties, including Mensheviks and Social Revolutionists, must be made more complete. For the same reason, moreover, we cannot afford the luxury of a factionally divided party. On Lenin's initiative, factions were ordered dissolved and factional strife within the Bolshevik party was prohibited, at least for the next period. The Congress, frightened by all that Kronstadt implied, concurred. The "juridical ground" was now laid for smashing all the later opposition groups in the party.

In the next few years, the Nep brought about a great economic relaxation, not only in agriculture but also in industry, which managed to approach the prewar level. It also brought with it new and gnawing problems, and crucial old ones. How these problems were dealt with by the regime finally installed by Stalin, is well enough known to obviate the need to detail it here. The new regime not only militarized the entire working population, as well as the Communist Party itself, but subjected it to a totalitarian organization, direction and control without equal in the history of despotism. Not only were the workers and what passed for unions (to say nothing of the peasants) deprived of the slightest possibility of "defense from their state," but the very membership of the privileged Communist Party were denied the possibility of defending themselves from the arbitrary rule of their leadership. The basic justification for this is embodied in the "Stalin Constitution," which proclaims that the state property, entirely controlled by a handful of rulers, is "the possession of the whole people." In 1936 Trotsky wrote that "this identification is the fundamental sophism of the official doctrine" of the Stalinists. In 1920 his identification of the Communist Party with the interests of the revolution, to the point where the workers did not need to negotiate with the state or defend themselves from it because it was already theirs, was more easily and openly argued, but not less easily refuted. But even the refutation by Lenin had its ambiguities and inconsistencies. Free from these defects was what Lenin wrote just before the revolution:

"It would be a fundamental mistake to suppose that the struggle for democracy can divert the proletariat from the socialist revolution, or obscure, or overshadow it, etc. On the contrary, just as socialism cannot be victorious unless it introduces complete democracy, so the proletariat will be unable to prepare for victory over the bourgeoisie unless it wages a many-sided, consistent and revolutionary struggle for democracy."

It is exactly forty-five years ago that these lines were written. The fact that they are honored only in the breach and not in the observance by his avowed followers today does not detract from their validity. It is tragic that Lenin and Trotsky did not observe them when it would have assured a different evolution.

France at a Turning Point*

By LEON TROTSKY

A New Translation by Max Shachtman

This book is devoted to a clarification of the methods of the proletariat's revolutionary policy in our epoch. The exposition bears a polemical character, like revolutionary policy itself. In winning the oppressed masses, polemics aimed against the ruling class are transformed at a certain moment into revolution.

A clear understanding of the social nature of modern society, of its state, of its law, of its ideology, constitutes the theoretical fundament of revolutionary policy. The bourgeoisie works with abstractions ("nation," "Fatherland," "democracy") in order to camouflage the exploitation which lies at the foundation of its rule. Le Temps, one of the most infamous newspapers on the globe, teaches patriotism and impartiality to the masses of the French people every day. Yet it is no secret to anyone that the impartiality of Le Temps is valued at a well-fixed international price scale.

The first act of revolutionary policy is to unmask the bourgeois fictions that poison the mind of the popular masses. These fictions become particularly malevolent when they are blended with the ideas of "socialism" and "revolution." Today more than at any other time the fabricators of this type of blend are setting the tone in the French workers' organizations.

The first edition of this work exercized a certain influence upon the formation of the French Communist Party: the author received a good deal of evidence of this—after all, it would not be difficult to find signs of it in L'Humanité[1] up until 1924. In the course of the ensuing twelve years the Communist International, after several feverish zigzags, underwent the process of a fundamental revision of values: it suffices to say that today this work

---

* Trotsky's Preface to a 1936 French edition of Terrorism and Communism.

[1] The principal newspaper of the French Communist Party.

figures on the index of prohibited books. In their ideas and their methods, the present leaders of the French Communist Party (we are forced to retain this name, which is in complete contradiction to reality) are distinguished in no principle from Kautsky, against whom this work is directed: they are, however, vastly more ignorant and cynical. The new access of reformism and of patriotism that Cachin[2] and Co. are undergoing might by itself alone justify a new edition of this book. However, there are other and more serious reasons for it: they have their roots in the profound prerevolutionary crisis that is shaking the regime of the Third Republic.

After an absence of eighteen years, the author of this work had the opportunity to spend two years in France (1933–35) as an ordinary observer, in the provinces to be sure, who was moreover the object of strict surveillance. During this period a little incident occurred in the Department of the Isère, where the author had occasion to live, which was no different from so many others of its kind but which nonetheless offers the key to the whole of French politics. In a sanatorium belonging to the Comité des Forges,[3] a young worker who was threatened with a serious operation took it upon himself to read a revolutionary newspaper (more exactly, the paper that he naïvely regarded as revolutionary was *L'Humanité*). The administration put this ultimatum to the imprudent patient and then to four other patients who shared his sympathies: either give up receiving undesirable publications or be thrown into the street. The patients pointed out in vain that clerical and reactionary propaganda was being carried on openly in the sanatorium, but this was obviously without effect. Since it was a matter of ordinary workers who were risking neither parliamentary mandates nor ministerial portfolios but simply their health and life, the ultimatum was not successful: five patients, one of them on the eve of being operated on, were shown the door of the sanatorium. Grenoble had a Socialist municipality at the time, headed by a Doctor Martin, one of those bourgeois conservatives who generally set the tone of the Socialist Party and of whom Léon Blum[4] is the consummate representative. The expelled workers tried to find support from the mayor. In vain: despite

---

[2] Marcel Cachin, leader of the Communist group in the Chamber of Deputies.
[3] The association of French steel companies.
[4] Then leader of the French Socialist Party and later premier.

their insistence, their letters, their applications, they were not even received. They turned to the local journal of the Left, *La Dépêche,* in which Radicals[5] and Socialists form an indissoluble cartel. When he learned that the sanatorium of the Comité des Forges was involved, the director of the journal refused categorically to intervene: anything you want, but not that. For having once before committed an imprudence toward this powerful organization, *La Dépêche* had been deprived of advertising and thereby suffered a loss of 20,000 francs. Unlike the proletarians, the director of the journal of the Left, as well as the mayor, did have something to lose: so they forewent an unequal struggle by abandoning the workers, with their sick intestines and kidneys, to their own fate.

Once or twice a week, the Socialist mayor, stirred by vague memories of his youth, delivers a speech to extol the advantages of socialism over capitalism. During the elections, *La Dépêche* supports the mayor and his party. All works out for the best. The Comité des Forges looks with an altogether liberal tolerance upon this species of socialism which does not do the slightest harm to the material interests of capital. For 20,000 francs worth of advertising per year (so cheap are these gentlemen to be had!), the feudalists of heavy industry and banking have their hold, practically speaking, on the devotion of a big journal of the Cartel! And not only of this journal: the Comité des Forges assuredly has enough means, direct and indirect, with which to influence Messrs. mayors, senators, and deputies, including the Socialist mayors, senators, and deputies. All of official France is placed under the dictatorship of finance capital. In the Larousse dictionary, this system is given the name of "democratic republic."

Messrs. deputies of the Left and the journalists, not only of the Isère but of all the departments of France, believed that their peaceful coexistence with capitalist reaction would never come to an end. They were wrong. Democracy, long since worm-eaten, suddenly felt a pistol barrel at its temple. Just as Hitler's armaments—a brutal material act—produced a veritable revolution in the relations between states by showing the vanity and illusory character of what is conventionally called "international law," so

---

[5] Members of the Radical Socialist Party, a middle-of-the-road party, led by Herriot and Daladier.

the armed bands of Colonel de La Rocque[6] have flung commotion into the internal relations of France by forcing all the parties, without exception, to reorganize, limit, and regroup themselves.

Friedrich Engels once wrote that the state, including the democratic republic, is armed bands for the defense of property; everything else serves only to embellish or mask this fact. The eloquent defenders of "law," of the type of Herriot and Blum, have always been shocked by this cynicism. But Hitler, like La Rocque— each in his own field—has again shown that Engels was right.

At the beginning of 1934, Daladier was president of the Council by the will of universal direct and secret suffrage: he carried national sovereignty in his pocket along with his handkerchief. But as soon as the bands of La Rocque, Maurras, and Co. showed that they had the audacity to fire revolver shots and hamstring the horses of the police, Daladier and his sovereignty gave way to the ineffectual policy prescribed by the chiefs of these bands. This fact has infinitely greater importance than all the electoral statistics, and it will not be possible to efface it from the recent history of France because it is an indication of the future.

To be sure, it is not within the power of *any group* armed with revolvers to change the political orientation of a country at any moment whatsoever. Only armed bands that are the organs of definite classes can, under *certain* circumstances, play a decisive rôle. Colonel de La Rocque and his supporters want to insure "order" against shocks. And since "order" in France signifies the domination of the whole of the bourgeoisie over the proletariat and the social strata close to it, the troops of La Rocque are quite simply armed bands of finance capital.

This idea is not a new one. It can even be found frequently in *Le Populaire*[7] and *L'Humanité*, even if they were not the first ones to formulate it. Yet, these publications tell only half the truth. The other half, no less important, is that Herriot and Daladier, along with their supporters, are also an agency of finance capital; otherwise the Radicals would not have been able to act as the governing party of France for dozens of years. If one does not want to play hide-and-seek, it is necessary to say that La Rocque and Daladier are working for the same boss. This does not mean, obviously, that

---

[6] Leader of the Croix de Feu, one of the armed fascist groups.

[7] The principal newspaper of the French Socialist Party.

there is a complete identity between them or their methods. Quite the contrary. They are fighting an implacable war, like two specialized agencies each of which possesses the secret of salvation. Daladier promises to maintain order by means of the old tricolored democracy. La Rocque considers that obsolete parliamentarism must be swept away in favor of an avowed military and police dictatorship. The political methods are antagonistic, but the social interests are the same.

The decay of the capitalist system, its incurable crisis, its decomposition—these form the historic basis of the antagonism that exists between La Rocque and Daladier (we take these two names only so as to facilitate the exposition). In spite of the constant progress in technique and the remarkable results of certain industrial branches, capitalism as a whole brakes the development of the productive forces; this determines an extreme instability of social and international relations. Parliamentary democracy is intimately linked with the epoch of free competition and international free trade. The bourgeoisie was able to tolerate the right to strike, of assembly, freedom of the press, so long as the productive forces were in full upward swing, as markets expanded, as the welfare of the masses, while restricted, nevertheless increased, and the capitalist nations were able to live and let live. But not any more. The imperialist epoch is characterized, except for the Soviet Union, by a stagnation and decline in the national income, by a chronic agrarian crisis and an organic unemployment. These internal phenomena are inherent in the present phase of capitalism, like gout and sclerosis at a certain age of the individual. To seek to explain the world economic chaos by the consequences of the last war is to display a hopelessly superficial mind like that of M. Caillaux, Count Sforza, and others. The war was nothing else but an attempt by the capitalist countries to shift on to the back of the adversary the crash that threatened at any moment. The attempt failed. The war only worsened the signs of decomposition whose subsequent sharpening is preparing a new war.

Poor as are French economic statistics, which deliberately pass over class antagonisms in silence, they cannot conceal the manifest marks of the decomposition. Parallel to the decline in national income, to the truly catastrophic fall in rural incomes, to the ruination of the little people of the towns, to the growth of unemployment, the giant enterprises with an annual turnover of 100 to 200 millions and even more are making brilliant profits. Finance capital, in all the accepted senses of the term, is sucking the blood of the French people. Such is the social basis of the ideology and the politics of the "National Union."

Alleviations and rifts in the process of decomposition are possible, even inevitable; but they will retain a character strictly conditioned by the conjuncture. As to the general tendency of our epoch, it places France, after many other countries, before this alternative: either the proletariat must overturn the fundamentally gangrened bourgeois order—or capital, aiming at its own preservation, must replace democracy by fascism. For how long? The fate of Mussolini and of Hitler will answer this question.

On February 6, 1934, the fascists fired upon the direct order of the Stock Exchange, the banks, and the trusts. From these same command positions, Daladier was summoned to turn over power to Doumergue. And if the Radical minister, the president of the Council, capitulated—with the pusillanimity that characterizes the Radicals—it is because he recognized in the bands of La Rocque the troops of his own boss. To put it in other words: Daladier, the sovereign minister, yielded power to Doumergue for the same reason that the director of *La Dépêche* and the mayor of Grenoble refused to denounce the odious cruelty of the agents of the Comité des Forges.

However, passing over from democracy to fascism leaves room for risks of social collisions. Hence the hesitations and the tactical disagreements that may be noted in the upper spheres of the bourgeoisie. All the magnates of capital are in favor of continuing to strengthen the armed bands that may constitute a beneficial reserve at the hour of danger. But what place should be granted these bands right at the present? Should they be permitted to shift immediately to the attack, or be kept in attendance as a means of intimidation? Many are the questions that are not yet resolved. Finance capital no longer believes it possible for the Radicals to hold behind them the masses of the petty bourgeoisie and, by means of the pressure of these masses, to keep the proletariat within the confines of "democratic" discipline. But neither does it believe that the fascist organizations, which are still lacking a genuine mass basis, are capable of seizing power and establishing a strong regime.

What brought the directors of the corridors an understanding of the need for caution was not parliamentary rhetoric, but the revolt of the workers, the attempt at a general strike, even though it was stifled from the start by the bureaucracy of Jouhaux,[8] and finally the local uprisings (Toulon, Brest). The fascists having been put back in their place a bit, the Radicals breathed more freely. *Le Temps,* which had already found the means, in a series of articles, of extending hand and heart to the "young generation," rediscovered the advantages of the liberal regime which harmonizes, it says, with the genius of France. In this way an unstable, transitory, bastard régime has been established, in harmony not with the genius of France but with the decline of the Third Republic. In this régime, the *Bonapartist* traits are the ones that appear with the highest clarity: independence of the government from the parties and programs, liquidation of the legislative power by means of plenary powers, with the government taking its place above the battling factions, that is, in point of fact, above the nation, so that it may play the part of "arbiter." The Doumergue, Flandin, Laval ministries, all three of them, with the unfailing participation of the humiliated and discredited Radicals, have represented tiny variations on one and the same theme.

When the Sarraut ministry was constituted, Léon Blum, whose perspicacity has two dimensions instead of three, announced: "The last effects of February 6[9] are destroyed on the parliamentary plane" (*Populaire,* February 2, 1936). That's what is called brushing the shadow of a carriage with the shadow of a brush! As if you could wipe out "on the parlimentary plane" the pressure of the armed bands of finance capital! As if Sarraut could fail to feel this pressure and not tremble under it! In reality, the Sarraut-Flandin government is a variety of this same semiparliamentarian "Bonapartism," however slightly inclined to the "Left." Sarraut himself, in refuting the accusation of having taken arbitrary measures, replied in parliament in a way that cannot be improved upon: "If my measures are arbitrary, that is because I want to be an arbiter." This aphorism would not have been out of place on the lips of Napoleon III. Sarraut does not feel himself the representative of a definite party or of a bloc of parties in power, as the

---

[8] Léon Jouhaux was the leader of the moderate trade unions.

[9] Date of the armed fascist attempt to overturn the parliamentary government in France in 1934.

rules of parliamentarism would have it, but an arbiter above the classes and the parties, as the laws of Bonapartism would have it.

The aggravation of the class struggle and above all the appearance on the scene of the armed bands of reaction have served no less to revolutionize the workers' organizations. The Socialist Party, which peaceably played the rôle of fifth wheel in the cart of the Third Republic, found itself constrained to repudiate half-way its cartelist traditions and even to break with its Right wing (Neos). At the same time, the Communists carried out a contrary evolution, only on an infinitely vaster scale. For years these gentlemen dreamed of barricades, of conquest of the streets, etc. . . . (this dream, to be sure, had a literary character, above all). After February 6, understanding that the affair was serious, the barricade-builders rushed off to the Right. The spontaneous reflex of these terrified phrasemongers coincided strikingly with the new international orientation of Soviet diplomacy.

In face of the danger represented by Hitlerite Germany, the Kremlin's policy turned toward France. *Statu quo* in international relations! *Statu quo* in the internal régime of France! Hopes for a socialist revolution? Chimeras! The leading circles of the Kremlin speak of French Communism only with contempt. So it is necessary to hold on to what exists in order not to have worse. Since parliamentary democracy in France is not conceivable without the Radicals, let us see to it that the Socialists support them; let us order the Communists not to embarrass the Blum-Herriot bloc; if possible, let us have them join in the bloc. No disturbances, no threats! That is the orientation of the Kremlin.

When Stalin repudiates the world revolution, the French bourgeois parties do not want to believe him. They are quite mistaken! In politics, blind confidence is obviously not a higher virtue. But blind distrust is worth no more. You must know how to compare words with deeds, and to discern the general trend of development for several years. The policy of Stalin, which is determined by the interests of the privileged Soviet bureaucracy, has become thoroughly conservative. The French bourgeoisie has every reason to place confidence in Stalin. The French proletariat has just as much reason to be distrustful.

At the Unity Congress of Toulouse, the "Communist" Racamond gave the policy of the People's Front a formula worthy of passing into posterity: "How are we to overcome the timidity of

the Radical Party?" How overcome the fear that the bourgeoisie
has of the proletariat? Very simply: the terrific revolutionists must
throw away the knife they clenched between their teeth, pomade
their hair, and assume the most charming smile of the odalisques:
Vaillant-Couturier[10] of the latest style will serve as their prototype.
Under the pressure of the pomaded "Communists" who bent all
their strength to drive to the Right the Socialists who were evolv-
ing to the Left, Blum had to change his orientation once again. He
did it, happily, in the customary sense. Thus the People's Front
was formed: an insurance company of Radical bankrupts at the
expense of the capital of the workers' organizations.

Radicalism is inseparable from Freemasonry. That says everything. In the course of the debates that took place in the Chamber
of Deputies on the Leagues, M. Xavier-Vallat recalled that Trotsky had once "prohibited" Communists from belonging to the
Masonic lodges. M. Jammy-Schmidt who is, it seems, an authority
in the matter, hastened to explain this prohibition by the incompatibility of despotic Bolshevism with the "spirit of freedom." We
do not see the need of a polemic on this theme with the Radical
deputy. But we consider to this day that the workers' representative who goes to seek his inspiration or consolation in the insipid
Masonic religion of class collaboration does not deserve the slightest confidence. It is not by chance that the Cartel has been supplemented by a wide participation of socialists in the Masonic
lodges. But the time has come for the repentant Communists themselves to put on the apron. After all, with the apron on, it will be
more comfortable for the newly initiated journeymen to serve the
old bosses of the Cartel.

The People's Front, we are told not without indignation, is not
at all a cartel but a mass movement. There is no lack of pompous
definitions, to be sure, but they change nothing of substance. The
aim of the Cartel has always been to *brake* the mass movement by
orienting it toward class collaboration. The People's Front has
exactly the same aim. The difference between them—and it is a
big one—is that the traditional Cartel was applied in the epochs
of stability and calm of the parliamentary régime. But today,
when the masses are impatient and ready to explode, a more solid
brake, joined in by the "Communists," has become indispensable.

---

[10] Paul Vaillant-Couturier, one of the leading Communist spokesmen.

xxviii

The joint meetings, the big theatrical processions, the solemn oaths, the union of the banner of the Commune with the banner of Versailles, the hurly-burly, the demagoguery—all this has but one aim: to contain and to demoralize the mass movement.

In order to justify himself before the right-wingers, Sarraut explained to the Chamber that his harmless concessions to the People's Front constitute nothing more than the *safety valve* of the régime. Such candor might have appeared imprudent. But the extreme Left smothered it in applause. So there was no ground for Sarraut to stand on ceremony. In any case, he succeeded in giving, perhaps involuntarily, a definition of the People's Front: a safety valve against the mass movement. In general, M. Sarraut is a good hand at aphorisms!

Foreign policy is a continuation of domestic policy. Having completely abandoned the standpoint of the proletariat, Blum, Cachin, and Co. adopt—under the mask of "collective security" and of "international law"—the standpoint of national imperialism. They are preparing the same policy of abdication and platitude they followed from 1914 to 1918, adding only this: "for the defense of the U.S.S.R." Yet, from 1918 to 1923, when Soviet diplomacy frequently found itself obliged to tack and veer and to sign agreements, it never occurred to a single section of the Communist International that it could make a bloc with its bourgeoisie! Is not this point, all by itself, enough proof of the sincerity of Stalin when he repudiates the world revolution?

For the same reasons that the present leaders of the Communist International cling to the udders of "democracy" in the period of its agony, they discover the radiant visage of the League of Nations when you can already hear its death rattle. Thus a joint platform on foreign policy has been created between the Radicals and the Soviet Union. The domestic program of the People's Front is a collection of commonplaces which permits as wide an interpretation as the Geneva Covenant. The general sense of the program is this: no change. But the masses do want a change and therein lies the heart of the political crisis.

In disarming the proletariat politically, the Blums, Paul Faures, Cachins, Thorezes, are concerned above all that it does not arm itself physically. The propaganda of these gentlemen is no different from religious sermons on the superiority of moral principles. Engels, who taught that the possession of state power is a matter of armed bands, Marx, who regarded insurrection as an art, appear to the present deputies, senators, and mayors of the People's Front like savages out of the Middle Ages. *Le Populaire* has printed for the hundredth time a cartoon showing an unarmed worker with this inscription: "You will learn that our naked fists are tougher than all your blackjacks." What splendid contempt for military technique! In this respect, the Negus himself has more advanced views. For these people, the *coups d'état* in Italy, in Germany, in Austria do not exist. Will they stop extolling the "naked fists" when La Rocque puts them in handcuffs? At times, one almost regrets that Messrs. leaders cannot be made to undergo this experience without the masses having to suffer from it!

From the standpoint of the bourgeois régime, the People's Front is an episode in the rivalry between Radicalism and fascism to win the attention and favors of big capital. By their theatrical fraternization with the Socialists and the Communists, the Radicals seek to show the boss that the régime is not as sick as the Right-wingers claim; that the danger of revolution is exaggerated; that Vaillant-Couturier himself has traded his knife for a collar; that the masses of workers can be disciplined by domesticated "revolutionists" and the parliamentary system be saved thereby from collapse.

Yet, not all the Radicals believe in this manoeuver; the more serious and more influential among them, with Herriot in the lead, prefer to adopt an attitude of watchful waiting. But in the last analysis, they cannot propose anything else. The crisis of parliamentarism is primarily a crisis of confidence of the voter with regard to Radicalism.

So long as nobody discovers the means of rejuvenating capitalism, there will be no recipe for saving the Radical party. It is left only with the choice between different kinds of political death. A relative success in the next elections would not for long prevent or even slow down its collapse.

The leaders of the Socialist party, the most carefree politicians of France, do not trouble themselves over the sociology of the People's Front: nobody can draw anything interesting out of the interminable monologues of Léon Blum. As for the Communists, who are extremely proud of having taken the initiative in the collaboration with the bourgeoisie, they present the People's Front as the *alliance of the proletariat with the middle classes*. What a parody on Marxism! No, the Radical party is not the party of the petty bourgeoisie. Neither is it a "bloc of the middle and the petty bourgeoisie," in the absurd definition of *Pravda*. Not only does the middle bourgeoisie exploit the petty bourgeoisie on the economic plane, but it is itself an agency of finance capital. To designate hierarchical political relations founded upon exploitation by the neutral term of "bloc," is to make a mockery of reality. A horseman is not a bloc between man and horse. If the party of Herriot-Daladier has roots in the petty-bourgeois masses and, to a certain point, down into the circles of the workers, it is solely with the aim of duping them in the interest of the capitalist régime. *The Radicals are the democratic party of French imperialism*—any other definition is a snare.

The crisis of the capitalist system disarms the Radicals by depriving them of the traditional means that enabled them to lull the petty bourgeoisie to sleep. The "middle classes" are beginning to feel, if not to understand, that the situation will not be saved by miserable reforms and that a bold remolding of the present régime has become necessary. But Radicalism and boldness go together like water and fire. Fascism feeds primarily upon the mounting distrust of the petty bourgeoisie toward Radicalism. It can be said without exaggerating that the political fate of France will soon be decided in large measure according to the way in which Radicalism is liquidated and whether it is fascism or the party of the proletariat that takes over its succession, that is, its influence over the petty-bourgeois masses.

It is an elementary principle of Marxian strategy that the alliance of the proletariat with the little people of town and country must be realized solely in the irreducible struggle against the traditional parliamentary representation of the petty bourgeoisie. In order to win the peasant over to the side of the worker it is necessary to detach him from the Radical politician who subjects him to finance capital. Contrary to this, the People's Front, a complot of the labor bureaucracy with the worst political exploiters of the middle classes, is simply capable of killing the faith of the masses in revolutionary methods and of hurling them into the arms of the fascist counterrevolution.

However difficult it may be to believe it, it is nonetheless a fact that a few cynics try to justify the policy of the People's Front by reference to Lenin who, it seems, demonstrated that you cannot do without "compromises" and, notably, agreements with other parties. For the leaders of the Communist International of today, to insult Lenin has become the rule; they trample upon the doctrine of the founder of the Bolshevik party and then go on to Moscow to bow before his mausoleum.

Lenin began on his task in Tsarist Russia, where not only the workers, the peasants, and the intellectuals but wide circles of the bourgeoisie were fighting against the old régime. If, generally speaking, the policy of the People's Front could have been justified, it would appear to be above all in a country which had not yet made its bourgeois revolution. Messrs. falsifiers would do well to point out in what phase, at what moment, and in what circumstances the Bolshevik party realized a simulacrum of the People's Front in Russia. Let them put their gray matter to work and rummage through the historical documents!

The Bolsheviks made agreements of a practical kind with petty-bourgeois revolutionary organizations for the joint clandestine transportation of revolutionary writings, sometimes for the joint organization of a street demonstration, or for thrusting back at pogrom gangs. During elections to the Duma, they resorted under certain circumstances and on the second level[11] to electoral blocs with the Mensheviks or with the Social Revolutionists. That's all. There were neither joint "programs," permanent organisms, nor renunciation of criticism of momentary allies. This sort of agreement and episodic compromise, strictly confined to specific aims— that is all Lenin had in mind—had nothing in common with the People's Front, which represents a conglomerate of heterogeneous organizations, a lasting alliance of different classes bound for a whole period—and what a period!—by a common policy and program: a policy of show, of declamation and of dust in the eyes. At the first serious test, the People's Front will shatter and all its constituent parts will emerge from it with deep cracks. The policy of the People's Front is a policy of betrayal.

The rule of Bolshevism insofar as blocs are concerned was the following: *March separately, strike together!* The rule of the leaders of the present Communist International is this: *March together so as to be struck down separately.* Let these gentlemen stick to Stalin and Dimitrov, but let them leave Lenin in peace.

---

[11] Elections to the Tsarist Duma were organized on the basis of electoral colleges on the second and third levels.

It is impossible not to grow indignant upon reading the declarations of the braggart chiefs who claim that the People's Front "saved" France from fascism; in reality this means quite simply that our terrified heroes saved themselves by their mutual encouragement from a greater fright. For how long? Between the first uprising of Hitler and his advent to power, ten years elapsed, marked by alternating ebbs and flows. At the time, the German Blums and Cachins proclaimed several times their "victory" over National Socialism. We did not believe them and we were not mistaken. Nevertheless, this experience taught the French cousins of Wels and Thaelmann nothing. To be sure, in Germany the Communists did not participate in the People's Front, which embraced the Social Democracy, the Left-wing bourgeoisie, and the Catholic Center ("alliance of the proletariat with the middle classes"!). In those days, the Communist International even rejected fighting agreements between workers' organizations against fascism. The results are known. Our warmest sympathy for Thaelmann as a prisoner of the executioners cannot prevent us from saying that his policy, that is, the policy of Stalin, did more for the victory of Hitler than the policy of Hitler himself. Now that it has made an about-face, the Communist International is applying in France the well-enough-known policy of the German Social Democracy. Is it really so hard to foresee its results?

The next parliamentary elections, whatever their outcome, will not, *by themselves,* yield any serious changes in the situation: after all, the voters are asked to choose between an arbiter of the Laval type and an arbiter of the Herriot-Daladier type. But since Herriot has collaborated peaceably with Laval, and Daladier has supported both of them, the difference that divides them, if measured on the scale of the historic problems that are posed, is insignificant.

To believe that Herriot-Daladier are capable of declaring war upon the "Two Hundred Families" who govern France, is to deceive the people impudently. The Two Hundred Families are not suspended between heaven and earth, they constitute the organic crowning of the system of finance capital. In order to triumph over the Two Hundred Families it is necessary to overturn the economic and political régime which Herriot and Daladier are no less interested in maintaining than are Tardieu and La Rocque. It is not a matter of the struggle of the "nation" against a few feudalists, as

L'Humanité depicts it, but of the struggle of the proletariat against the bourgeoisie, of the class struggle that can only be clinched by the revolution. The antilabor plot of the leaders of the People's Front has become the main obstacle on this road.

It cannot be said in advance for how long a time the semiparliamentary, semi-Bonapartist ministries will continue to follow upon each other in France and through just what phases the country will pass in the course of the next period. That will depend upon the national and the world economic conjuncture, the international atmosphere, the situation in the U.S.S.R., the degree of stability of Italian and German fascism, the course of events in Spain, and finally—this is not the least important factor—upon the clearsightedness and activity of the advanced elements of the French proletariat. The convulsions of the franc may hasten the dénouement. A closer co-operation of France with England could slow it down. At all events, the agony of "democracy" may last a much longer time in France than the prefascist period of Bruening-Papen-Schleicher lasted in Germany; but that will not make it stop being an agony. Democracy will be swept away. The question is solely one of knowing who will sweep it away.

The struggle against the "Two Hundred Families," against fascism and war—for peace, bread, freedom, and other fine things—is either a snare or a struggle to overturn capitalism. The problem of the revolutionary conquest of power is posed before the French workers not as a remote objective but as a task of the period which is opening up. Yet the Socialist and Communist leaders not only refuse to proceed with the revolutionary mobilization of the proletariat, but they oppose it with all their strength. At the same time that they fraternize with the bourgeoisie, they hound and expel the Bolsheviks. Such is the violence of their hatred of the revolution and of the fear it inspires in them! In this situation, the worst rôle is played by pseudo-revolutionists of the Marceau Pivert[12] type who promise to overturn the bourgeoisie but not otherwise than with the permission of Léon Blum!

The whole march of the French workers' movement in the course of these last dozen years has placed on the order of the day the need of creating a *new revolutionary party!*

To try guessing whether events will leave "enough" time in

---

[12] Leader of a Left-wing group in the French Socialist Party.

which to form the new party is to engage in the most sterile of endeavors. The resources of history in matters of various possibilities, transitional forms, stages, accelerations and delays are inexhaustible. Under the sway of economic difficulties, fascism may take the offensive prematurely and suffer a defeat. A lasting respite would be the result. On the other hand, it might, out of caution, adopt an attitude of watchful waiting and by virtue of this offer new opportunities to the revolutionary organizations. The People's Front may go to pieces on its contradictions before fascism is capable of engaging in general battle: the result would be a period of regroupings and splits in the workers' parties and a rapid crystallization of a revolutionary vanguard. The spontaneous movements of the masses, following the example of Toulon and Brest, may take on large scope and create a reliable fulcrum for the revolutionary lever. Finally, even a victory of fascism in France, which is theoretically not impossible, does not signify that it would remain in power for a thousand years, as Hitler proclaims, nor that this victory would vouchsafe it a period like the one enjoyed by Mussolini. If the twilight of fascism were to fall in Italy or in Germany, it would not be long before it spread to France. Under the least favorable hypothesis, the building of a revolutionary party would mean to speed the hour of revenge. The wiseacres who duck away from this urgent task by claiming that "conditions are not ripe" only show that they themselves are not ripe for these conditions.

The French Marxists, like those of all countries, must recommence from the beginning in a sense, but upon an infinitely higher plane than that of their predecessors. The fall of the Communist International, more shameful than the fall of the Social Democracy in 1914, considerably impedes the start of the forward march. The recruiting of new cadres takes place slowly in the course of a cruel struggle within the working class against the united front of the reactionary and patriotic bureaucracy. On the other hand, these difficulties, which did not fall upon the proletariat by chance, constitute an important factor favoring a good selection and a solid tempering of the first phalanxes of the new party and the new International.

Only a tiny portion of the cadres of the Communist International began its revolutionary education at the beginning of the war, before the October revolution. All of them, almost without exception, now find themselves outside the Third International

Their succession adhered to the October Revolution after it had already triumphed: that was easier. But even of this succession there does not remain very much. The major portion of the present cadres of the Communist International adhered not to the Bolshevik program, not to the revolutionary flag, but to the Soviet bureaucracy. They are not fighters but docile functionaries, aides-de-camp, grooms. That is why the Third International is disintegrating so ingloriously in a historic situation so rich in grand revolutionary possibilities.

The Fourth International lifts itself on to the shoulders of its three forerunners. It receives blows, from the front, the side, and the rear. One part of it, sectarians and adventurers, will leave it, as is inevitable at the start, to the extent that the movement grows. Let the pedants and skeptics shrug their shoulders about "little" organizations that publish "little" papers and issue challenges to the entire world. The serious revolutionists will pass them by with contempt. The October Revolution too began to walk in baby shoes. . . .

The powerful Russian Social Revolutionary and Menshevik parties who for months formed a "People's Front" with the Kadets, fell apart into dust under the blows of a "handful of fanatics" of Bolshevism. The German Social Democracy, the German Communist Party, and the Austrian Social Democracy met a death without glory under the blows of fascism. The epoch which is about to begin for European humanity will not leave a trace in the labor movement of all that is ambiguous and gangrened. All the Jouhauxs, Citrines, Blums, Cachins, Vanderveldes, and Caballeros are nothing but phantoms. The sections of the Second and Third Internationals will depart the scene without a sound, one after the other. A new and grand regrouping of the workers' ranks is inevitable. The young revolutionary cadres will acquire flesh and blood. Victory is conceivable only on the basis of Bolshevik methods, to the defense of which the present work is devoted.

March 28, 1936

Introduction to the Second English Edition

by LEON TROTSKY

THIS book was written in 1920 in the car of a military train and amid the flames of civil war. This circumstance the reader must keep before his eyes if he wishes rightly to understand not only the basic material of the book, but also its harsh allusions, and particularly the tone in which it is written.

The book was written as an attack on Karl Kautsky. To the younger generation this name does not mean much, although indeed Kautsky is still alive among us: not long ago he kept his eightieth birthday. Kautsky at one time wielded a very great authority in the ranks of the Second International as the theorist of Marxism. The war soon showed that his Marxism was only a method for a passive interpretation of the process of history, but not a method of revolutionary action. So long as the class struggle flowed between the peaceful shores of parliamentarism, Kautsky, like thousands of others, indulged himself in the luxury of revolutionary criticism and bold perspectives: in practice these did not bind him to anything. But when the war and the after-war period brought the problems of revolution onto the field, Kautsky took up his position definitively on the other side of the barricade. Without breaking away from Marxist phraseology he made himself, instead of the champion of the proletarian revolution, the advocate of passivity of a crawling capitulation before Imperialism.

In the period before the war Karl Kautsky and the leaders of the British Labour Party seemed to be standing at opposite poles of the Second International. Our generation, which then was young, in the fight against the opportunism of MacDonald, Henderson, and their brethren, not seldom made use of weapons taken from Kautsky's arsenal. But in truth even in those days we went a great deal further than that wavering and ambiguous teacher was willing to go. Even before the war, Rosa Luxemburg, who had a closer knowledge of Kautsky than others, had ruthlessly exposed the pinchbeck in his radicalism. These last years, anyhow, have thrown a full light on the facts: politically Kautsky belongs to the same camp as Henderson. If the former still goes on quoting from Marx, while the latter chooses rather the psalms of King David, this difference in habits does no harm whatever to their solidarity. All that is essentially uttered in this book against Kautsky can likewise almost unreservedly be applied to the leaders of the British trade union movement and of the Labour Party.

One of the chapters in the book is given to the so-called Austrian school of Marxism (Otto Bauer, Karl Renner, and others). Essentially this school fulfilled the same function: with the help of sterilised formulae from Marxism it gave shelter to a policy of cowering opportunism and, coward-like, it refused to make those bold decisions which were inevitably called for by the course of the class struggle. Events put both Kautskianism and Austrian Marxism to a ruthless test. The once powerful social-democratic parties of Germany and Austria, raised (against their own will) by the revolutionary movement in 1918 to the heights of power, freely yielded up bit by bit their positions to the bourgeoisie, until they were seen to have been ruthlessly crushed by it. The history of these two parties will be found to be a priceless illustration in the question of the part played by revolutionary and counter-revolutionary violence in history.

For the sake of continuity I have kept the title for the book under which the first English edition came out: "The Defence of Terrorism." But it must at once be said here that this title, which is that of the original publishers and not the author's, is too wide and may even give grounds for misunderstanding. What we are concerned with is not at all the defence of "terrorism" as such. Methods of compulsion and terrorisation down to the physical extirpation of its opponents have up to now advantaged, and continue to advantage in an infinitely higher degree the cause of reaction, as represented by the outworn exploiting classes, than they do the cause of historical progress, as represented by the proletariat. The jury of moralists who condemn "terrorism" of whatever kind have their gaze fixed really on the revolutionary deeds of the persecuted who are seeking to set themselves free. The best example of this is Mr. Ramsay MacDonald. In the name of the eternal principles of morality and religion he was unwearied in condemning violence. But when the collapse of the capitalist system and the sharpening of the class struggle made the revolutionary fight of the proletariat for power an actual and living question for England also, MacDonald left the Labour camp for that of the Conservative bourgeoisie with just as little bother as when a passenger changes from a smoking compartment to a non-smoking. To-day the pious enemy of terrorism is keeping up by the help of organized violence a "peaceful" system of unemployment, colonial oppression, armed forces and preparation for fresh wars.

The present work, therefore, is far away from any thought of defending terrorism in general. It champions the historical justification of the proletarian revolution. The root idea of the book is this: that history down to now has not thought out any other way of carrying mankind forward than that of setting up always the revolutionary violence of the progressive class against the conservative violence of the outworn classes.

The incurable Fabians, it is true, keep on saying that, if the arguments of this book are true for backward Russia, they are utterly without application to advanced lands, especially to old democracies like Great Britain. This consoling illusion may have worn a cloak of persuasiveness up to fifteen or ten years ago. But since then a wave of Fascist or militarised police dictatorships has overwhelmed a great part of the European states. The day after I was exiled from the Soviet Union, on February 25, 1929, I wrote— not for the first time, indeed—with reference to the situation in Europe: "Democratic institutions have shown that they cannot withstand the pressure of present-day antagonisms both international and national—more often, both together. . . . On the analogy with electrical science democracy may be defined as a system of safety switches and fuses to guard against too strong currents of national or social hostility. There has never been one period in the history of mankind even within the slightest degree so filled with antagonisms as our own. The overloading of the current shows itself more and more at various points in the European system. Under the too high tension of class and international oppositions the safety switches of democracy fuse or burst. This is the essence of the short-circuit of dictatorship. The first to give way, of course, are the weakest switches. Internal and world oppositions, however, are not losing strength, but growing. It is hardly a ground for consolation that the process has taken hold only of the edge of the capitalistic world; gout begins with the big toe, but, once it has begun, it reaches the heart."

In the six years that have gone by since these lines were written the "short-circuits" of dictatorship have arisen in Germany, Austria, and Spain—in this last after a short-lived revolutionary flowering of democracy. All those democratic illusionary dreamers who tried to explain Italian Fascism as a passing phenomenon that had arisen in a relatively backward land as the result of an after-war psychosis, met with the sternest refutation from the facts themselves. Among the great European countries the parliamentary regime is now left only in France and in England. But after what has happened in Europe anyone would have to be extraordinarily blind if he believes France and England to be safe from civil war and dictatorship. On February 6, 1934, French parliamentarianism was given its first warning.

Extraordinarily superficial is the idea that the comparatively strong resisting power of the British political system arises out of the great age of its parliamentary traditions, and that as the years go on it automatically draws fresh strength from these for resistance. It has nowhere been found that old things, other circumstances being the same, are set firmer than new things. The fact is that British parliamentarianism holds together better than the others amid the crisis of the capitalist system only because their former world domination allowed the ruling classes of Great Britain to heap up an immense wealth, which now goes on lighting up the gloom of their days. In other words: the British parliamentary democracy holds together not through a mystic power of tradition, but from the plump savings which have been handed down from thriving times.

The future lot of British democracy depends not on its inner characteristics, but on the lot of British and world capitalism. If the jugglers and wonder-workers in power were really to find out the secret of giving youth to capitalism there is no doubt that along with it bourgeois democracy would find its own youth again. But we see no grounds for believing in the jugglers and wonder-workers. The last imperialistic war, indeed, came as an expression, and at the same time a proof, of the historical truth that world capitalism has drunk its progressive mission to the last drop. The development of the productive powers comes to rest against two reactionary barriers: private ownership of the means of production and the frontiers of the national state. Unless these two barriers are swept away, that is to say, unless the means of production are

concentrated in the hands of the community, and unless there is
an organized planned economy which can gradually enfold the
whole world, the economic and cultural collapse of mankind is
foredoomed. Further short-circuitings by reactionary dictatorships
would in such a case inevitably spread to Great Britain also; the
successes won by Fascism are seen to be no more than the political
expression of the decay of the capitalist system. In other words:
even in England a political state of things is not impossible wherein
some coxcomb such as Mosley, will be able to play an historical
part like that played by his teachers Mussolini and Hitler.

From the Fabians we may hear it objected that the English
proletariat have it quite in their own hands to come to power by
way of Parliament, to carry through peacefully, within the law
and step by step, all the changes called for in the capitalist system,
and by so doing not only to make revolutionary terrorism needless,
but also to dig the ground away under the feet of counter-revolutionary adventurers. An outlook such as this has at first sight a
particular persuasiveness in the light of the Labour Party's very
important successes in the elections—but only at first sight, and
that a very superficial one. The Fabian hope must, I fear, be held
from the very beginning to be out of the question. I say "I fear,"
since a peaceful, parliamentary change over to a new social structure would undoubtedly offer highly important advantages from
the standpoint of the interests of culture, and therefore those of
socialism. But in politics nothing is more dangerous than to mistake what we wish for what is possible. On the one hand, a victory
for the Labour Party at the elections would by no means bring with
it the immediate concentration of real power in its hands. On the
other hand, the Labour Party does not, indeed, aim at full power,
for, as represented by its leaders, it has no wish to expropriate the
bourgeoisie. Henderson, Lansbury, and the others have nothing
about them of the great social reformers; they are nothing else
than small bourgeois conservatives. We have seen social democracy
in power in Austria and Germany. In England we have twice be-
held a so-called Labour Government. To-day there are social
democratic governments at the head of Denmark and of Sweden.
In all these cases not one hair has fallen from the head of capitalism. A Henderson-Lansbury Government would not differ in the
slightest from a Hermann Müller Government in Germany. It
would not dare to lay a finger on the property of the bourgeoisie,

and would be doomed to try paltry reforms, which, while disappointing the workers, would irritate the bourgeoisie. Far-reaching social reforms cannot be carried out amid the conditions of crumbling capitalism. The workers would be more and more insistent in demanding more determined measures from the Government. In the parliamentary section of the Labour Party the revolutionary wing would split off, the right wing would be drawn more and more openly to a capitulation on the MacDonald pattern. As a counterweight to the Labour Government and a safeguard against revolutionary action by the masses, big capital would set about energetically supporting (this it has already begun to do) the Fascist movement. The Crown, the House of Lords, the bourgeois minority in the House of Commons, the bureaucracy, the military and naval commands, the banks, the trusts, the main body of the Press, would merge into a counterrevolutionary bloc, ever ready to bring up the bands of Mosley or of some other more efficient adventurer to help the regular armed forces. In other words the "parliamentary outlook" would inevitably and fatally lead along the road to civil war, a civil war which, the less the leaders of the Labour Party were ready for it, would threaten the more to take on a long-drawn, embittered, and for the proletariat, unfavourable character.

The conclusion to be drawn from all this is that the British proletariat must not reckon on any historic privileges. It will have to struggle for power by the road of revolution and keep it in its hands by crushing the fierce resistance of the exploiters. There is no other way leading to Socialism. The problems of revolutionary violence, or "terrorism," therefore have their practical interest for England also. That is why I agreed to a new English edition of this book.

At the Geneva conference (1922) the French representative Cobrat stated: "Soviet Russia, which has brought the land to the brink of an economic crash, has no right to teach the other countries Socialism." But to-day he would find it hard to repeat these words. The Soviet Union since then has succeeded in showing in practice how great are the economic possibilities that lie in the nationalisation of the means of production. This proof is the more striking since we have to do with a backward land, and one without any reserves of trained workers and technicians.

At the time of the civil war, when this book was written, the Soviets were still under the flag of "military Communism." This system was not an "illusion"—as the Philistines often maintained afterwards—but an iron necessity. The question was how the wretched resources were to be applied, mainly for the needs of the war, and how production, on however small a scale, was to be kept alive for these same ends and without any possibility of the work being paid for. Military communism fulfilled its mission in so far as it made victory a possibility in the civil war. "Illusions," so far as this word has any application at all here, are rather what we may call those economic hopes which were bound up with the development of the world revolution. The common and inseparable conviction of the whole party at that time was that the speedy victory of the proletariat in the West, beginning with Germany, would reveal vast technical and cultural possibilities, and thereby leave the ground free for a direct passage from military Communism to a Socialistic system of production. The idea of five-year plans was not only formulated in that period, but in some economic departments it was also technically worked out.

The slow development of the revolution in the West brought about a far-reaching change in the economic methods of the Soviets. The period of the New Economic Policy started. It led on the one hand to a general quickening of the economic life, and on the other to a new birth of the small bourgeoisie, especially of the kulaks. The Soviet bureaucracy for the first time felt itself less dependent on the proletariat. It was now standing "between the classes," regulating their relations to one another. At the same time as this it was losing piece by piece its trust and interest in the Western proletariat. It is from the autumn of 1924 that Stalin, in utter contradiction with the party traditions and with what he wrote himself as late as the spring of the same year, puts forward for the first time the theory of "Socialism in one country." Bukharin supplements it by a theory of the "gradual growth of the kulak into Socialism." Stalin and Bukharin go along arm in arm.

The difficulties of the revolution, the deprivations, the sacrifices, the death of the best workers during the civil war, the slow coming of economic successes led in those days to an inevitable reaction among the masses of the population. The loss of hope in the European workers made greater the dependence of the Russian workers on their own bureaucracy. On the other hand the reaction arising out of weariness among the masses favoured a further growth of independence in the machinery of government. Taking its stand on the conservative forces among the small bourgeoisie, and making every use of the defeat of the world proletariat and of the fallen spirit among the Soviet masses, Stalin's section, that staff of the bureaucracy, comes down with a heavy hand on the so-called left opposition ("the Trotskyites"). The October revolution enters on the stage of bureaucratic degeneration.

But the kulak is not at all allured by the vision of a "peaceful growth into Socialism." What he wishes is the restoration of freedom to trade. He accumulates in his hands the wheat supplies and refuses them to the Government. He demands payment against the notes he was given by the bureaucracy during the struggle with the opposition of the left. From an ally he becomes a foe.

The bureaucracy is driven to defend itself. It starts a campaign against the kulak, whose existence it had yesterday denied, and against the right wing of the party, its ally in the struggle with the opposition of the left. The new political course which was set in 1928 threw a strong light on the dependence of the Soviet bureaucracy upon the economic foundations laid by the October revolution. Unwillingly and always struggling, it was forced to take the road of industrialisation and collectivisation. Here for the first time it brings to light those unbounded productive possibilities that are the necessary results of the concentration of the means of production in the hands of the State.

The wonderful, though very uneven, successes of the five-year plan naturally raised the self-confidence of the bureaucracy. The collectivisation of millions of small peasant holdings gave it at the same time a new social basis. The defeats suffered by the world proletariat, the growth of Fascist and Bonapartist dictatorships in Europe all helped towards the success of the doctrine of "Socialism in one country." The bureaucracy succeeded, indeed, in breaking up the Bolshevist Party and the Soviets, too, which were left only in name. The power passed from the masses, from the party, to a centralised bureaucracy; from this to a close supreme authority; and in the end to one man as the embodiment of an unchecked bureaucracy.

Many onlookers are astounded and repelled by the worship of the "leader," which so humiliatingly brings the Soviet system of to-day not far away from Hitler's system. The "party" in Russia and

Germany alike has one, and only one, right: the right to agree with the leader. The party meetings become nothing else than demonstrations of a unanimity that is assured beforehand. In what way is the Soviet order of things better than the Fascist? is the question put by the democrats, the pacifists, the idealists, who are none of them capable of looking below the political superstructure. Without in the slightest wishing to defend the bureaucratic caricature of the Soviet system, we will answer this one-sided criticism of it by pointing to its social basis. Hitler's system is seen to be the last and truly desperate form of self-defence taken by a capitalism rotting to destruction. Stalin's system is seen to be the misshapen bureaucratic form of self-defence taken by a Socialism that is rising. These two are not the same.

In so far as the Soviet bureaucracy is forced in its own interest to preserve the frontiers and the institutions of the Russian Soviet republic against foes without and within, and to give heed to the development of the nationalised productive forces, this bureaucracy is still fulfilling a progressive historical task, and has so far a right to the support of the workers of the world. But the root of the matter is this: that the farther ahead the tasks of economic and cultural construction lie, the less capable are they of being carried through by bureaucratic methods. The distribution of productive forces and materials is now carried out by the authorities under orders from above, without any share by the workers in deciding those questions on which their labor and their life depend. Cases where there is a lack of proportion or ill-adjustment in management grow more and more. The raising of the standard of life among the masses goes on exceedingly slowly and unevenly, and lags far behind technical achievements and the output of energy by the workers. Thus, economic successes, while for a time they strengthen the bureaucratic autocracy, in their further development turn more and more against it.

The Socialistic economy must be directed to ensuring the satisfaction of every possible human need. Such a problem it is impossible to solve by way of commands only. The greater the scale of the productive forces, the more involved the technique; the more complex the needs, then the more indispensable is a wide and free creative initiative of the organized producers and consumers. The Socialist culture implies the utmost development of the human personality. Progress along this path is made possible not through a standardised cringing before irresponsible "leaders," but only through a fully conscious and critical participation by all in a Socialistic creative activity. The youthful generations stand in need of independence, which is wholly consistent with a firm leadership but rules out any police regimentation. Thus the bureaucratic system in crushing the Soviets and the party is coming ever more clearly into opposition with the basic needs of economic and cultural development.

The workers' state has come into existence for the first time in history. Neither its forms and methods, nor the stages it must go through could be, and they cannot now be, laid down beforehand. Bourgeois society developed itself in the course of centuries and came into power by stepping into the place of scores of political systems. There are good grounds for believing that the Socialist society will reach its full development by an incomparably shorter and more economical road. But it would, anyhow, be a poor kind of illusion to imagine that an "enlightened bureaucracy" is capable of leading mankind by the bridle in a straight line to Socialism. The workers' state will more than once again reform its methods before it becomes dissolved in a Communist society. The great historical reform whose turn has now come demands that the Soviet state be set free from bureaucratic absolutism; in other words: the restoration of the creative character of the Soviets on new and deeper economic and cultural foundations. This task cannot be carried through unless the working masses take up the fight against the usurping bureaucracy.

The historical part played by government violence naturally changes along with changes in the character of the workers' state. So far as bureaucratic violence, however grim it may sometimes be, is defending the social foundations of the new system, it is historically justified. But to defend the Soviet state and to defend the positions of bureaucracy within the Soviet state is not one and the same thing. As time goes on the bureaucracy has recourse more and more cynically to terror against the party and the working class, so as to defend its economic and political privileges. Its object, of course, is to make its caste defence look like the defence of the highest interests of Socialism. Hence comes the ever-growing falseness of the official ideology, the repulsive worship of the leaders, and the downright deception of the working masses through political and legal forgeries.

It is the policy of the Soviet bureaucracy in relation to the international proletariat that has a peculiarly criminal character. Having in reality long ago given up any hopes for a world revolution, the bureaucracy is keeping sections of the Communist International in a purely military subordination, and turning them into auxiliary instruments for its diplomacy. The revolutionary defence of the Soviet Union has long been exchanged for the lawyers' defence of all the actions of the ruling Soviet heads. The leaders of the Comintern more and more show themselves to the workers as officials independent of the masses.

The German Communist party, which had seemed so imposing, was found, when it was brought against real danger, to be a political cipher. Blind obedience is not a thing to be proud of in a revolutionary. The Comintern has been robbed of life, personality, and soul. If in England in spite of the highly favourable conditions, the Communist party is still an organization without importance, without influence, without authority, and without a future, then the responsibility for this lies above all with the Soviet bureaucracy.

Everything in England is heading for a revolutionary explosion. A happy issue from the economic crisis—and this is quite a possibility in itself and even inevitable—could never have more than a transitory character, and would quickly yield once more to a fresh and devastating crisis. There is no way to salvation through capitalism. The coming into power of the Labour party will have only this meaning for progress, that once more it will show—infinitely clearer even than before—the bankruptcy of the methods and illusions of parliamentarianism amidst the crumbling ruins of the capitalist system. And so the absolute need for a new, a truly revolutionary party will stand forth clear-cut before our eyes. The British proletariat will enter upon a period of political crisis and theoretical criticism. The problems of revolutionary violence will stand in their full height before it. The teachings of Marx and Lenin for the first time will find the masses as their audience. Such being the case, it may be also that the present book will turn out to be not without its use.

January 10, 1935

CONTENTS

Introduction

THE origin of this book was the learned brochure by Kautsky with the same name. My work was begun at the most intense period of the struggle with Denikin and Yudenich, and more than once was interrupted by events at the front. In the most difficult days, when the first chapters were being written, all the attention of Soviet Russia was concentrated on purely military problems. We were obliged to defend first of all the very possibility of Socialist economic reconstruction. We could busy ourselves little with industry, further than was necessary to maintain the front. We were obliged to expose Kautsky's economic slanders mainly by analogy with his political slanders. The monstrous assertions of Kaustky—to the effect that the Russian workers were incapable of labor discipline and economic self-control—could, at the beginning of this work, nearly a year ago, be combatted chiefly by pointing to the high state of discipline and heroism in battle of the Russian workers at the front created by the civil war. That experience was more than enough to explode these bourgeois slanders. But now a few months have gone by, and we can turn to facts and conclusions drawn directly from the economic life of Soviet Russia.

As soon as the military pressure relaxed after the defeat of Kolchak and Yudenich and the infliction of decisive blows on Denikin, after the conclusion of peace with Esthonia and the beginning of negotiations with Lithuania and Poland, the whole country turned its mind to things economic. And this one fact, of a swift and concentrated transference of attention and energy from one set of problems to another—very different, but requiring not less sacrifice—is incontro-

vertible evidence of the mighty vigor of the Soviet order.
In spite of political tortures, physical sufferings and horrors,
the laboring masses are infinitely distant from political decomposition, from moral collapse, or from apathy. Thanks to
a regime which, though it has inflicted great hardships upon
them, has given their life a purpose and a high goal, they
preserve an extraordinary moral stubbornness and ability
unexampled in history, and concentrate their attention and
will on collective problems. To-day, in all branches of industry, there is going on an energetic struggle for the establishment of strict labor discipline, and for the increase of the
productivity of labor. The party organizations, the trade
unions, the factory and workshop administrative committees,
rival one another in this respect, with the undivided support
of the public opinion of the working class as a whole. Factory
after factory willingly, by resolution at its general meeting,
increases its working day. Petrograd and Moscow set the
example, and the provinces emulate Petrograd. Communist
Saturdays and Sundays—that is to say, voluntary and unpaid
work in hours appointed for rest—spread ever wider and wider,
drawing into their reach many, many hundreds of thousands
of working men and women. The industry and productivity
of labor at the Communist Saturdays and Sundays, according
to the report of experts and the evidence of figures, is of a
remarkably high standard.

Voluntary mobilizations for labor problems in the party
and in the Young Communist League are carried out with
just as much enthusiasm as hitherto for military tasks. Voluntarism supplements and gives life to universal labor service.
The Committees for universal labor service recently set up
have spread all over the country. The attraction of the population to work on a mass scale (clearing snow from the roads,
repairing railway lines, cutting timber, chopping and bringing
up of wood to the towns, the simplest building operations,
the cutting of slate and of peat) become more and more widespread and organized every day. The ever increasing employment of military formations on the labor front would be
quite impossible in the absence of elevated enthusiasm for
labor.

True, we live in the midst of a very difficult period of

economic depression—exhausted, poverty-stricken, and hungry. But this is no argument against the Soviet regime. All periods of transition have been characterized by just such tragic features. Every class society (serf, feudal, capitalist), having exhausted its vitality, does not simply leave the arena, but is violently swept off by an intense struggle, which immediately brings to its participants even greater privations and sufferings than those against which they rose.

The transition from feudal economy to bourgeois society—a step of gigantic importance from the point of view of progress—gave us a terrifying list of martyrs. However the masses of serfs suffered under feudalism, however difficult it has been, and is, for the proletariat to live under capitalism, never have the sufferings of the workers reached such a pitch as at the epochs when the old feudal order was being violently shattered, and was yielding place to the new. The French Revolution of the eighteenth century, which attained its titanic dimensions under the pressure of the masses exhausted with suffering, itself deepened and rendered more acute their misfortunes for a prolonged period and to an extraordinary extent. Can it be otherwise?

Palace revolutions, which end merely by personal reshufflings at the top, can take place in a short space of time, having practically no effect on the economic life of the country. Quite another matter are revolutions which drag into their whirlpool millions of workers. Whatever be the form of society, it rests on the foundation of labor. Dragging the mass of the people away from labor, drawing them for a prolonged period into the struggle, thereby destroying their connection with production, the revolution in all these ways strikes deadly blows at economic life, and inevitably lowers the standard which it found at its birth. The more perfect the revolution, the greater are the masses it draws in; and the longer it is prolonged, the greater is the destruction it achieves in the apparatus of production, and the more terrible inroads does it make upon public resources. From this there follows merely the conclusion which did not require proof—that a civil war is harmful to economic life. But to lay this at the door of the Soviet economic system is like accusing a new-born human being of the birth-pangs of the mother who brought him into the world. The problem is to make a civil war a short one; and this is attained only by resoluteness in action. But it is just against revolutionary resoluteness that Kautsky's whole book is directed.

* * *

Since the time that the book under examination appeared, not only in Russia, but throughout the world—and first of all in Europe—the greatest events have taken place, or processes of great importance have developed, undermining the last buttresses of Kautskianism.

In Germany, the civil war has been adopting an ever fiercer character. The external strength in organization of the old party and trade union democracy of the working class has not only not created conditions for a more peaceful and "humane" transition to Socialism—as follows from the present theory of Kautsky—but, on the contrary, has served as one of the principal reasons for the long-drawn-out character of the struggle, and its constantly growing ferocity. The more German Social-Democracy became a conservative, retarding force, the more energy, lives, and blood have had to be spent by the German proletariat, devoted to it, in a series of systematic attacks on the foundation of bourgeois society, in order, in the process of the struggle itself, to create an actually revolutionary organization, capable of guiding the proletariat to final victory. The conspiracy of the German generals, their fleeting seizure of power, and the bloody events which followed, have again shown what a worthless and wretched masquerade is so-called democracy, during the collapse of imperialism and a civil war. This democracy that has outlived itself has not decided one question, has not reconciled one contradiction, has not healed one wound, has not warded off risings either of the Right or of the Left; it is helpless, worthless, fraudulent, and serves only to confuse the backward sections of the people, especially the lower middle classes.

The hope expressed by Kautsky, in the conclusion of his book, that the Western countries, the "old democracies" of France and England—crowned as they are with victory—will afford us a picture of a healthy, normal, peaceful, truly Kautskian development of Socialism, is one of the most puerile illusions possible. The so-called Republican democracy of victorious France, at the present moment, is nothing but the most reactionary, grasping government that has ever existed in the world. Its internal policy is built upon fear, greed, and violence, in just as great a measure as its external policy. On the other hand, the French proletariat, misled more than any other class has ever been misled, is more and more entering on the path of direct action. The repressions which the government of the Republic has hurled upon the General Confederation of Labor show that even syndicalist Kautskianism—*i.e.*, hypocritical compromise—has no legal place within the framework of bourgeois democracy. The revolutionizing of the masses, the growing ferocity of the propertied classes, and the disintegration of intermediate groups—three parallel processes which determine the character and herald the coming of a cruel civil war—have been going on before our eyes in full blast during the last few months in France.

In Great Britain, events, different in form, are moving along the self-same fundamental road. In that country, the ruling class of which is oppressing and plundering the whole world more than ever before, the formulæ of democracy have lost their meaning even as weapons of parliamentary swindling. The specialist best qualified in this sphere, Lloyd George, appeals now not to democracy, but to a union of Conservative and Liberal property holders against the working class. In his arguments there remains not a trace of the vague democracy of the "Marxist" Kautsky. Lloyd George stands on the ground of class realities, and for this very reason speaks in the language of civil war. The British working class, with that ponderous learning by experience which is its distinguishing feature, is approaching that stage of its struggle before which the most heroic pages of Chartism will fade, just as the Paris Commune will grow pale before the coming victorious revolt of the French proletariat.

Precisely because historical events have, with stern energy, been developing in these last months their revolutionary logic, the author of this present work asks himself: Does it still require to be published? Is it still necessary to confute Kautsky theoretically? Is there still theoretical necessity to justify revolutionary terrorism?

Unfortunately, yes. Ideology, by its very essence, plays

in the Socialist movement an enormous part. Even for practical England the period has arrived when the working class must exhibit an ever-increasing demand for a theoretical statement of its experiences and its problems. On the other hand, even the proletarian psychology includes in itself a terrible inertia of conservatism—the more that, in the present case, there is a question of nothing less than the traditional ideology of the parties of the Second International which first roused the proletariat, and recently were so powerful. After the collapse of official social-patriotism (Scheidemann, Victor Adler, Renaudel, Vandervelde, Henderson, Plekhanov, etc.), international Kautskianism (the staff of the German Independents, Friedrich Adler, Longuet, a considerable section of the Italians, the British Independent Labor Party, the Martov group, etc.) has become the chief political factor on which the unstable equilibrium of capitalist society depends. It may be said that the will of the working masses of the whole of the civilized world, directly influenced by the course of events, is at the present moment incomparably more revolutionary than their consciousness, which is still dominated by the prejudices of parliamentarism and compromise. The struggle for the dictatorship of the working class means, at the present moment, an embittered struggle with Kautskianism within the working class. The lies and prejudices of the policy of compromise, still poisoning the atmosphere even in parties tending towards the Third International, must be thrown aside. This book must serve the ends of an irreconcilable struggle against the cowardice, half-measures, and hypocrisy of Kautskianism in all countries.

* * *

P. S.—To-day (May, 1920) the clouds have again gathered over Soviet Russia. Bourgeois Poland, by its attack on the Ukraine, has opened the new offensive of world imperialism against the Soviet Republic. The gigantic perils again growing up before the revolution, and the great sacrifices again imposed on the laboring masses by the war, are once again pushing Russian Kautskianism on to the path of open opposition to the Soviet Government—i.e., in reality, on to the path of assistance to the world murderers of Soviet Russia. It is the fate of Kautskianism to try to help the proletarian revolution when it is in satisfactory circumstances, and to raise all kinds of obstacles in its way when it is particularly in need of help. Kautsky has more than once foretold our destruction, which must serve as the best proof of his, Kautsky's, theoretical rectitude. In his fall, this "successor of Marx" has reached a stage at which his sole serious political programme consists in speculations on the collapse of the proletarian dictatorship.

He will be once again mistaken. The destruction of bourgeois Poland by the Red Army, guided by Communist working men, will appear as a new manifestation of the power of the proletarian distatorship, and will thereby inflict a crushing blow on bourgeois scepticism (Kautskianism) in the working class movement. In spite of mad confusion of external forms, watchwords, and appearances, history has extremely simplified the fundamental meaning of its own process, reducing it to a struggle of imperialism against Communism. Pilsudsky is fighting, not only for the lands of the Polish magnates in the Ukraine and in White Russia, not only for capitalist property and for the Catholic Church, but also for parliamentary democracy and for evolutionary Socialism, for the Second International, and for the right of Kautsky to remain a critical hanger-on of the bourgeoisie. We are fighting for the Communist International, and for the international proletarian revolution. The stakes are great on either side. The struggle will be obstinate and painful. We hope for the victory, for we have every historical right to it.

L. TROTSKY.

Moscow, May 29, 1920.

Terrorism and Communism

A Reply to Karl Kautsky

By LEON TROTSKY

I

THE BALANCE OF POWER

THE argument which is repeated again and again in
criticisms of the Soviet system in Russia, and particularly in criticisms of revolutionary attempts to set
up a similar structure in other countries, is the argument based
on the balance of power. The Soviet regime in Russia is
utopian—"because it does not correspond to the balance of
power." Backward Russia cannot put objects before itself
which would be appropriate to advanced Germany. And for
the proletariat of Germany it would be madness to take political
power into its own hands, as this "at the present moment"
would disturb the balance of power. The League of Nations
is imperfect, but still corresponds to the balance of power.
The struggle for the overthrow of imperialist supremacy is
utopian—the balance of power only requires a revision of
the Versailles Treaty. When Longuet hobbled after Wilson
this took place, not because of the political decomposition of
Longuet, but in honor of the law of the balance of power.
The Austrian president, Seitz, and the chancellor, Renner,
must, in the opinion of Friedrich Adler, exercise their bourgeois impotence at the central posts of the bourgeois republic,
for otherwise the balance of power would be infringed. Two

years before the world war, Karl Renner, then not a chancellor, but a "Marxist" advocate of opportunism, explained to me that the regime of June 3—that is, the union of landlords and capitalists crowned by the monarchy—must inevitably maintain itself in Russia during a whole historical period, as it answered to the balance of power.

What is this balance of power after all—that sacramental formula which is to define, direct, and explain the whole course of history, wholesale and retail? Why exactly is it that the formula of the balance of power, in the mouth of Kautsky and his present school, inevitably appears as a justification of indecision, stagnation, cowardice and treachery?

By the balance of power they understand everything you please: the level of production attained, the degree of differentiation of classes, the number of organized workers, the total funds at the disposal of the trade unions, sometimes the results of the last parliamentary elections, frequently the degree of readiness for compromise on the part of the ministry, or the degree of effrontery of the financial oligarchy. Most frequently, it means that summary political impression which exists in the mind of a half-blind pedant, or a so-called realist politician, who, though he has absorbed the phraseology of Marxism, in reality is guided by the most shallow manœuvres, bourgeois prejudices, and parliamentary "tactics." After a whispered conversation with the director of the police department, an Austrian Social-Democratic politician in the good, and not so far off, old times always knew exactly whether the balance of power permitted a peaceful street demonstration in Vienna on May Day. In the case of the Eberts, Scheidemanns and Davids, the balance of power was, not so very long ago, calculated exactly by the number of fingers which were extended to them at their meeting in the Reichstag with Bethmann-Hollweg, or with Ludendorff himself.

According to Friedrich Adler, the establishment of a Soviet dictatorship in Austria would be a fatal infraction of the balance of power; the Entente would condemn Austria to starvation. In proof of this, Friedrich Adler, at the July congress of Soviets, pointed to Hungary, where at that time the Hungarian Renners had not yet, with the help of the Hungarian Adlers, overthrown the dictatorship of the Soviets.

At the first glance, it might really seem that Friedrich Adler was right in the case of Hungary. The proletarian dictatorship was overthrown there soon afterwards, and its place was filled by the ministry of the reactionary Friedrich. But it is quite justifiable to ask: Did the latter correspond to the balance of power? At all events, Friedrich and his Huszar might not even temporarily have seized power had it not been for the Roumanian army. Hence, it is clear that, when discussing the fate of the Soviet Government in Hungary, it is necessary to take account of the "balance of power," at all events in two countries—in Hungary itself, and in its neighbor, Roumania. But it is not difficult to grasp that we cannot stop at this. If the dictatorship of the Soviets had been set up in Austria before the maturing of the Hungarian crisis, the overthrow of the Soviet regime in Budapest would have been an infinitely more difficult task. Consequently, we have to include Austria also, together with the treacherous policy of Friedrich Adler, in that balance of power which determined the temporary fall of the Soviet Government in Hungary.

Friedrich Adler himself, however, seeks the key to the balance of power, not in Russia and Hungary, but in the West, in the countries of Clemenceau and Lloyd George. They have in their hands bread and coal—and really bread and coal, especially in our time, are just as foremost factors in the mechanism of the balance of power as cannon in the constitution of Lassalle. Brought down from the heights, Adler's idea consists, consequently, in this: that the Austrian proletariat must not seize power until such time as it is permitted to do so by Clemenceau (or Millerand—*i.e.*, a Clemenceau of the second order).

However, even here it is permissible to ask: Does the policy of Clemenceau himself really correspond to the balance of power? At the first glance it may appear that it corresponds well enough, and, if it cannot be proved, it is, at least, guaranteed by Clemenceau's gendarmes, who break up working-class meetings, and arrest and shoot Communists. But here we cannot but remember that the terrorist measures of the Soviet Government—that is, the same searches, arrests, and executions, only directed against the counter-revolutionaries—are considered by some people as a proof that the Soviet Government does *not* correspond to the balance of power. In vain would we, however, begin to seek in our time, anywhere in the world, a regime which, to preserve itself, did not have recourse to measures of stern mass repression. This means that hostile class forces, having broken through the framework of every kind of law—including that of "democracy"—are striving to find their new balance by means of a merciless struggle.

When the Soviet system was being instituted in Russia, not only the capitalist politicians, but also the Socialist opportunists of all countries proclaimed it an insolent challenge to the balance of forces. On this score, there was no quarrel between Kautsky, the Austrian Count Czernin, and the Bulgarian Premier, Radoslavov. Since that time, the Austro-Hungarian and German monarchies have collapsed, and the most powerful militarism in the world has fallen into dust. The Soviet regime has held out. The victorious countries of the Entente have mobilized and hurled against it all they could. The Soviet Government has stood firm. Had Kautsky, Friedrich Adler, and Otto Bauer been told that the system of the dictatorship of the proletariat would hold out in Russia—first against the attack of German militarism, and then in a ceaseless war with the militarism of the Entente countries—the sages of the Second International would have considered such a prophecy a laughable misunderstanding of the "balance of power."

The balance of political power at any given moment is determined under the influence of fundamental and secondary factors of differing degrees of effectiveness, and only in its most fundamental quality is it determined by the stage of the development of production. The social structure of a people is extraordinarily behind the development of its productive forces. The lower middle classes, and particularly the peasantry, retain their existence long after their economic methods have been made obsolete, and have been condemned, by the technical development of the productive powers of society. The consciousness of the masses, in its turn, is extraordinarily behind the development of their social relations, the consciousness of the old Socialist parties is a whole epoch behind the state of mind of the masses, and the consciousness of the old parliamentary and trade union leaders, more reactionary than the consciousness of their party, represents a petrified mass which history has been unable hitherto either to digest or reject. In the parliamentary epoch, during the period of stability of social relations, the psychological factor—without great error—was the foundation upon which all current calculations were based. It was considered that parliamentary elections reflected the balance of power with sufficient exactness. The imperialist war, which upset all bourgeois society, displayed the complete uselessness of the old criteria. The latter completely ignored those profound historical factors which had gradually been accumulating in the preceeding period, and have now, all at once, appeared on the surface, and have begun to determine the course of history.

The political worshippers of routine, incapable of surveying the historical process in its complexity, in its internal clashes and contradictions, imagined to themselves that history was preparing the way for the Socialist order simultaneously and systematically on all sides, so that concentration of production and the development of a Communist morality in the producer and the consumer mature simultaneously with the electric plough and a parliamentary majority. Hence the purely mechanical attitude towards parliamentarism, which, in the eyes of the majority of the statesmen of the Second International, indicated the degree to which society was prepared for Socialism as accurately as the manometer indicates the pressure of steam. Yet there is nothing more senseless than this mechanized representation of the development of social relations.

If, beginning with the productive bases of society, we ascend the stages of the superstructure—classes, the State, laws, parties, and so on—it may be established that the weight of each additional part of the superstructure is not simply to be added to, but in many cases to be multiplied by, the weight of all the preceding stages. As a result, the political consciousness of groups which long imagined themselves to be among the most advanced, displays itself, at a moment of change, as a colossal obstacle in the path of historical development. To-day it is quite beyond doubt that the parties of the

Second International, standing at the head of the proletariat, which dared not, could not, and would not take power into their hands at the most critical moment of human history, and which led the proletariat along the road of mutual destruction in the interests of imperialism, proved a *decisive factor* of the counter-revolution.

The great forces of production—that shock factor in historical development—were choked in those obsolete institutions of the superstructure (private property and the national State) in which they found themselves locked by all preceding development. Engendered by capitalism, the forces of production were knocking at all the walls of the bourgeois national State, demanding their emancipation by means of the Socialist organization of economic life on a world scale. The stagnation of social groupings, the stagnation of political forces, which proved themselves incapable of destroying the old class groupings, the stagnation, stupidity and treachery of the directing Socialist parties, which had assumed to themselves in reality the defense of bourgeois society—all these factors led to an elemental revolt of the forces of production, in the shape of the imperialist war. Human technical skill, the most revolutionary factor in history, arose with the might accumulated during scores of years against the disgusting conservatism and criminal stupidity of the Scheidemanns, Kautskies, Renaudels, Vanderveldes and Longuets, and, by means of its howitzers, machine-guns, dreadnoughts and aeroplanes, it began a furious pogrom of human culture.

In this way the cause of the misfortunes at present experienced by humanity is precisely that the development of the technical command of men over nature has *long ago* grown ripe for the socialization of economic life. The proletariat has occupied a place in production which completely guarantees its dictatorship, while the most intelligent forces in history—the parties and their leaders—have been discovered to be still wholly under the yoke of the old prejudices, and only fostered a lack of faith among the masses in their own power. In quite recent years Kautsky used to understand this. "The proletariat at the present time has grown so strong," wrote Kautsky in his pamphlet, *The Path to Power*, "that it can calmly await the coming war. There can be no more talk of a *premature revolution,* now that the proletariat has drawn from the present structure of the State such strength as could be drawn therefrom, and now that its reconstruction has become a condition of the proletariat's further progress." From the moment that the development of productive forces, outgrowing the framework of the bourgeois national State, drew mankind into an epoch of crises and convulsions, the consciousness of the masses was shaken by dread shocks out of the comparative equilibrium of the preceding epoch. The routine and stagnation of its mode of living, the hypnotic suggestion of peaceful legality, had already ceased to dominate the proletariat. But it had not yet stepped, consciously and courageously, on to the path of open revolutionary struggle. It wavered, passing through the last moment of unstable equilibrium. At such a moment of psychological change, the part played by the summit—the State, on the one hand, and the revolutionary Party on the other—acquires a colossal importance. A determined push from left or right is sufficient to move the proletariat, for a certain period, to one or the other side. We saw this in 1914, when, under the united pressure of imperialist governments and Socialist patriotic parties, the working class was all at once thrown out of its equilibrium and hurled on to the path of imperialism. We have since seen how the experience of the war, the contrasts between its results and its first objects, is shaking the masses in a revolutionary sense, making them more and more capable of an open revolt against capitalism. In such conditions, the presence of a revolutionary party, which renders to itself a clear account of the motive forces of the present epoch, and understands the exceptional role amongst them of a revolutionary class; which knows its inexhaustible, but unrevealed, powers; which believes in that class and believes in itself; which knows the power of revolutionary method in an epoch of instability of all social relations; which is ready to employ that method and carry it through to the end—the presence of such a party represents a factor of incalculable historical importance.

And, on the other hand, the Socialist party, enjoying traditional influence, which does *not* render itself an account of what is going on around it, which does *not* understand the revolutionary situation, and, therefore, finds no key to it, which does *not* believe in either the proletariat or itself—such a party in our time is the most mischievous stumbling block in history, and a source of confusion and inevitable chaos.

Such is now the role of Kautsky and his sympathizers. They teach the proletariat not to believe in itself, but to believe its reflection in the crooked mirror of democracy which has been shattered by the jack-boot of militarism into a thousand fragments. The decisive factor in the revolutionary policy of the working class must be, in their view, not the international situation, not the actual collapse of capitalism, not that social collapse which is generated thereby, not that concrete necessity of the supremacy of the working class for which the cry arises from the smoking ruins of capitalist civilization—not all this must determine the policy of the revolutionary party of the proletariat—but that counting of votes which is carried out by the capitalist tellers of parliamentarism. Only a few years ago, we repeat, Kautsky seemed to understand the real inner meaning of the problem of revolution. "Yes, the proletariat represents the sole revolutionary class of the nation," wrote Kautsky in his pamphlet, *The Path to Power*. It follows that every collapse of the capitalist crder, whether it be of a moral, financial, or military character, implies the bankruptcy of all the bourgeois parties responsible for it, and signifies that the sole way out of the blind alley is the establishment of the power of the *proletariat*. And to-day the party of prostration and cowardice, the party of Kautsky, says to the working class: "The question is not whether you to-day are the sole creative force in history; whether you are capable of throwing aside that ruling band of robbers into which the propertied classes have developed; the question is not whether anyone else can accomplish this task on your behalf; the question is not whether history allows you any postponement (for the present condition of bloody chaos threatens to bury you yourself, in the near future, under the last ruins of capitalism). The problem is for the ruling imperialist bandits to succeed—yesterday or to-day—to deceive, violate, and swindle public opinion, by collecting 51 per cent. of the votes against your 49. Perish the world, but long live the parliamentary majority!"

2

The Dictatorship of the Proletariat

"MARX and Engels hammered out the idea of the dictatorship of the proletariat, which Engels stubbornly defended in 1891, shortly before his death—the idea that the political autocracy of the proletariat is the sole form in which it can realize its control of the state."

That is what Kautsky wrote about ten years ago. The sole form of power for the proletariat he considered to be not a Socialist majority in a democratic parliament, but the political autocracy of the proletariat, its dictatorship. And it is quite clear that, if our problem is the abolition of private property in the means of production, the only road to its solution lies through the concentration of State power in its entirety in the hands of the proletariat, and the setting up for the transitional period of an exceptional regime—a regime in which the ruling class is guided, not by general principles calculated for a prolonged period, but by considerations of revolutionary policy.

The dictatorship is necessary because it is a case, not of partial changes, but of the very existence of the bourgeoisie. No agreement is possible on this ground. Only force can be the deciding factor. The dictatorship of the proletariat does not exclude, of course, either separate agreements, or considerable concessions, especially in connection with the lower middle class and the peasantry. But the proletariat can only conclude these agreements after having gained possession of the apparatus of power, and having guaranteed to itself the possibility of independently deciding on which points to yield and on which to stand firm, in the interests of the general Socialist task.

Kautsky now repudiates the dictatorship of the proletariat

at the very outset, as the "tyranny of the minority over the majority." That is, he discerns in the revolutionary regime of the proletariat those very features by which the honest Socialists of all countries invariably describe the dictatorship of the exploiters, albeit masked by the forms of democracy.

Abandoning the idea of a revolutionary dictatorship, Kautsky transforms the question of the conquest of power by the proletariat into a question of the conquest of a majority of votes by the Social-Democratic Party in one of the electoral campaigns of the future. Universal suffrage, according to the legal fiction of parliamentarism, expresses the will of the citizens of all classes in the nation, and, consequently, gives a possibility of attracting a majority to the side of Socialism. While the theoretical possibility has not been realized, the Socialist minority must submit to the bourgeois majority. This fetishism of the parliamentary majority represents a brutal repudiation, not only of the dictatorship of the proletariat, but of Marxism and of the revolution altogether. If, in principle, we are to subordinate Socialist policy to the parliamentary mystery of majority and minority, it follows that, in countries where formal democracy prevails, there is no place at all for the revolutionary struggle. If the majority elected on the basis of universal suffrage in Switzerland pass draconian legislation against strikers, or if the executive elected by the will of a formal majority in Northern America shoots workers, have the Swiss and American workers the "right" of protest by organizing a general strike? Obviously, no. The political strike is a form of extra-parliamentary pressure on the "national will," as it has expressed itself through universal suffrage. True, Kautsky himself, apparently, is ashamed to go as far as the logic of his new position demands. Bound by some sort of remnant of the past, he is obliged to acknowledge the possibility of correcting universal suffrage by action. Parliamentary elections, at all events in principle, never took the place, in the eyes of the Social-Democrats, of the real class struggle, of its conflicts, repulses, attacks, revolts; they were considered merely as a contributory fact in this struggle, playing a greater part at one period, a smaller at another, and no part at all in the period of dictatorship.

In 1891, that is, not long before his death, Engels, as
we just heard, obstinately defended the dictatorship of the
proletariat as the only possible form of its control of the
State. Kautsky himself more than once repeated this definition. Hence, by the way, we can see what an unworthy forgery
is Kautsky's present attempt to throw back the dictatorship
of the proletariat at us as a purely Russian invention.

Who aims at the end cannot reject the means. The
struggle must be carried on with such intensity as actually to
guarantee the supremacy of the proletariat. If the Socialist
revolution requires a dictatorship—"the sole form in which
the proletariat can achieve control of the State"—it follows
that the dictatorship must be guaranteed at all cost.

To write a pamphlet about dictatorship one needs an ink-
pot and a pile of paper, and possibly, in addition, a certain
number of ideas in one's head. But in order to establish and
consolidate the dictatorship, one has to prevent the bourgeoisie
from undermining the State power of the proletariat. Kautsky
apparently thinks that this can be achieved by tearful pam-
phlets. But his own experience ought to have shown him
that it is not sufficient to have lost all influence with the
proletariat, to acquire influence with the bourgeoisie.

It is only possible to safeguard the supremacy of the
working class by forcing the bourgeoisie accustomed to rule,
to realize that it is too dangerous an undertaking for it to
revolt against the dictatorship of the proletariat, to undermine it by conspiracies, sabotage, insurrections, or the calling
in of foreign troops. The bourgeoisie, hurled from power,
must be forced to obey. In what way? The priests used to
terrify the people with future penalties. We have no such
resources at our disposal. But even the priests' hell never
stood alone, but was always bracketed with the material fire
of the Holy Inquisition, and with the scorpions of the democratic State. Is it possible that Kautsky is leaning to the
idea that the bourgeoisie can be held down with the help
of the categorical imperative, which in his last writings plays
the part of the Holy Ghost? We, on our part, can only promise
him our material assistance if he decides to equip a Kantian-
humanitarian mission to the realms of Denikin and Kolchak.
At all events, there he would have the possibility of convincing

himself that the counter-revolutionaries are not naturally devoid of character, and that, thanks to their six years' existence in the fire and smoke of war, their character has managed to become thoroughly hardened. Every White Guard has long ago acquired the simple truth that it is easier to hang a Communist to the branch of a tree than to convert him with a book of Kautsky's. These gentlemen have no superstitious fear, either of the principles of democracy or of the flames of hell—the more so because the priests of the church and of official learning act in collusion with them, and pour their combined thunders exclusively on the heads of the Bolsheviks. The Russian White Guards resemble the German and all other White Guards in this respect—that they cannot be convinced or shamed, but only terrorized or crushed.

The man who repudiates terrorism in principle—*i.e.*, repudiates measures of suppression and intimidation towards determined and armed counter-revolution, must reject all idea of the political supremacy of the working class and its revolutionary dictatorship. The man who repudiates the dictatorship of the proletariat repudiates the Socialist revolution, and digs the grave of Socialism.

* * *

At the present time, Kautsky has no theory of the social revolution. Every time he tries to generalize his slanders against the revolution and the dictatorship of the proletariat, he produces merely a réchauffé of the prejudices of Jaurèsism and Bernsteinism.

"The revolution of 1789," writes Kaustky, "itself put an end to the most important causes which gave it its harsh and violent character, and prepared the way for milder forms of the future revolution." (Page 140.)* Let us admit this, though to do so we have to forget the June days of 1848 and the horrors of the suppression of the Commune. Let us admit that the great revolution of the eighteenth century,

---

* Translator's Note—For convenience sake, the references throughout have been altered to fall in the English translation of Kautsky's book. Mr. Kerridge's translation, however, has not been adhered to.

which by measures of merciless terror destroyed the rule of absolutism, of feudalism, and of clericalism, really prepared the way for more peaceful and milder solutions of social problems. But, even if we admit this purely liberal standpoint, even here our accuser will prove to be completely in the wrong; for the Russian Revolution, which culminated in the dictatorship of the proletariat, began with just that work which was done in France at the end of the eighteenth century. Our forefathers, in centuries gone by, did not take the trouble to prepare the democractic way—by means of revolutionary terrorism—for milder manners in our revolution. The ethical mandarin, Kautsky, ought to take these circumstances into account, and accuse our forefathers, not us.

Kautsky, however, seems to make a little concession in this direction. "True," he says, "no man of insight could doubt that a military monarchy like the German, the Austrian, or the Russian could be overthrown only by violent methods. But in this connection there was always less thought" (amongst whom?). "of the bloody use of arms, and more of the working class weapon peculiar to the proletariat—the mass strike. And that a considerable portion of the proletariat, after seizing power, would again—as at the end of the eighteenth century—give vent to its rage and revenge in bloodshed could not be expected. This would have meant a complete negation of all progress." (Page 147.)

As we see, the war and a series of revolutions were required to enable us to get a proper view of what was going on in reality in the heads of some of our most learned theoreticians. It turns out that Kautsky did not think that a Romanoff or a Hohenzollern could be put away by means of conversations; but at the same time he seriously imagined that a military monarchy could be overthrown by a general strike—*i.e.*, by a peaceful demonstration of folded arms. In spite of the Russian revolution, and the world discussion of this question, Kautsky, it turns out, retains the anarcho-reformist view of the general strike. We might point out to him that, in the pages of its own journal, the *Neue Zeit*, it was explained twelve years ago that the general strike is only a mobilization of the proletariat and its setting up against its enemy, the State; but that the strike in itself cannot produce the solution of the problem, because it exhausts the forces of the proletariat sooner than those of its enemies, and this, sooner or later, forces the workers to return to the factories. The general strike acquires a decisive importance only as a preliminary to a conflict between the proletariat and the armed forces of the opposition—*i.e.*, to the open revolutionary rising of the workers. Only by breaking the will of the armies thrown against it can the revolutionary class solve the problem of power—the root problem of every revolution. The general strike produces the mobilization of both sides, and gives the first serious estimate of the powers of resistance of the counter-revolution. But only in the further stages of the struggle, after the transition to the path of armed insurrection, can that bloody price be fixed which the revolutionary class has to pay for power. But that it will have to pay with blood, that, in the struggle for the conquest of power and for its consolidation, the proletariat will have not only to be killed, but also to kill—of this no serious revolutionary ever had any doubt. To announce that the existence of a determined life-and-death struggle between the proletariat and the bourgeoisie "is a complete negation of all progress," means simply that the heads of some of our most reverend theoreticians take the form of a camera-obscura, in which objects are represented upside down.

But, even when applied to more advanced and cultured countries with established democractic traditions, there is absolutely no proof of the justice of Kautsky's historical argument. As a matter of fact, the argument itself is not new. Once upon a time the Revisionists gave it a character more based on principle. They strove to prove that the growth of proletarian organizations under democractic conditions guaranteed the gradual and imperceptible—reformist and evolutionary—transition to Socialist society—without general strikes and risings, without the dictatorship of the proletariat.

Kautsky, at that culminating period of his activity, showed that, in spite of the forms of democracy, the class contradictions of capitalist society grew deeper, and that this process must inevitably lead to a revolution and the conquest of power by the proletariat.

No one, of course, attempted to reckon up beforehand the number of victims that will be called for by the revolutionary insurrection of the proletariat, and by the regime of its dictatorship. But it was clear to all that the number of victims will vary with the strength of resistance of the propertied classes. If Kautsky desires to say in his book that a democractic upbringing has not weakened the class egoism of the bourgeoisie, this can be admitted without further parley.

If he wishes to add that the imperialist war, which broke out and continued for four years, *in spite of* democracy, brought about a degradation of morals and accustomed men to violent methods and action, and completely stripped the bourgeoisie of the last vestige of awkwardness in ordering the destruction of masses of humanity—here also he will be right.

All this is true on the face of it. But one has to struggle in real conditions. The contending forces are not proletarian and bourgeois manikins produced in the retort of Wagner-Kautsky, but a real proletariat against a real bourgeoisie, as they have emerged from the last imperialist slaughter.

In this fact of merciless civil war that is spreading over the whole world, Kautsky sees only the result of a fatal lapse from the "experienced tactics" of the Second International.

"In reality, since the time," he writes, "that Marxism has dominated the Socialist movement, the latter, up to the world war, was, in spite of its great activities, preserved from great defeats. And the idea of insuring victory by means of terrorist domination had completely disappeared from its ranks.

"Much was contributed in this connection by the fact that, at the time when Marxism was the dominating Socialist teaching, democracy threw out firm roots in Western Europe, and began there to change from an end of the struggle to a trustworthy basis of political life." (Page 145.)

In this "formula of progress" there is not one atom of Marxism. The real process of the struggle of classes and their material conflicts has been lost in Marxist propaganda, which, thanks to the conditions of democracy, guarantees, forsooth, a painless transition to a new and "wiser" order. This is the most vulgar liberalism, a belated piece of rationalism in the spirit of the eighteenth century—with the difference that the ideas of Condorcet are replaced by a vulgarisation of the Communist Manifesto. All history resolves itself into an endless sheet of printed paper, and the centre of this "humane" process proves to be the well-worn writing table of Kautsky.

We are given as an example the working-class movement in the period of the Second International, which, going forward under the banner of Marxism, never sustained great defeats whenever it deliberately challenged them. But did not the whole working-class movement, the proletariat of the whole world, and with it the whole of human culture, sustain an incalculable defeat in August, 1914, when history cast up the accounts of all the forces and possibilities of the Socialist parties, amongst whom, we are told, the guiding role belonged to Marxism, "on the firm footing of democracy"? *Those parties proved bankrupt.* Those features of their previous work which Kautsky now wishes to render permanent—self-adaptation, repudiation of "illegal" activity, repudiation of the open fight, hopes placed in democracy as the road to a painless revolution—all these fell into dust. In their fear of defeat, holding back the masses from open conflict, dissolving the general strike discussions, the parties of the Second International were preparing their own terrifying defeat; for they were not able to move one finger to avert the greatest catastrophe in world history, the four years' imperialist slaughter, which foreshadowed the violent character of the civil war. Truly, one has to put a wadded nightcap not only over one's eyes, but over one's nose and ears, to be able to-day, after the inglorious collapse of the Second International, after the disgraceful bankruptcy of its leading party—the German Social Democracy—after the bloody lunacy of the world slaughter and the gigantic sweep of the civil war, to set up in contrast to us, the profundity, the loyalty, the peacefulness and the sobriety of the Second International, the heritage of which we are still liquidating.

3

DEMOCRACY

"EITHER DEMOCRACY, OR CIVIL WAR"

KAUTSKY has a clear and solitary path to salvation: *democracy.* All that is necessary is that every one should acknowledge it and bind himself to support it. The Right Socialists must renounce the sanguinary slaughter with which the have been carrying out the will of the bourgeoisie. The bourgeoisie itself must abandon the idea of using its Noskes and Lieutenant Vogels to defend its privileges to the last breath. Finally, the proletariat must once and for all reject the idea of overthrowing the bourgeoisie by means other than those laid down in the Constitution. If the conditions enumerated are observed, the social revolution will painlessly melt into democracy. In order to succeed it is sufficient, as we see, for our stormy history to draw a nightcap over its head, and take a pinch of wisdom out of Kautsky's snuffbox.

"There exist only two possibilties," says our sage, "either democracy, or civil war." (Page 220.) Yet, in Germany, where the formal elements of "democracy" are present before our eyes, the civil war does not cease for a moment. "Unquestionably," agrees Kautsky, "under the present National Assembly Germany cannot arrive at a healthy condition. But that process of recovery will not be assisted, but hindered, if we transform the struggle against the present Assembly into a struggle against the democratic franchise." (Page 230.) As if the question in Germany really did reduce itself to one of electoral forms and not to one of the real possession of power!

The present National Assembly, as Kautsky admits, cannot "bring the country to a healthy condition." Therefore let us begin the game again at the beginning. But will the partners agree? It is doubtful. If the rubber is not favorable to us, obviously it is so to them. The National Assembly which "is incapable of bringing the country to a healthy condition," is quite capable, through the mediocre dictatorship of Noske, of preparing the way for the dictatorship of Ludendorff. So it was with the Constituent Assembly which prepared the way for Kolchak. The historical mission of Kautsky consists precisely in having waited for the revolution to write his (n + 1th) book, which should explain the collapse of the revolution by all the previous course of history, from the ape to Noske, and from Noske to Ludendorff. The problem before the revolutionary party is a difficult one: its problem is to foresee the peril in good time, and to forestall it by *action*. And for this there is no other way at present than to tear the power out of the hands of its real possessors, the agrarian and capitalist magnates, who are only temporarily hiding behind Messrs. Ebert and Noske. Thus, from the present National Assembly, the path divides into two: either the dictatorship of the imperialist clique, or the dictatorship of the proletariat. On neither side does the path lead to "democracy." Kautsky does not see this. He explains at great length that democracy is of great importance for its political development and its education in organization of the masses, and that through it the proletariat can come to complete emancipation. One might imagine that, since the day on which the Erfurt Programme was written, nothing worthy of notice had ever happened in the world!

Yet meanwhile, for decades, the proletariat of France, Germany, and the other most important countries has been struggling and developing, making the widest possible use of the institutions of democracy, and building up on that basis powerful political organizations. This path of the education of the proletariat through democracy to Socialism proved, however, to be interrupted by an event of no inconsiderable importance—the world imperialist war. The class state at the moment when, thanks to its machinations, the war broke out succeeded in enlisting the assistance of the guiding organizations of Social-Democracy to deceive the proletariat and draw it into the whirl-pool. So that, taken as they stand, the methods of democracy, in spite of the incontestable bene-

fits which they afford at a certain period, displayed an extremely limited power of action; with the result that two generations of the proletariat, educated under conditions of democracy, by no means guaranteed the necessary political preparation for judging accurately an event like the world imperialist
war. That experience gives us no reasons for affirming that,
if the war had broken out ten or fifteen years later, the
proletariat would have been more prepared for it. The bourgeois democratic state not only creates more favorable conditions for the political education of the workers, as compared
with absolutism, but also sets a limit to that development
in the shape of bourgeois legality, which skilfully accumulates
and builds on the upper strata of the proletariat opportunist
habits and law-abiding prejudices. The school of democracy
proved quite insufficient to rouse the German proletariat to
revolution when the catastrophe of the war was at hand.
The barbarous school of the war, social-imperialist ambitions,
colossal military victories, and unparalleled defeats were required. After these events, which made a certain amount of
difference in the universe, and even in the Erfurt Programme,
to come out with common-places as to meaning of democratic
parliamentarism for the education of the proletariat signifies
a fall into political childhood. This is just the misfortune
which has overtaken Kautsky.

"Profound disbelief in the political struggle of the proletariat," he writes, "and in its participation in politics, was the
characteristic of Proudhonism. To-day there arises a similar (!!) view, and it is recommended to us as the new
gospel of Socialist thought, as the result of an experience
which Marx did not, and could not, know. In reality, it is
only a variation of an idea which half a century ago Marx
was fighting, and which he in the end defeated." (Page 79.)

Bolshevism proves to be warmed-up Proudhonism! From
a purely theoretical point of view, this is one of the most
brazen remarks in the pamphlet.

The Proudhonists repudiated democracy for the same
reason that they repudiated the political struggle generally.
They stood for the economic organization of the workers
without the interference of the State, without revolutionary
outbreaks—for self-help of the workers on the basis of produc-

tion for profit. As far as they were driven by the course of events on to the path of the political struggle, they, as lower middle class theoreticians, preferred democracy, not only to plutocracy, but to revolutionary dictatorship. What thoughts have they in common with us? While we repudiate democracy in the name of the concentrated power of the proletariat, the Proudhonists, on the other hand, were prepared to make their peace with democracy, diluted by a federal basis, in order to avoid the revolutionary monopoly of power by the proletariat. With more foundation Kautsky might have compared us with the opponents of the Proudhonists, the *Blanquists,* who understood the meaning of a revolutionary government, but did not superstitiously make the question of seizing it depend on the formal signs of democracy. But in order to put the comparison of the Communists with the Blanquists on a reasonable footing, it would have to be added that, in the Workers' and Soldiers' Councils, we had at our disposal such an organization for revolution as the Blanquists could not even dream of; in our party we had, and have, an invaluable organization of political leadership with a perfected programme of the social revolution. Finally, we had, and have, a powerful apparatus of economic transformation in our trade unions, which stand as a whole under the banner of Communism, and support the Soviet Government. Under such conditions, to talk of the renaissance of Proudhonist prejudices in the shape of Bolshevism can only take place when one has lost all traces of theoretical honesty and historical understanding.

THE IMPERIALIST TRANSFORMATION OF DEMOCRACY

It is not for nothing that the word "democracy" has a double meaning in the political vocabulary. On the one hand, it means a state system founded on universal suffrage and the other attributes of formal "popular government." On the other hand, by the word "democracy" is understood the mass of the people itself, in so far as it leads a political existence. In the second sense, as in the first, the meaning of democracy rises above class distinctions. This peculiarity of terminology has its profound political significance. Democracy as a political system is the more perfect and unshakable the greater is the part played in the life of the country by the intermediate and less differentiated mass of the population—the lower middle class of the town and the country. Democracy achieved its highest expression in the nineteenth century in Switzerland and the United States of North America. On the other side of the ocean the democratic organization of power in a federal republic was based on the agrarian democracy of the farmers. In the small Helvetian Republic, the lower middle classes of the towns and the rich peasantry constituted the basis of the conservative democracy of the united cantons.

Born of the struggle of the Third Estate against the powers of feudalism, the democratic State very soon becomes the weapon of defence against the class antagonisms generated within bourgeois society. Bourgeois society succeeds in this the more, the wider beneath it is the layer of the lower middle class, the greater is the importance of the latter in the economic life of the country, and the less advanced, consequently, is the development of class antagonism. However, the intermediate classes become ever more and more helplessly behind historical development, and, thereby, become ever more and more incapable of speaking in the name of the nation. True, the lower middle class doctrinaires (Bernstein and Company) used to demonstrate with satisfaction that the disappearance of the middle classes was not taking place with that swiftness that was expected by the Marxian school. And, in reality, one might agree that, numerically, the middle-class elements in the town, and especially in the country, still maintain an extremely prominent position. But the chief meaning of evolution has shown itself in the decline in importance on the part of the middle classes from the point of view of production: the amount of values which this class brings to the general income of the nation has fallen incomparably more rapidly than the numerical strength of the middle classes. Correspondingly, falls their social, political, and cultural importance. Historical development has been relying more and more, not on these conservative elements inherited from the past, but on the polar classes of society—i. e., the capitalist bourgeoisie and the proletariat.

The more the middle classes lost their social importance, the less they proved capable of playing the part of an authoritative arbitral judge in the historical conflict between capital and labor. Yet the very considerable numerical proportion of the town middle classes, and still more of the peasantry, continues to find direct expression in the electoral statistics of parliamentarism. The formal equality of all citizens as electors thereby only gives more open indication of the incapacity of democratic parliamentarism to settle the root questions of historical evolution. An "equal" vote for the proletariat, the peasant, and the manager of a trust formally placed the peasant in the position of a mediator between the two antagonists; but, in reality, the peasantry, socially and culturally backward and politically helpless, has in all countries always provided support for the most reactionary, filibustering, and mercenary parties which, in the long run, always supported capital against labor.

Absolutely contrary to all the prophecies of Bernstein, Sombart, Tugan-Baranovsky, and others, the continued existence of the middle classes has not softened, but has rendered to the last degree acute, the revolutionary crisis of bourgeois society. If the proletarization of the lower middle classes and the peasantry had been proceeding in a chemically purified form, the peaceful conquest of power by the proletariat through the democratic parliamentary apparatus would have been much more probable than we can imagine at present. Just the fact that was seized upon by the partisans of the lower middle class—its longevity—has proved fatal even for the external forms of political democracy, now that capitalism has undermined its essential foundations. Occupying in parliamentary politics a place which it has lost in production, the middle class has finally compromised parliamentarism, and has transformed it into an institution of confused chatter and legislative obstruction. From this fact alone, there grew up before the proletariat the problem of seizing the apparatus of state power as such, independently of the middle class, and even against it—not against its interests, but against its stupidity and its policy, impossible to follow in its helpless contortions.

"Imperialism," wrote Marx of the Empire of Napoleon

34

III, "is the most prostituted, and, at the same time, perfected form of the state which the bourgeoisie, having attained its fullest development, transforms into a weapon for the enslavement of labor by capital." This definition has a wider significance than for the French Empire alone, and includes the latest form of imperialism, born of the world conflict between the national capitalisms of the great powers. In the economic sphere, imperialism pre-supposed the final collapse of the rule of the middle class; in the political sphere, it signified the complete destruction of democracy by means of an internal molecular transformation, and a universal subordination of all democracy's resources to its own ends. Seizing upon all countries, independently of their previous political history, imperialism showed that all political prejudices were foreign to it, and that it was equally ready and capable of making use, after their transformation and subjection, of the monarchy of Nicholas Romanoff or Wilhelm Hohenzollern, of the presidential autocracy of the United States of North America, and of the helplessness of a few hundred chocolate legislators in the French parliament. The last great slaughter —the bloody font in which the bourgeois world attempted to be re-baptised—presented to us a picture, unparalleled in history, of the mobilization of all state forms, systems of government, political tendencies, religious, and schools of philosophy, in the service of imperialism. Even many of those pedants who slept through the preparatory period of imperialist development during the last decades, and continued to maintain a traditional attitude towards ideas of democracy and universal suffrage, began to feel during the war that their accustomed ideas had become fraught with some new meaning. Absolutism, parliamentary monarchy, democracy—in the presence of imperialism (and, consequently, in the presence of the revolution rising to take its place), all the state forms of bourgeois supremacy, from Russian Tsarism to North American quasi-democratic federalism, have been given equal rights, bound up in such combinations as to supplement one another in an indivisible whole. Imperialism succeeded by means of all the resources it had at its disposal, including parliamentarism, irrespective of the electoral arithmetic of voting, to subordinate for its own purposes at the critical moment the lower middle classes of the towns and country and even the upper layers of the proletariat. The national idea, under the watchword of which the Third Estate rose to power, found in the imperialist war its re-birth in the watchword of national defence. With unexpected clearness, national ideology flamed up for the last time at the expense of class ideology. The collapse of imperialist illusions, not only amongst the vanquished, but—after a certain delay—amongst the victorious also, finally laid low what was once national democracy, and, with it, its main weapon, the democratic parliament. The flabbiness, rottenness, and helplessness of the middle classes and their parties everywhere became evident with terrifying clearness. In all countries the question of the control of the State assumed first-class importance as a question of an open measuring of forces between the capitalist clique, openly or secretly supreme and disposing of hundreds of thousands of mobilized and hardened officers, devoid of all scruple, and the revolting, revolutionary proletariat; while the intermediate classes were living in a state of terror, confusion, and prostration. Under such conditions, what pitiful nonsense are speeches about the peaceful conquest of power by the proletariat by means of democratic parliamentarism!

The scheme of the political situation on a world scale is quite clear. The bourgeoisie, which has brought the nations, exhausted and bleeding to death, to the brink of destruction—particularly the victorious bourgeoisie—has displayed its complete inability to bring them out of their terrible situation, and, thereby, its incompatibility with the future development of humainty. All the intermediate political groups, including here first and foremost the social-patriotic parties, are rotting alive. The proletariat they have deceived is turning against them more and more every day, and is becoming strengthened in its revolutionary convictions as the only power that can save the peoples from savagery and destruction. However, history has not at all secured, just at this moment, a formal parliamentary majority on the side of the party of the social revolution. In other words, history has not transformed the nation into a debating society solemnly voting the transition to the social revolution by a majority of votes. On the contrary, the violent revolution has become a necessity precisely because the imminent requirements of history are helpless to find a road through the apparatus of parliamentary democracy. The capitalist bourgeois calculates: "while I have in my hands lands, factories, workshops, banks; while I possess newspapers, universities, schools; while—and this most important of all—I retain control of the army: the apparatus of democracy, however, you reconstruct it, will remain obedient to my will. I subordinate to my interests spiritually the stupid, conservative, characterless lower middle class, just as it is subjected to me materially. I oppress, and will oppress, its imagination by the gigantic scale of my buildings, my transactions, my plans, and my crimes. For moments when it is dissatisfied and murmurs, I have created scores of safety-valves and lightning-conductors. At the right moment I will bring into existence opposition parties, which will disappear to-morrow, but which to-day accomplish their mission by affording the possibility of the lower middle class expressing their indignation without hurt therefrom for capitalism. I shall hold the masses of the people, under cover of compulsory general education, on the verge of complete ignorance, giving them no opportunity of rising above the level which my experts in spiritual slavery consider safe. I will corrupt, deceive, and terrorize the more privileged or the more backward of the proletariat itself. By means of these measures, I shall not allow the vanguard of the working class to gain the ear of the majority of the working class, while the necessary weapons of mastery and terrorism remain in my hands."

To this the revolutionary proletarian replies: "Consequently, the first condition of salvation is to tear the weapons of domination out of the hands of the bourgeoisie. It is hopeless to think of a peaceful arrival to power while the bourgeoisie retains in its hands all the apparatus of power. Three times over hopeless is the idea of coming to power by the path which the bourgeoisie itself indicates and, at the same time, barricades—the path of parliamentary democracy. There is only one way: to seize power, taking away from the bourgeoisie the material apparatus of government. Independently of the superficial balance of forces in parliament, I shall take over for social administration the chief forces and resources of production. I shall free the mind of the lower middle class from their capitalist hypnosis. I shall show them in practice what is the meaning of Socialist production. Then even the most backward, the most ignorant, or most terrorized sections of the nation will support me, and willingly and intelligently will join in the work of social construction."

When the Russian Soviet Government dissolved the Constituent Assembly, that fact seemed to the leading Social-Democrats of Western Europe, if not the beginning of the end of the world, at all events a rude and arbitrary break with all the previous developments of Socialism. In reality, it was only the inevitable outcome of the new position resulting from imperialism and the war. If Russian Communism was the first to enter the path of casting up theoretical and practical accounts, this was due to the same historical reasons which forced the Russian proletariat to be the first to enter the path of the struggle for power.

All that has happened since then in Europe bears witness to the fact that we drew the right conclusion. To imagine that democracy can be restored in its general purity means that one is living in a pitiful, reactionary utopia.

THE METAPHYSICS OF DEMOCRACY

Feeling the historical ground shaking under his feet on the question of democracy, Kautsky crosses to the ground of metaphysics. Instead of inquiring into what is, he deliberates about what ought to be.

The principles of democracy—the sovereignty of the people, universal and equal suffrage, personal liberties—appear, as presented to him, in a halo of moral duty. They are turned from their historical meaning and presented as unalterable and sacred things-in-themselves. This metaphysical fall from grace is not accidental. It is instructive that the late Plekhanov, a merciless enemy of Kantism at the best period of his activity, attempted at the end of his life, when the wave of patriotism had washed over him, to clutch at the straw of the categorical imperative.

That real democracy with which the German people is now making practical acquaintance Kautsky confronts with a kind of ideal democracy, as he would confront a common phenomenon with the thing-in-itself. Kautsky indicates with certitude not one country in which democracy is really capable of guaranteeing a painless transition to Socialism. But he does know, and firmly, that such democracy ought to exist. The present German National Assembly, that organ of helplessness, reactionary malice, and degraded solicitations, is confronted by Kautsky with a different, real, true National Assembly, which possesses all virtues—excepting the small virtue of reality.

The doctrine of formal democracy is not scientific Socialism, but the theory of so-called natural law. The essence of the latter consists in the recognition of eternal and unchanging standards of law, which among different peoples and at different periods find a different, more or less limited and distorted expression. The natural law of the latest history— *i.e.*, as it emerged from the middle ages—included first of all a protest against class privileges, the abuse of despotic legislation, and the other "artificial" products of feudal positive law. The theoreticians of the, as yet, weak Third Estate expressed its class interests in a few ideal standards, which later on developed into the teaching of democracy, acquiring at the same time an individualist character. The individual is absolute; all persons have the right of expressing their thoughts in speech and print; every man must enjoy equal electoral rights. As a battle cry against feudalism, the demand for democracy had a progressive character. As time went on, however, the metaphysics of natural law (the theory of formal democracy) began to show its reactionary side—the establishment of an ideal standard to control the real demands of the laboring masses and the revolutionary parties.

If we look back to the historical sequence of world concepts, the theory of natural law will prove to be a paraphrase of Christian spiritualism freed from its crude mysticism. The Gospels proclaimed to the slave that he had just the same soul as the slave-owner, and in this way established the equality of all men before the heavenly tribunal. In reality, the slave remained a slave, and obedience became for him a religious duty. In the teaching of Christianity, the slave found an expression for his own ignorant protest against his degraded condition. Side by side with the protest was also the consolation. Christianity told him:—"You have an immortal soul, although you resemble a pack-horse." Here sounded the note of indignation. But the same Christianity said:—"Although you are like a pack-horse, yet your immortal soul has in store for it an eternal reward." Here is the voice of consolation. These two notes were found in historical Christianity in different proportions at different periods and amongst different classes. But as a whole, Christianity, like all other religions, became a method of deadening the consciousness of the oppressed masses.

Natural law, which developed into the theory of democracy, said to the worker: "all men are equal before the law, independently of their origin, their property, and their position; every man has an equal right in determining the fate of the people." This ideal criterion revolutionized the consciousness of the masses in so far as it was a condemnation of absolutism, aristocratic privileges, and the property qualification. But the longer it went on, the more it sent the consciousness to sleep, legalizing poverty, slavery and degradation: for how could one revolt against slavery when every man has an equal right in determining the fate of the nation?

Rothschild, who has coined the blood and tears of the world into the gold napoleons of his income, has one vote at the parliamentary elections. The ignorant tiller of the soil who cannot sign his name, sleeps all his life without taking his clothes off, and wanders through society like an underground mole, plays his part, however, as a trustee of the nation's sovereignty, and is equal to Rothschild in the courts and at the elections. In the real conditions of life, in the economic process, in social relations, in their way of life, people became more and more unequal; dazzling luxury was accumulated at one pole, poverty and hopelessness at the other. But in the sphere of the legal edifice of the State, these glaring contradictions disappeared, and there penetrated thither only unsubstantial legal shadows. The landlord, the laborer, the capitalist, the proletarian, the minister, the bootblack—all are equal as "citizens" and as "legislators." The mystic equality of Christianity has taken one step down from the heavens in the shape of the "natural," "legal" equality of democracy. But it has not yet reached earth, where lie the economic foundations of society. For the ignorant day-laborer, who all his life remains a beast of burden in the service of the bourgeoisie, the ideal right to influence the fate of the nations by means of the parliamentary elections remained little more real than the palace which he was promised in the kingdom of heaven.

In the practical interests of the development of the working class, the Socialist Party took its stand at a certain period on the path of parliamentarism. But this did not mean in the slightest that it accepted in principle the metaphysical theory of democracy, based on extra-historical, super-class rights. The proletarian doctrines examined democracy as the instrument of bourgeois society entirely adapted to the problems and requirements of the ruling classes; but as bourgeois society lived by the labor of the proletariat and could not deny it the legalization of a certain part of its class struggle without destroying itself, this gave the Socialist Party the possibility of utilizing, at a certain period, and within certain limits, the mechanism of democracy, without taking an oath to do so as an unshakable principle.

The root problem of the party, at all periods of its struggle, was to create the conditions for real, economic, living equality for mankind as members of a united human commonwealth. It was just for this reason that the theoreticians of the proletariat had to expose the metaphysics of democracy as a philosophic mask for political mystification.

The democratic party at the period of its revolutionary enthusiasm, when exposing the enslaving and stupefying lie of church dogma, preached to the masses:—"You are lulled to sleep by promises of eternal bliss at the end of your life, while here you have no rights and you are bound with the chains of tyranny." The Socialist Party, a few decades later, said to the same masses with no less right:—"You are lulled to sleep with the fiction of civic equality and political rights, but you are deprived of the possibility of realizing those rights. Conditional and shadowy legal equality has been transformed into the convicts' chain with which each of you is fastened to the chariot of capitalism."

In the name of its fundamental task, the Socialist Party mobilized the masses on the parliamentary ground as well as on others; but nowhere and at no time did any party bind itself to bring the masses to Socialism only through the gates of democracy. In adapting ourselves to the parliamentary regime, we stopped at a theoretical exposure of democracy, because we were still too weak to overcome it in practice. But the path of Socialist ideas which is visible through all deviations, and even betrayals, foreshadows no other outcome but this: to throw democracy aside and replace it by the mechanism of the proletariat, at the moment when the latter is strong enough to carry out such a task.

We shall bring one piece of evidence, albeit a sufficiently striking one. "Parliamentarism," wrote Paul Lafargue in the Russian review, *Sozialdemokrat,* in 1888, "is a system of government in which the people acquires the illusion that it is controlling the forces of the country itself, when, in reality, the actual power is concentrated in the hands of the bourgeoisie—and not even of the whole bourgeoisie, but only of certain sections of that class. In the first period of its supremacy the bourgeoisie does not understand, or, more correctly, does not feel, the necessity for making the people believe in the illusion of self-government. Hence it was that all the parliamentary countries of Europe began with a limited franchise. Everywhere the right of influencing the policy of the country by means of the election of deputies belonged at first only to more or less large property holders, and was only gradually extended to less substantial citizens, until finally in some countries it became from a privilege the universal right of all and sundry.

"In bourgeois society, the more considerable becomes the amount of social wealth, the smaller becomes the number of individuals by whom it is appropriated. The same takes place with power: in proportion as the mass of citizens who possess political rights increases, and the number of elected rulers increases, the actual power is concentrated and becomes the monopoly of a smaller and smaller group of individuals." Such is the secret of the majority.

For the Marxist, Lafargue, parliamentarism remains as long as the supremacy of the bourgeoisie remains. "On the

42

day," writes Lafargue, "when the proletariat of Europe and America seizes the State, it will have to organize a revolutionary government, and govern society as a dictatorship, until the bourgeoisie has disappeared as a class."

Kautsky in his time knew this Marxist estimate of parliamentarism, and more than once repeated it himself, although with no such Gallic sharpness and lucidity. The theoretical apostasy of Kautsky lies just in this point: having recognized the principle of democracy as absolute and eternal, he has stepped back from materialist dialectics to natural law. That which was exposed by Marxism as the passing mechanism of the bourgeoisie, and was subjected only to temporary utilization with the object of preparing the proletarian revolution, has been newly sanctified by Kautsky as the supreme principle standing above classes, and unconditionally subordinating to itself the methods of the proletarian struggle. The counter-revolutionary degeneration of parliamentarism finds its most perfect expression in the deification of democracy by the decaying theoreticians of the Second International.

THE CONSTITUENT ASSEMBLY

Speaking generally, the attainment of a majority in a democratic parliament by the party of the proletariat is not an absolute impossibility. But such a fact, even if it were realized, would not introduce any new principle into the course of events. The intermediate elements of the intelligentsia, under the influence of the parliamentary victory of the proletariat, might possibly display less resistance to the new regime. But the fundamental resistance of the bourgeoisie would be decided by such facts as the attitude of the army, the degree to which the workers were armed, the situation in the neighboring states: and the civil war would develop under the pressure of these most real circumstances, and not by the mobile arithmetic of parliamentarism.

Our party has never refused to lead the way for proletarian dictatorship through the gates of democracy, having clearly summed up in its mind certain agitational and political advantages of such a "legalized" transition to the new regime. Hence, our attempt to call the Constituent Assembly. The

Russian peasant, only just awakened by the revolution to political life, found himself face to face with half a dozen parties, each of which apparently had made up its mind to confuse his mind. The Constituent Assembly placed itself across the path of the revolutionary movement, and was swept aside.

The opportunist majority in the Constituent Assembly represented only the political reflection of the mental confusion and indecision which reigned amidst the middle classes in the town and country and amidst the more backward elements of the proletariat. If we take the viewpoint of isolated historical possibilities, one might say that it would have been more painless if the Constituent Assembly had worked for a year or two, had finally discredited the Socialist-Revolutionaries and the Mensheviks by their connection with the Cadets, and had thereby led to the formal majority of the Bolsheviks, showing the masses that in reality only two forces existed: the revolutionary proletariat, led by the Communists, and the counter-revolutionary democracy, headed by the generals and the admirals. But the point is that the pulse of the internal relations of the revolution was beating not at all in time with the pulse of the development of its external relations. If our party had thrown all responsibility on to the objective formula of "the course of events" the development of military operations might have forestalled us. German imperialism might have seized Petrograd, the evacuation of which the Kerensky Government had already begun. The fall of Petrograd would at that time have meant a death-blow to the proletariat, for all the best forces of the revolution were concentrated there, in the Baltic Fleet and in the Red capital.

Our party may be accused, therefore, not of going against the course of historical development, but of having taken at a stride several political steps. It stepped over the heads of the Mensheviks and the Socialist-Revolutionaries, in order not to allow German imperialism to step across the head of the Russian proletariat and conclude peace with the Entente on the back of the revolution before it was able to spread its wings over the whole world.

From the above it will not be difficult to deduce the answers to the two questions with which Kautsky pestered us. Firstly: Why did we summon the Constituent Assembly when we had in view the dictatorship of the proletariat? Secondly: If the first Constituent Assembly which we summoned proved backward and not in harmony with the interests of the revolution, why did we reject the idea of a new Assembly? The thought at the back of Kautsky's mind is that we repudiated democracy, not on the ground of principle, but only because it proved against us. In order to seize this insinuation by its long ears, let us establish the facts.

The watchword, "All power to the Soviets," was put forward by our Party at the very beginning of the revolution— *i.e.*, long before, not merely the decree as to the dissolution of the Constituent Assembly, but the decree as to its convocation. True, we did not set up the Soviets in opposition to the future Constituent Assembly, the summoning of which was constantly postponed by the Government of Kerensky, and consequently became more and more problematical. But in any case, we did not consider the Constituent Assembly, after the manner of the democrats, as the future master of the Russian land, who would come and settle everything. We explained to the masses that the Soviets, the revolutionary organizations of the laboring masses themselves, can and must become the true masters. If we did not formally repudiate the Constituent Assembly beforehand, it was only because it stood in contrast, not to the power of the Soviets, but to the power of Kerensky himself, who, in his turn, was only a screen for the bourgeoisie. At the same time we did decide beforehand that, if, in the Constituent Assembly, the majority proved in our favor, that body must dissolve itself and hand over the power to the Soviets—as later on the Petrograd Town Council did, elected as it was on the basis of the most democratic electoral franchise. In my book on the October Revolution, I tried to explain the reasons which made the Constituent Assembly the out-of-date reflection of an epoch through which the revolution had already passed. As we saw the organization of revolutionary power only in the Soviets, and as the moment of the summoning of the Constituent Assembly the Soviets were already the de facto power, the question was inevitably decided for us in the sense of the violent dissolution of the Constituent Assembly, since it would not dissolve itself in favor of the Government of the Soviets.

"But why," asks Kautsky, "did you not summon a new Constituent Assembly?"

Because we saw no need for it. If the first Constituent Assembly could still play a fleeting progressive part, conferring a sanction upon the Soviet regime in its first days, convincing for the middle-class elements, now, after two years of victorious proletarian dictatorship and the complete collapse of all democratic attempts in Siberia, on the shores of the White Sea, in the Ukraine, and in the Caucasus, the power of the Soviets truly does not need the blessing of the faded authority of the Constituent Assembly. "Are we not right in that case to conclude," asks Kautsky in the tone of Lloyd George, "that the Soviet Government rules by the will of the minority, since it avoids testing its supremacy by universal suffrage?" Here is a blow that misses its mark.

If the parliamentary regime, even in the period of "peaceful," stable development, was a rather crude method of discovering the opinion of the country, and in the epoch of revolutionary storm completely lost its capacity to follow the course of the struggle and the development of revolutionary consciousness, the Soviet regime, which is more closely, straightly, honestly bound up with the toiling majority of the people, does achieve meaning, not in statically reflecting a majority, but in dynamically creating it. Having taken its stand on the path of revolutionary dictatorship, the working class of Russia has thereby declared that it builds its policy in the period of transition, not on the shadowy art of rivalry with chameleon-hued parties in the chase for peasant votes, but on the actual attraction of the peasant masses, side by side with the proletariat, into the work of ruling the country in the real interests of the laboring masses. Such democracy goes a little deeper down than parliamentarism.

To-day, when the main problem—the question of life and death—of the revolution consists in the military repulse of the various attacks of the White Guard bands, does Kautsky imagine that any form of parliamentary "majority" is capable of guaranteeing a more energetic, devoted, and successful organization of revolutionary defence? The conditions of the struggle are so defined, in a revolutionary country throttled by the criminal ring of the blockade, that all the middle-class groups are confronted only with the alternative of Denikin or the Soviet Government. What further proof is needed when even parties, which stand for compromise in principle, like the Mensheviks and the Socialist-Revolutionaries, have split along that very line?

When suggesting to us the election of a Constituent Assembly, does Kautsky propose the stopping of the civil war for the purpose of the elections? By whose decision? If he intends for this purpose to bring into motion the authority of the Second International, we hasten to inform him that that institution enjoys in Denikin's camp only a little more authority than it does in ours. But to the extent that the civil war between the Workers' and Peasants' Army and the inperialist bands is still going on, the elections must of necessity be limited to Soviet territory. Does Kautsky desire to insist that we should allow the parties which support Denikin to come out into the open? Empty and contemptible chatter! There is not one government, at any time and under any conditions, which would allow its enemies to mobilize hostile forces in the rear of its armies.

A not unimportant place in the discussion of the question is occupied by the fact that the flower of the laboring population is at present on active service. The foremost workers and the most class-conscious peasants, who take the first place at all elections, as in all important political activities, directing the public opinion of the workers, are at present fighting and dying as commanders, commissars, or rank and file in the Red Army. If the most "democratic" governments in the bourgeois states, whose regime is founded on parliamentarism, consider it impossible to carry on elections to parliament in wartime, it is all the more senseless to demand such elections during the war of the Soviet Republic, the regime of which is not for one moment founded on parliamentarism. It is quite sufficient that the revolutionary government of Russia, in the most difficult months and times, never stood in the way of periodic re-elections of its *own* elective institutions—the local and central Soviets.

Finally, as a last argument—the last and the least—we

have to present to the notice of Kautsky that even the Russian Kautskians, the Mensheviks like Martov and Dan, do not consider it possible to put forward at the present moment a demand for a Constituent Assembly, postponing it to better times in the future. Will there be any need of it then? Of this one may be permitted to doubt. When the civil war is over, the dictatorship of the working class will disclose all its creative energy, and will, in practice, show the most backward masses what it can give them. By means of a systematically applied universal labor service, and a centralized organization of distribution, the whole population of the country will be drawn into the general Soviet system of economic arrangement and self-government. The Soviets themselves, at present the organs of government, will gradually melt into purely economic organizations. Under such conditions it is doubtful whether any one will think of erecting, over the real fabric of Socialist society, an archaic crown in the shape of the Constituent Assembly, which would only have to register the fact that everything necessary has already been "constituted" before it and without it. *

---

* In order to charm us in favor of a Constituent Assembly Kautsky brings forward an argument based on the rate of exchange to the assistance of his argument, based on the categorical imperative. "Russia requires," he writes, "the help of foreign capital, but this help will not come to the Soviet Republic if the latter does not summon a Constituent Assembly, and does not give freedom of the Press; not because the capitalists are democratic idealists—to Tsarism they gave without any hesitation many milliards—but because they have no business faith in a revolutionary government." (Page 218.)

There are scraps of truth in this rubbish. The Stock Exchange did really support the government of Kolchak when it relied for support on the Constituent Assembly. From its experience of Kolchak the Stock Exchange became confirmed in its conviction that the mechanism of bourgeois democracy can be utilized in capitalist interests, and then thrown aside like a worn-out pair of puttees. It is quite possible that the Stock Exchange would again give a parliamentary loan on the guarantee of a Constituent Assembly, believing, on the basis of its former experience, that such a body would prove only an intermediate step to capitalist dictatorship. We do not propose to buy the "business faith" of the Stock Exchange at such a price, and decidedly prefer the "faith" which is aroused in the realist Stock Exchange by the weapon of the Red Army.

TERRORISM.

THE chief theme of Kautsky's book is terrorism. The view that terrorism is of the essence of revolution Kautsky proclaims to be a widespread delusion. It is untrue that he who desires revolution must put up with terrorism. As far as he, Kautsky, is concerned, he is, generally speaking, for revolution, but decidedly against terrorism. From there, however, complications begin.

"The revolution brings us," Kautsky complains, "a bloody terrorism carried out by Socialist governments. The Bolsheviks in Russia first stepped on to this path, and were, consequently, sternly condemned by all Socialists who had not adopted the Bolshevik point of view, including the Socialists of the German Majority. But as soon as the latter found themselves threatened in their supremacy, they had recourse to the methods of the same terrorist regime which they attacked in the East." (Page 9.) It would seem that from this follows the conclusion that terrorism is much more profoundly bound up with the nature of revolution than certain sages think. But Kautsky makes an absolutely opposite conclusion. The gigantic development of White and Red terrorism in all the last revolutions—the Russian, the German, the Austrian, and the Hungarian—is evidence to him that these revolutions turned aside from their true path and turned out to be not the revolution they ought to have been according to the theoretical visions of Kautsky. Without going into the question whether terrorism "as such" is "immanent" to the revolution "as such," let us consider a few of the revolutions as they pass before us in the living history of mankind.

Let us first regard the religious Reformation, which proved the watershed between the Middle Ages and modern

48

history: the deeper were the interests of the masses that it involved, the wider was its sweep, the more fiercely did the civil war develop under the religious banner, and the more merciless did the terror beccme on the other side.

In the seventeenth century England carried out two revolutions. The first, which brought forth great social upheavals and wars, brought amongst other things the execution of King Charles I, while the second ended happily with the accession of a new dynasty. The British bourgeoisie and its historians maintain quite different attitudes to these two revolutions: the first is for them a rising of the mob—the "Great Rebellion"; the second has been handed down under the title of the "Glorious Revolution." The reason for this difference in estimates was explained by the French historian, Augustin Thierry. In the first English revolution, in the "Great Rebellion," the active force was the people; while in the second it was almost "silent." Hence, it follows that, in surroundings of class slavery, it is difficult to teach the oppressed masses good manners. When provoked to fury they use clubs, stones, fire, and the rope. The court historians of the exploiters are offended at this. But the great event in modern "bourgeois" history is, none the less, not the "Glorious Revolution," but the "Great Rebellion."

The greatest event in modern history after the Reformation and the "Great Rebellion," and far surpassing its two predecessors in significance, was the great French Revolution of the eighteenth century. To this classical revolution there was a corresponding classical terrorism. Kautsky is ready to forgive the terrorism of the Jacobins, acknowledging that they had no other way of saving the republic. But by this justification after the event no one is either helped or hindered. The Kautskies of the end of the eighteenth century (the leaders of the French Girondists) saw in the Jacobins the personification of evil. Here is a comparison, sufficiently instructive in its banality, between the Jacobins and the Girondists from the pen of one of the bourgeois French historians: "Both one side and the other desired the republic." But the Girondists "desired a free, legal, and merciful republic. The Montagnards desired a despotic and terrorist republic. Both stood for the supreme power of the people; but the Girondist justly

50

understood all by the people, while the Montagnards considered only the working class to be the people. That was why only to such persons, in the opinion of the Montagnards, did the supremacy belong." The antithesis between the noble champions of the Constituent Assembly and the bloodthirsty agents of the revolutionary dictatorship is here outlined fairly clearly, although in the political terms of the epoch.

The iron dictatorship of the Jacobins was evoked by the monstrously difficult position of revolutionary France. Here is what the bourgeois historian says of this period: "Foreign troops had entered French territory from four sides. In the north, the British and the Austrians, in Alsace, the Prussians, in Dauphine and up to Lyons, the Piedmontese, in Roussillon the Spaniards. And this at a time when civil war was raging at four different points: in Normandy, in the Vendée, at Lyons, and at Toulon." (Page 176). To this we must add internal enemies in the form of numerous secret supporters of the old regime, ready by all methods to assist the enemy.

The severity of the proletarian dictatorship in Russia, let us point out here, was conditioned by no less difficult circumstances. There was one continuous front, on the north and south, in the east and west. Besides the Russian White Guard armies of Kolchak, Denikin and others, there are attacking Soviet Russia, simultaneously or in turn: Germans, Austrians, Czecho-Slovaks, Serbs, Poles, Ukrainians, Roumanians, French, British, Americans, Japanese, Finns, Esthonians, Lithuanians.... In a country throttled by a blockade and strangled by hunger, there are conspiracies, risings, terrorist acts, and destruction of roads and bridges.

"The government which had taken on itself the struggle with countless external and internal enemies had neither money, nor sufficient troops, nor anything except boundless energy, enthusiastic support on the part of the revolutionary elements of the country, and the gigantic courage to take all measures necessary for the safety of the country, however arbitrary and severe they were." In such words did once upon a time Plekhanov describe the government of the—Jacobins. (*Sozial-demokrat,* a quarterly review of literature and politics. Book I, February, 1890, London. The article on "The Centenary of the Great Revolution," pages 6-7).

Let us now turn to the revolution which took place in the second half of the nineteenth century, in the country of "democracy"—in the United States of North America. Although the question was not the abolition of property altogether, but only of the abolition of property in negroes, nevertheless, the institutions of democracy proved absolutely powerless to decide the argument in a peaceful way. The southern states, defeated at the presidential elections in 1860, decided by all possible means to regain the influence they had hitherto exerted in the question of slave-owning; and uttering, as was right, the proper sounding words about freedom and independence, rose in a slave-owners' insurrection. Hence inevitably followed all the later consequences of civil war. At the very beginning of the struggle, the military government in Baltimore imprisoned in Fort MacHenry a few citizens, sympathizers with the slave-holding South, in spite of Habeas Corpus. The question of the lawfulness or the unlawfulness of such action became the object of fierce disputes between so-called "high authorities." The judge of the Supreme Court, decided that the President had neither the right to arrest the operation of Habeas Corpus nor to give plenipotentiary powers to that end to the military authorities. "Such, in all probability, is the correct Constitutional solution of the question," says one of the first historians of the American Civil War. "But the state of affairs was to such a degree critical, and the necessity of taking decisive measures against the population of Baltimore so great, that not only the Government but the people of the United States also supported the most energetic measures." *

Some goods that the rebellious South required were secretly supplied by the merchants of the North. Naturally, the Northerners had no other course but to introduce methods of repression. On August 6, 1861, the President confirmed a resolution of Congress as to "the confiscation of property used for insurrectionary purposes." The people, in the shape of the most democratic elements, were in favor of extreme measures. The Republican Party had a decided majority in the

* (The History of the American War, by Fletcher, Lieut.-Colonel in the Scots Guards, St. Petersburg, 1867, page 95.)

North, and persons suspected of secessionism, *i.e.*, of sympathizing with the rebellious Southern states, were subjected to violence. In some northern towns, and even in the states of New England, famous for their order, the people frequently burst into the offices of newspapers which supported the revolting slave-owners and smashed their printing presses. It occasionally happened that reactionary publishers were smeared with tar, decorated with feathers, and carried in such array through the public squares until they swore an oath of loyalty to the Union. The personality of a planter smeared in tar bore little resemblance to the "end-in-itself;" so that the categorical imperative of Kautsky suffered in the civil war of the states a considerable blow. But this is not all. "The government, on its part," the historian tells us, "adopted repressive measures of various kinds against publications holding views opposed to its own: and in a short time the hitherto free American press was reduced to a condition *scarcely superior to that prevailing in the autocratic European States.*" The same fate overtook the freedom of speech. "In this way," Lieut.-Colonel Fletcher continues, "the American people at this time denied itself the greater part of its freedom. It should be observed," he moralizes, "that *the majority of the people* was to such an extent occupied with the war, and to such a degree imbued with the readiness for any kind of sacrifice to attain its end, that it not only did not regret its vanished liberties, but scarcely even noticed their disappearance." *

Infinitely more ruthlessly did the bloodthirsty slave-owners of the South employ their uncontrollable hordes. "Wherever there was a majority in favor of slavery," writes the Count of Paris, "public opinion behaved despotically to the minority. All who expressed pity for the national banner... were forced to be silent. But soon this itself became insufficient; as in all revolutions, the indifferent were forced to express their loyalty to the new order of things.... Those who did not agree to this were given up as a sacrifice to the hatred and violence of the mass of the people.... In each centre of growing civilization (South-Western states) vigil-

---

* Fletcher's History of the American War, pages 162-164.

ance committees were formed, composed of all those who had been distinguished by their extreme views in the electoral struggle.... A tavern was the usual place of their sessions, and a noisy orgy was mingled with a contemptible parody of public forms of justice. A few madmen sitting around a desk on which gin and whisky flowed judged their present and absent fellow-citizens. The accused, even before having been questioned, could see the rope being prepared. He who did not appear at the court learned his sentence when falling under the bullets of the executioner concealed in the forest..." This picture is extremely reminiscent of the scenes which day by day took place in the camps of Denikin, Kolchak, Yudenich, and the other heroes of Anglo-Franco-American "democracy."

We shall see later how the question of terrorism stood in regard to the Paris Commune of 1871. In any case, the attempts of Kautsky to contrast the Commune with us are false at their very root, and only bring the author to a juggling with words of the most petty character.

The institution of hostages apparently must be recognized as "immanent'" in the terrorism of the civil war. Kautsky is against terrorism and against the institution of hostages, but in favor of the Paris Commune. (N. B.—The Commune existed fifty years ago.) Yet the Commune took hostages. A difficulty arises. But what does the art of exegesis exist for?

The decree of the Commune concerning hostages and their execution in reply to the atrocities of the Versaillese arose, according to the profound explanation of Kautsky, "from a striving to preserve human life, not to destroy it." A marvellous discovery! It only requires to be developed. It could, and must, be explained that in the civil war we destroyed White Guards in order that they should not destroy the workers. Consequently, our problem is not the destruction of human life, but its preservation. But as we have to struggle for the preservation of human life with arms in our hands, it leads to the destruction of human life—a puzzle the dialectical secret of which was explained by old Hegel, without reckoning other still more ancient sages.

The Commune could maintain itself and consolidate its position only by a determined struggle with the Versaillese.

The latter, on the other hand, had a large number of agents in Paris. Fighting with the agents of Thiers, the Commune could not abstain from destroying the Versaillese at the front and in the rear. If its rule had crossed the bounds of Paris, in the provinces it would have found—during the process of the civil war with the Army of the National Assembly—still more determined foes in the midst of the peaceful population. The Commune when fighting the royalists could not allow freedom of speech to royalist agents in the rear.

Kautsky, in spite of all the happenings in the world to-day, completely fails to realize what war is in general, and the civil war in particular. He does not understand that every, or nearly every, sympathizer with Thiers in Paris was not merely an "opponent" of the Communards in ideas, but an agent and spy of Thiers, a ferocious enemy ready to shoot one in the back. The enemy must be made harmless, and in wartime this means that he must be destroyed.

The problem of revolution, as of war, consists in breaking the will of the foe, forcing him to capitulate and to accept the conditions of the conqueror. The will, of course, is a fact of the physical world, but in contradistiction to a meeting, a dispute, or a congress, the revolution carries out its object by means of the employment of material resources—though to a less degree than war. The bourgeoisie itself conquered power by means of revolts, and consolidated it by the civil war. In the peaceful period, it retains power by means of a system of repression. As long as class society, founded on the most deep-rooted antagonisms, continues to exist, repression remains a necessary means of breaking the will of the opposing side.

Even if, in one country or another, the dictatorship of the proletariat grew up within the external framework of democracy, this would by no means avert the civil war. The question as to who is to rule the country, *i.e.*, of the life or death of the bourgeoisie, will be decided on either side, not by references to the paragraphs of the constitution, but by the employment of all forms of violence. However deeply Kautsky goes into the question of the food of the anthropopithecus (see page 122 et seq. of his book) and other immediate and remote conditions which determine the cause of human cruelty, he will find in history no other way of breaking the class will of the enemy except the systematic and energetic use of violence.

The degree of ferocity of the struggle depends on a series of internal and international circumstances. The more ferocious and dangerous is the resistance of the class enemy who have been overthrown, the more inevitably does the system of repression take the form of a system of terror.

But here Kautsky unexpectedly takes up a new position in his struggle with Soviet terrorism. He simply waves aside all reference to the ferocity of the counter-revolutionary opposition of the Russian bourgeoisie.

"Such ferocity," he says, "could not be noticed in November, 1917, in Petrograd and Moscow, and still less more recently in Budapest." (Page 149.) With such a happy formulation of the question, revolutionary terrorism merely proves to be a product of the bloodthirstiness of the Bolsheviks, who simultaneously abandoned the traditions of the vegetarian anthropopithecus and the moral lessons of Kautsky.

The first conquest of power by the Soviets at the beginning of November, 1917 (new style), was actually accomplished with insignificant sacrifices. The Russian bourgeoisie found itself to such a degree estranged from the masses of the people, so internally helpless, so compromised by the course and the result of the war, so demoralized by the regime of Kerensky, that it scarcely dared show any resistance. In Petrograd the power of Kerensky was overthrown almost without a fight. In Moscow its resistance was dragged out, mainly owing to the indecisive character of our own actions. In the majority of the provincial towns, power was transferred to the Soviet on the mere receipt of a telegram from Petrograd or Moscow. If the matter had ended there, there would have been no word of the Red Terror. But in November, 1917, there was already evidence of the beginning of the resistance of the propertied classes. True, there was required the intervention of the imperialist governments of the West in order to give the Russian counter-revolution faith in itself, and to add ever-increasing power to its resistance.

This can be shown from facts, both important and insignificant, day by day during the whole epoch of the Soviet revolution.

Kerensky's "Staff" felt no support forthcoming from the mass of the soldiery, and was inclined to recognize the Soviet Government, which had begun negotiations for an armistice with the Germans. But there followed the protest of the military missions of the Entente, followed by open threats. The Staff was frightened; incited by "Allied" officers, it entered the path of opposition. This led to armed conflict and to the murder of the chief of the field staff, General Dukhonin, by a group of revolutionary sailors.

In Petrograd, the official agents of the Entente, especially the French Military Mission, hand in hand with the S.R.s and the Mensheviks, openly organized the opposition, mobilizing, arming, inciting against us the cadets, and the bourgeois youth generally, from the second day of the Soviet revolution. The rising of the junkers on November 10 brought about a hundred times more victims than the revolution of November 7. The campaign of the adventurers Kerensky and Krasnov against Petrograd, organized at the same time by the Entente, naturally introduced into the struggle the first elements of savagery. Nevertheless, General Krasnov was set free on his word of honor. The Yaroslav rising (in the summer of 1918) which involved so many victims, was organized by Savinkov on the instructions of the French Embassy, and with its resources. Archangel was captured according to the plans of British naval agents, with the help of British warships and aeroplanes. The beginning of the empire of Kolchak, the nominee of the American Stock Exchange, was brought about by the foreign Czecho-Slovak Corps maintained by the resources of the French Government. Kaledin and Krasnov (liberated by us), the first leaders of the counter-revolution on the Don, could enjoy partial success only thanks to the open military and financial aid of Germany. In the Ukraine the Soviet power was overthrown in the beginning of 1918 by German militarism. The Volunteer Army of Denikin was created with the financial and technical help of Great Britain and France. Only in the hope of British intervention and of British military support was Yudenich's army created. The politicians, the diplomats, and the journalists of the Entente have for two years on end been debating with complete frankness the question of whether the financing of the civil war in Russia is a sufficiently profitable enterprise. In such circumstances, one needs truly a brazen forehead to seek the reason for the sanguinary character of the civil war in Russia in the malevolence of the Bolsheviks, and not in the international situation.

The Russian proletariat was the first to enter the path of the social revolution, and the Russian bourgeoisie, politically helpless, was emboldened to struggle against its political and economic expropriation only because it saw its elder sister in all countries still in power, and still maintaining economic, political, and, to a certain extent, military supremacy.

If our November revolution had taken place a few months, or even a few weeks, after the establishment of the rule of the proletariat in Germany, France, and England, there can be no doubt that our revolution would have been the most "peaceful," the most "bloodless" of all possible revolutions on this sinful earth. But this historical sequence—the most "natural" at the first glance, and, in any case, the most beneficial for the Russian working class—found itself infringed—not through our fault, but through the will of events. Instead of being the last, the Russian proletariat proved to be the first. It was just this circumstance, after the first period of confusion, that imparted desperation to the character of the resistance of the classes which had ruled in Russia previously, and forced the Russian proletariat, in a moment of the greatest peril, foreign attacks, and internal plots and insurrections, to have recourse to severe measures of State terror. No one will now say that those measures proved futile. But, perhaps, we are expected to consider them "intolerable"?

The working class, which seized power in battle, had as its object and its duty to establish that power unshakeably, to guarantee its own supremacy beyond question, to destroy its enemies' hankering for a new revolution, and thereby to make sure of carrying out Socialist reforms. Otherwise there would be no point in seizing power.

The revolution "logically" does not demand terrorism,

just as "logically" it does not demand an armed insurrection. What a profound commonplace! But the revolution does require of the revolutionary class that it should attain its end by all methods at its disposal—if necessary, by an armed rising: if required, by terrorism. A revolutionary class which has conquered power with arms in its hands is bound to, and will, suppress, rifle in hand, all attempts to tear the power out of its hands. Where it has against it a hostile army, it will oppose to it its own army. Where it is confronted with armed conspiracy, attempt at murder, or rising, it will hurl at the heads of its enemies an unsparing penalty. Perhaps Kautsky has invented other methods? Or does he reduce the whole question to the *degree* of repression, and recommend in all circumstances imprisonment instead of execution?

The question of the form of repression, or of its degree, of course, is not one of "principle." It is a question of expediency. In a revolutionary period, the party which has been thrown from power, which does not reconcile itself with the stability of the ruling class, and which proves this by its desperate struggle against the latter, cannot be terrorized by the threat of imprisonment, as it does not believe in its duration. It is just this simple but decisive fact that explains the widespread recourse to shooting in a civil war.

Or, perhaps, Kautsky wishes to say that execution is not expedient, that "classes cannot be cowed." This is untrue. Terror is helpless—and then only "in the long run"—if it is employed by reaction against a historically rising class. But terror can be very efficient against a reactionary class which does not want to leave the scene of operations. *Intimidation* is a powerful weapon of policy, both internationally and internally. War, like revolution, is founded upon intimidation. A victorious war, generally speaking, destroys only an insignificant part of the conquered army, intimidating the remainder and breaking their will. The revolution works in the same way: it kills individuals, and intimidates thousands. In this sense, the Red Terror is not distinguishable from the armed insurrection, the direct continuation of which it represents. The State terror of a revolutionary class can be condemned "morally" only by a man who, as a principle, rejects (in words) every form of violence whatsoever—

consequently, every war and every rising. For this one has to be merely and simply a hypocritical Quaker.

"But, in that case, in what do your tactics differ from the tactics of Tsarism?" we are asked, by the high priests of Liberalism and Kautskianism.

You do not understand this, holy men? We shall explain to you. The terror of Tsarism was directed against the proletariat. The gendarmerie of Tsarism throttled the workers who were fighting for the Socialist order. Our Extraordinary Commissions shoot landlords, capitalists, and generals who are striving to restore the capitalist order. Do you grasp this...distinction? Yes? For us Communists it is quite sufficient.

"FREEDOM OF THE PRESS"

One point particularly worries Kautsky, the author of a great many books and articles—the freedom of the Press. Is it permissible to suppress newspapers?

During war all institutions and organs of the State and of public opinion become, directly or indirectly, weapons of warfare. This is particularly true of the Press. No government carrying on a serious war will allow publications to exist on its territory which, openly or indirectly, support the enemy. Still more so in a civil war. The nature of the latter is such that each of the struggling sides has in the rear of its armies considerable circles of the population on the side of the enemy. In war, where both success and failure are repaid by death, hostile agents who penetrate into the rear are subject to execution. This is inhumane, but no one ever considered war a school of humanity—still less civil war. Can it be seriously demanded that, during a civil war with the White Guards of Denikin, the publications of parties supporting Denikin should come out unhindered in Moscow and Petrograd? To propose this in the name of the "freedom" of the Press is just the same as, in the name of open dealing, to demand the publication of military secrets. "A besieged city," wrote a Communard, Arthur Arnould of Paris, "cannot permit within its midst that hopes for its fall should openly be expressed, that the fighters defending it should be incited to treason, that the movements of its troops should be communicated to the enemy. Such was the position of Paris

under the Commune." Such is the position of the Soviet
Republic during the two years of its existence.

Let us, however, listen to what Kautsky has to say in
this connection.

"The justification of this system (*i.e.,* repressions in
connection with the Press) is reduced to the naive idea that
an absolute truth (!) exists, and that only the Communists
posses it (!). Similarly," continues Kautsky, "it reduces
itself to another point of view, that all writers are by nature
liars (!) and that only Communists are fanatics for truth (!).
In reality, liars and fanatics for what they consider truth are
to be found in all camps." And so on, and so on, and so on.
(Page 176.)

In this way, in Kautsky's eyes, the revolution, in its most
acute phase, when it is a question of the life and death of
classes, continues as hitherto to be a literary discussion with
the object of establishing...the truth. What profundity!...
Our "truth," of course, is not absolute. But as in its name
we are, at the present moment, shedding our blood, we have
neither cause nor possibility to carry on a literary discussion
as to the relativity of truth with those who "criticize" us
with the help of all forms of arms. Similarly, our problem
is not to punish liars and to encourage just men amongst
journalists of all shades of opinion, but to throttle the class
lie of the bourgeoisie and to achieve the class truth of the
proletariat, irrespective of the fact that in both camps there
are fanatics and liars.

"The Soviet Government," Kautsky thunders, "has destroyed the sole remedy that might militate against corruption: the freedom of the Press. Control by means of unlimited
freedom of the Press alone could have restrained those bandits
and adventurers who will inevitably cling like leeches to
every unlimited, uncontrolled power." (Page 188.) And
so on.

The Press as a trusty weapon of the struggle with corruption! This liberal recipe sounds particularly pitiful when
one remembers the two countries with the greatest "freedom"
of the Press—North America and France—which, at the same
time, are countries of the most highly developed stage of
capitalist corruption.

Feeding on the old scandal of the political ante-rooms of the Russian revolution, Kautsky imagines that without Cadet and Menshevik freedom the Soviet apparatus is honeycombed with "bandits" and "adventurers." Such was the voice of the Mensheviks a year or eighteen months ago. Now even they will not dare to repeat this. With the help of Soviet control and party selection, the Soviet Government, in the intense atmosphere of the struggle, has dealt with the bandits and adventurers who appeared on the surface at the moment of the revolution incomparably better than any government whatsoever, at any time whatsoever.

We are fighting. We are fighting a life-and-death struggle. The Press is a weapon not of an abstract society, but of two irreconcilable, armed and contending sides. We are destroying the Press of the counter-revolution, just as we destroyed its fortified positions, its stores, its communications, and its intelligence system. Are we depriving ourselves of Cadet and Menshevik criticisms of the corruption of the working class? In return we are victoriously destroying the very foundations of capitalist corruption.

But Kautsky goes further to develop his theme. He complains that we suppress the newspapers of the S.R.s and the Mensheviks, and even—such things have been known—arrest their leaders. Are we not dealing here with "shades of opinion" in the proletarian or the Socialist movement? The scholastic pedant does not see facts beyond his accustomed words. The Mensheviks and S.R.s for him are simply tendencies in Socialism, whereas, in the course of the revolution, they have been transformed into an organization which works in active co-operation with the counter-revolution and carries on against us an open war. The army of Kolchak was organized by Socialist Revolutionaries (how that name savours to-day of the charlatan!), and was supported by Mensheviks. Both carried on—and carry on—against us, for a year and a half, a war on the Northern front. The Mensheviks who rule the Caucasus, formerly the allies of Hohenzollern, and to-day the allies of Lloyd George, arrested and shot Bolsheviks hand in hand with German and British officers. The Mensheviks and S.R.s of the Kuban Rada organized the army of Denikin. The Esthonian Mensheviks who participate in their government were directly concerned in the last advance of Yudenich against Petrograd. Such are these "tendencies" in the Socialist movement. Kautsky considers that one can be in a state of open and civil war with the Mensheviks and S.R.s, who, with the help of the troops they themselves have organized for Yudenich, Kolchak and Denikin, are fighting for their "shade of opinions" in Socialism, and at the same time to allow those innocent "shades of opinion" freedom of the Press in our rear. If the dispute with the S.R.s and the Mensheviks could be settled by means of persuasion and voting—that is, if there were not behind their backs the Russian and foreign imperialists—there would be no civil war.

Kautsky, of course, is ready to "condemn"—an extra drop of ink—the blockade, and the Entente support of Denikin, and the White Terror. But in his high impartiality he cannot refuse the latter certain extenuating circumstances. The White Terror, you see, does not infringe their own principles, while the Bolsheviks, making use of the Red Terror, betray the principle of "the sacredness of human life which they themselves proclaimed." (Page 210.)

What is the meaning of the principle of the sacredness of human life in practice, and in what does it differ from the commandment, "Thou shalt not kill," Kautsky does not explain. When a murderer raises his knife over a child, may one kill the murderer to save the child? Will not thereby the principle of the "sacredness of human life" be infringed? May one kill the murderer to save oneself? Is an insurrection of oppressed slaves against their masters permissible? Is it permissible to purchase one's freedom at the cost of the life of one's jailers? If human life in general is sacred and inviolable, we must deny ourselves not only the use of terror, not only war, but also revolution itself. Kautsky simply does not realize the counter-revolutionary meaning of the "principle" which he attempts to force upon us. Elsewhere we shall see that Kautsky accuses us of concluding the Brest-Litovsk peace: in his opinion we ought to have continued war. But what then becomes of the sacredness of human life? Does life cease to be sacred when it is a question of people talking another language, or does Kautsky consider that mass murders organized on principles of strategy and tactics are not murders at all? Truly it is difficult to put forward in our age a principle more hypocritical and more stupid. As long as human labor power, and, consequently, life itself, remain articles of sale and purchase, of exploitation and robbery, the principle of the "sacredness of human life" remains a shameful lie, uttered with the object of keeping the oppressed slaves in their chains.

We used to fight against the death penalty introduced by Kerensky, because that penalty was inflicted by the courts-martial of the old army on soldiers who refused to continue the imperialist war. We tore this weapon out of the hands of the old courts-martial, destroyed the courts-martial themselves, and demobilized the old army which had brought them forth. Destroying in the Red Army, and generally throughout the country, counter-revolutionary conspirators who strive by means of insurrections, murders, and disorganization, to restore the old regime, we are acting in accordance with the iron laws of a war in which we desire to guarantee our victory.

If it is a question of seeking formal contradictions, then obviously we must do so on the side of the White Terror, which is the weapon of classes which consider themselves "Chrisitian," patronize idealist philosophy, and are firmly convinced that the individuality (their own) is an end-in-itself. As for us, we were never concerned with the Kantian-priestly and vegetarian-Quaker prattle about the "sacredness of human life." We were revolutionaries in opposition, and have remained revolutionaries in power. To make the individual sacred we must destroy the social order which crucifies him. And this problem can only be solved by blood and iron.

There is another difference between the White Terror and the Red, which Kautsky to-day ignores, but which in the eyes of a Marxist is of decisive significance. The White Terror is the weapon of the historically reactionary class. When we exposed the futility of the repressions of the bourgeois State against the proletariat, we never denied that by arrests and executions the ruling class, under certain conditions, might temporarily retard the development of the social revolution. But we were convinced that they would not be able to bring it to a halt. We relied on the fact that the proletariat is the historically rising class, and that bourgeois society could not develop without increasing the forces of the proletariat. The bourgeoisie to-day is a falling class. It not only no longer plays an essential part in production, but by its imperialist methods of appropriation is destroying the economic structure of the world and human culture generally. Nevertheless, the historical persistence of the bourgeoisie is colossal. It holds to power, and does not wish to abandon it. Thereby it threatens to drag after it into the abyss the whole of society. We are forced to tear it off, to chop it away. The Red Terror is a weapon utilized against a class, doomed to destruction, which does not wish to perish. If the White Terror can only retard the historical rise of the proletariat, the Red Terror hastens the destruction of the bourgeoisie. This hastening—a pure question of acceleration—is at certain periods of decisive importance. Without the Red Terror, the Russian bourgeoisie, together with the world bourgeoisie, would throttle us long before the coming of the revolution in Europe. One must be blind not to see this, or a swindler to deny it.

The man who recognizes the revolutionary historic importance of the very fact of the existence of the Soviet system must also sanction the Red Terror. Kautsky, who, during the last two years, has covered mountains of paper with polemics against Communism and Terrorism, is obliged, at the end of his pamphlet, to recognize the facts, and unexpectedly to admit that the Russian Soviet Government is to-day the most important factor in the world revolution. "However one regards the Bolshevik methods," he writes, "the fact that a proletarian government in a large country has not only reached power, but has retained it for two years up to the present time, amidst great difficulties, extraordinarily increases the sense of power amongst the proletariat of all countries. For the actual revolution the Bolsheviks have thereby accomplished a great work—*grosses geleistet.* (Page 233.)

This announcement stuns us as a completely unexpected recognition of historical truth from a quarter whence we had long since ceased to await it. The Bolsheviks have accomplished a great historical task by existing for two years against the united capitalist world. But the Bolsheviks held out not only by ideas, but by the sword. Kautsky's admission is an involuntary sanctioning of the methods of the Red Terror, and at the same time the most effective condemnation of his own critical concoction.

THE INFLUENCE OF THE WAR

Kautsky sees one of the reasons for the extremely bloody character of the revolution in the war and in its hardening influence on manners. Quite undeniable. That influence, with all the consequences that follow from it, might have been foreseen earlier—approximately in the period when Kautsky was not certain whether one ought to vote for the war credits or against them.

"Imperialism has violently torn society out of its condition of unstable equilibrium," he wrote five years ago in our German book—*The War and the International.* "It has blown up the sluices with which Social Democracy held back the current of the revolutionary energy of the proletariat, and has directed that current into its own channels. This monstrous historical experiment, which at one blow has broken the back of the Socialist International, represents a deadly danger for bourgeoisie society itself. The hammer has been taken from the hand of the worker, and has been replaced by the sword. The worker, bound hand and foot by the mechanism of capitalist society, has suddenly burst out of its midst, and is learning to put the aims of the community higher than his own domestic happiness and than life itself.

"With this weapon, which he himself has forged, in his hand, the worker is placed in a position in which the political destiny of the State depends directly on him. Those who in former times oppressed and despised him now flatter and caress him. At the same time he is entering into intimate relations with those same guns which, according to Lassalle, constitute the most important integral part of the constitution. He crosses the boundaries of states, participates in violent requisitions, and under his blows towns pass from hand to hand. Changes take place such as the last generation did not dream of.

"If the most advanced workers were aware that force

was the mother of law, their political thought still remained saturated with the spirit of opportunism and self-adaptation to bourgeois legality. To-day the worker has learned in practice to despise that legality, and violently to destroy it. The static moments in his psychology are giving place to the dynamic. Heavy guns are knocking into his head the idea that, in cases where it is impossible to avoid an obstacle, there remains the possibility of destroying it. Nearly the whole adult male population is passing through this school of war, terrible in its social realism, which is bringing forth a new type of humanity.

"Over all the criteria of bourgeois society—its law, its morality, its religion—is now raised the fist of iron necessity. 'Necessity knows no law' was the declaration of the German Chancellor (August 4, 1914). Monarchs come out into the market place to accuse one another of lying in the language of fishwives; governments break promises they have solemnly made, while the national church binds its Lord God like a convict to the national cannon. Is it not obvious that these circumstances must create important alterations in the psychology of the working class, radically curing it of that hypnosis of legality which was created by the period of political stagnation? The propertied classes will soon, to their sorrow, have to be convinced of this. The proletariat, after passing through the school of war, at the first serious obstacle within its own country will feel the necessity of speaking with the language of force. 'Necessity knows no law,' he will throw in the face of those who attempt to stop him by laws of bourgeois legality. And the terrible economic necessity which will arise during the course of this war, and particularly at its end, will drive the masses to spurn very many laws." (Page 56-57.)

All this is undeniable. But to what is said above one must add that the war has exercised no less influence on the psychology of the ruling classes. As the masses become more insistent in their demands, so the bourgeoisie has become more unyielding.

In times of peace, the capitalists used to guarantee their interests by means of the "peaceful" robbery of hired labor. During the war they served those same interests by means of the destruction of countless human lives. This has imparted to their consciousness as a master class a new "Napoleonic" trait. The capitalists during the war became accustomed to send to their death millions of slaves—fellow-countrymen and colonials—for the sake of coal, railway, and other profits.

During the war there emerged from the ranks of the bourgeoisie—large, middle, and small—hundreds of thousands of officers, professional fighters, men whose character has received the hardening of battle, and has become freed from all external restraints: qualified soldiers, ready and able to defend the privileged position of the bourgeoisie which produced them with a ferocity which, in its way, borders on heroism.

The revolution would probably be more humane if the proletariat had the possibility of "buying off all this band," as Marx once put it. But capitalism during the war has imposed upon the toilers too great a load of debt, and has too deeply undermined the foundations of production, for us to be able seriously to contemplate a ransom in return for which the bourgeoisie would silently make its peace with the revolution. The masses have lost too much blood, have suffered too much, have become too savage, to accept a decision which economically would be beyond their capacity.

To this there must be added other circumstances working in the same direction. The bourgeoisie of the conquered countries has been embittered by defeat, the responsibility for which it is inclined to throw on the rank and file—on the workers and peasants who proved incapable of carrying on "the great national war" to a victorious conclusion. From this point of view, one finds very instructive those explanations, unparalleled for their effrontery, which Ludendorff gave to the Commission of the National Assembly. The bands of Ludendorff are burning with the desire to take revenge for their humiliation abroad on the blood of their own proletariat. As for the bourgeoisie of the victorious countries, it has become inflated with arrogance, and is more than ever ready to defend its social position with the help of the bestial methods which guaranteed its victory. We have seen that the bourgeoisie is incapable of organizing the division of the booty amongst its own ranks without war and destruction. Can it, without a fight, abandon its booty altogether? The experience of the last five years leaves no doubt whatsoever on this score: if even previously it was absolutely utopian to expect that the expropriation of the propertied classes—thanks to "democracy"—would take place imperceptibly and painlessly, without insurrections, armed conflicts, attempts at counter-revolution, and severe repression, the state of affairs we have inherited from the imperialist war predetermines, doubly and trebly, the tense character of the civil war and the dictatorship of the proletariat.

5

The Paris Commune and Soviet Russia.

"The short episode of the first revolution carried out by the proletariat for the proletariat ended in the triumph of its enemy. This episode—from March 18 to May 28—lasted seventy-two days."—"The Paris Commune" of March 18, 1871, P. L. Lavrov, Petrograd. 'Kolos' Publishing House, 1919, pp. 160.

THE IMMATURITY OF THE SOCIALIST PARTIES IN THE COMMUNE.

THE Paris Commune of 1871 was the first, as yet weak, historic attempt of the working class to impose its supremacy. We cherished the memory of the Commune in spite of the extremely limited character of its experience, the immaturity of its participants, the confusion of its programme, the lack of unity amongst its leaders, the indecision of their plans, the hopeless panic of its executive organs, and the terrifying defeat fatally precipitated by all these. We cherish in the Commune, in the words of Lavrov, "the first, though still pale, dawn of the proletarian republic." Quite otherwise with Kautsky. Devoting a considerable part of his book to a crudely tendencious contrast between the Commune and the Soviet power, he sees the main advantages of the Commune in features that we find are its misfortune and its fault.

Kautsky laboriously proves that the Paris Commune of 1871 was not "artifically" prepared, but emerged unexpectedly, taking the revolutionaries by surprise—in contrast to the November revolution, which was carefully prepared by our party. This is incontestable. Not daring clearly to formulate his profundly reactionary ideas, Kautsky does not say outright whether the Paris revolutionaries of 1871 deserve praise for not having foreseen the proletarian insurrection, and for not having foreseen the inevitable and consciously gone to meet it. However, all Kautsky's picture was built up in such a way as to produce in the reader just this idea: the Communards were simply overtaken by misfortune (the Bavarian philistine, Vollmar, once expressed his regret that the Communards had not gone to bed instead of taking power into their hands), and, therefore, deserve pity. The Bolsheviks consciously went to meet misfortune (the conquest of power), and, therefore, there is no forgiveness for them either in this or the future world. Such a formulation of the question may seem incredible in its internal inconsistency. None the less, it follows quite inevitably from the position of the Kautskian "Independents," who draw their heads into their shoulders in order to see and foresee nothing; and, if they do move forward, it is only after having received a preliminary stout blow in the rear.

"To humiliate Paris,' writes Kautsky, "not to give it self-government, to deprive it of its position as capital, to disarm it in order afterwards to attempt with greater confidence a monarchist *coup d'état*—such was the most important task of the National Assembly and the chief of the executive power it elected, Thiers. Out of this situation arose the conflict which led to the Paris insurrection.

"It is clear how different from this was the character of the *coup d'état* carried out by the Bolsheviks, which drew its strength from the yearning for peace; which had the peasantry behind it; which had in the National Assembly against it, not monarchists, but S.R.s and Menshevik Social Democrats.

"The Bolsheviks came to power by means of a well-prepared *coup d'état,* which at one blow handed over to them the whole machinery of the State—immediately utilized in the most energetic and merciless manner for the purpose of suppressing their opponents, amongst them their proletarian opponents.

"No one, on the other hand, was more surprised by the insurrection of the Commune than the revolutionaries themselves, and for a considerable number amongst them the conflict was in the highest degree undesirable." (Page 56.)

In order more clearly to realize the actual sense of what Kautsky has written here of the Communards, let us bring forward the following evidence.

"On March 1, 1871," writes Lavrov, in his very instructive book on the Commune, "six months after the fall of the Empire, and a few days before the explosion of the Commune, the guiding personalities in the Paris International still had no definite political programme." (Pages 64-65.)

"After March 18," writes the same author, "Paris was in the hands of the proletariat, but its leaders, overwhelmed by their unexpected power, did not take the most elementary measures." (Page 71.)

" 'Your part is too big for you to play, and your sole aim is to get rid of responsibility,' said one member of the Central Committee of the National Guard. In this was a great deal of truth," writes the Communard and historian of the Commune, Lissagaray. "But at the moment of action itself the absence of preliminary organization and preparation is very often a reason why parts are assigned to men which are too big for them to play." (Brussels, 1876; page 106.)

From this one can already see (later on it will become still more obvious) that the absence of a direct struggle for power on the part of the Paris Socialists was explained by their theoretical shapelessness and political helplessness, and not at all by higher considerations of tactics.

We have no doubt that Kautsky's own loyalty to the traditions of the Commune will be expressed mainly in that extraordinary surprise with which he will greet the proletarian revolution in Germany as "a conflict in the highest degree undesirable." We doubt, however, whether this will be ascribed by posterity to his credit. In reality, one must describe his historical analogy as a combination of confusion, omission, and fraudulent suggestion.

The intentions which were entertained by Thiers towards Paris were entertained by Miliukov, who was openly supported by Tseretelli and Chernov, towards Petrograd. All of them, from Kornilov to Potressov, affirmed day after day that Petrograd had alienated itself from the country, had nothing in common with it, was completely corrupted, and was attempting to impose its will upon the community. To overthrow and humiliate Petrograd was the first task of Miliukov and his assistants. And this took place at a period when Petrograd was the true centre of the revolution, which had not yet been able to consolidate its position in the rest of the country. The former president of the Duma, Rodzianko, openly talked about handing over Petrograd to the Germans for educative purposes, as Riga had been handed over. Rodzianko only called by its name what Miliukov was trying to carry out, and what Kerensky assisted by his whole policy.

Miliukov, like Thiers, wished to disarm the proletariat. More than that, thanks to Kerensky, Chernov, and Tseretelli, the Petrograd proletariat was to a considerable extent disarmed in July, 1917. It was partially re-armed during Kornilov's march on Petrograd in August. And this new arming was a serious element in the preparation of the November insurrection. In this way, it is just the points in which Kautsky contrasts our November revolution to the March revolt of the Paris workers that, to a very large extent, coincide.

In what, however, lies the difference between them? First of all, in the fact that Thiers' criminal plans succeeded: Paris was throttled by him, and tens of thousands of workers were destroyed. Miliukov, on the other hand, had a complete fiasco: Petrograd remained an impregnable fortress of the proletariat, and the leader of the bourgeoisie went to the Ukraine to petition that the Kaiser's troops should occupy Russia. For this difference we were to a considerable extent responsible—and we are ready to bear the responsibility. There is a capital difference also in the fact—that this told more than once in the further course of events—that, while the Communards began mainly with considerations of patriotism, we were invariably guided by the point of view of the international revolution. The defeat of the Commune led to the practical collapse of the First International. The victory of the Soviet power has led to the creation of the Third International.

But Marx—on the eve of the insurrection—advised the Communards not to revolt, but to create an organization! One might understand Kautsky if he adduced this evidence in order to show that Marx had insufficiently gauged the acuteness of the situation in Paris. But Kautsky attempts to exploit Marx's advice as a proof of his condemnation of insurrection in general. Like all the mandarins of German Social Democracy, Kautsky sees in organization first and foremost a method of hindering revolutionary action.

But limiting ourselves to the question of organization as such, we must not forget that the November revolution was preceded by nine months of Kerensky's Government, during which our party, not without success, devoted itself not only to agitation, but also to organization. The November revolution took place after we had achieved a crushing majority in the Workers' and Soldiers' Councils of Petrograd, Moscow, and all the industrial centres in the country, and had transformed the Soviets into powerful organizations directed by our party. The Communards did nothing of the kind. Finally, we had behind us the heroic Commune of Paris, from the defeat of which we had drawn the deduction that revolutionaries must foresee events and prepare for them. For this also we are to blame.

Kautsky requires his extensive comparison of the Commune and Soviet Russia only in order to slander and humiliate a living and victorious dictatorship of the proletariat in the interests of an attempted dictatorship, in the already fairly distant past.

Kautsky quotes with extreme satisfaction the statement of the Central Committee of the National Guard on March 19 in connection with the murder of the two generals by the soldiery. "We say indignantly: the bloody filth with the help of which it is hoped to stain our honor is a pitiful slander. We never organized murder, and never did the National Guard take part in the execution of crime."

Naturally, the Central Committee had no cause to assume responsibility for murders with which it had no concern. But the sentimental, pathetic tone of the statement very clearly characterises the political timorousness of these men in the face of bourgeois public opinion. Nor is this surprising. The representatives of the National Guard were men in most cases with a very modest revolutionary past. "Not one well-known name," writes Lissagaray. "They were pettybourgeois shopkeepers, strangers to all but limited circles, and, in most cases, strangers hitherto to politics." (Page 70.)

"The modest and, to some extent, fearful sense of terrible

historical responsibility, and the desire to get rid of it as soon as possible," writes Lavrov of them, "is evident in all the proclamations of this Central Committee, into the hands of which the destiny of Paris had fallen." (Page 77.)

After bringing forward, to our confusion, the declamation concerning bloodshed, Kautsky later on follows Marx and Engels in criticizing the indecision of the Commune. "If the Parisians (*i.e.*, the Communards) had persistently followed up the tracts of Thiers, they would, perhaps, have managed to seize the government. The troops falling back from Paris would not have shown the least resistance... but they let Thiers go without hindrance. They allowed him to lead away his troops and reorganize them at Versailles, to inspire a new spirit in, and strengthen, them." (Page 49.)

Kautsky cannot understand that it was the same men, and for the very same reasons, who published the statement of March 19 quoted above, who allowed Thiers to leave Paris with impunity and gather his forces. If the Communards had *conquered* with the help of resources of a purely moral character, their statement would have acquired great weight. But this did not take place. In reality, their sentimental humaneness was simply the obverse of their revolutionary passivity. The men who, by the will of fate, had received power in Paris, could not understand the necessity of immediately utilizing that power to the end, of hurling themselves after Thiers, and, before he recovered his grasp of the situation, of crushing him, of concentrating the troops in their hands, of carrying out the necessary weeding-out of the officer class, of seizing the provinces. Such men, of course, were not inclined to severe measures with counter-revolutionary elements. The one was closely bound up with the other. Thiers could not be followed up without arresting Thiers' agents in Paris and shooting conspirators and spies. When one considered the execution of counter-revolutionary generals as an indelible "crime," one could not develop energy in following up troops who were under the direction of counter-revolutionary generals.

In the revolution in the highest degree of energy is the highest degree of humanity. "Just the men," Lavrov justly remarks, "who hold human life and human blood dear must strive to organize the possibility for a swift and decisive victory, and then to act with the greatest swiftness and energy, in order to crush the enemy. For only in this way can we achieve the minimum of inevitable sacrifice and the minimum of bloodshed." (Page 225.)

The statement of March 19 will, however, be considered with more justice if we examine it, not as an unconditional confession of faith, but as the expression of transient moods the day after an unexpected and bloodless victory. Being an absolute stranger to the understanding of the dynamics of revolution, and the internal limitations of its swiftly-developing moods, Kautsky thinks in lifeless schemes, and distorts the perspective of events by arbitrarily selected analogies. He does not understand that soft-hearted indecision is generally characteristic of the masses in the first period of the revolution. The workers pursue the offensive only under the pressure of iron necessity, just as they have recourse to the Red Terror only under the threat of destruction by the White Guards. That which Kautsky represents as the result of the peculiarly elevated moral feeling of the Parisian proletariat in 1871 is, in reality, merely a characteristic of the first stage of the civil war. A similar phenomenon could have been witnessed in our case.

In Petrograd we conquered power in November, 1917, almost without bloodshed, and even without arrests. The ministers of Kerensky's Government were set free very soon after the revolution. More, the Cossack General, Krasnov, who had advanced on Petrograd together with Kerensky after the power had passed to the Soviet, and who had been made prisoner by us at Gatchina, was set free on his word of honor the next day. This was "generosity" quite in the spirit of the first measures of the Commune. But it was a mistake. Afterwards, General Krasnov, after fighting against us for about a year in the South, and destroying many thousands of Communists, again advanced on Petrograd, this time in the ranks of Yudenich's army. The proletarian revolution assumed a more severe character only after the rising of the junkers in Petrograd, and particularly after the rising of the Czecho-Slovaks on the Volga organized by the Cadets, the S.R.s, and the Mensheviks, after their mass executions of Communists, the attempt on Lenin's life, the murder of Uritsky, etc., etc.

The same tendencies, only in an embryonic form, we see in the history of the Commune.

Driven by the logic of the struggle, it took its stand in principle on the path of intimidation. The creation of the Committee of Public Safety was dictated, in the case of many of its supporters, by the idea of the Red Terror. The Committee was apopinted "to cut off the heads of traitors" (Journal Officiel" No. 123), "to avenge treachery" (No. 124). Under the head of "intimidatory" decrees we must class the order to seize the property of Thiers and of his ministers. to destroy Thiers' house, to destroy the Vendome column, and especially the decree on hostages. For every captured Communard or sympathizer with the Commune shot by the Versaillese, three hostages were to be shot. The activity of the Prefecture of Paris controlled by Raoul Rigault had a purely terroristic, though not always a useful, purpose.

The effect of all these measures of intimidation was paralyzed by the helpless opportunism of the guiding elements in the Commune, by their striving to reconcile the bourgeoisie with the *fait accompli* by the help of pitiful phrases, by their vacillations between the fiction of democracy and the reality of dictatorship. The late Lavrov expresses the latter idea splendidly in his book on the Commune.

"The Paris of the rich bourgeois and the poor proletarians, as a political community of different classes, demanded, in the name of liberal principles, complete freedom of speech, of assembly, of criticism of the government, etc. The Paris which had accomplished the revolution in the interests of the proletariat, and had before it the task of realizing this revolution in the shape of institutions, Paris, as the community of the emancipated working-class proletariat, demanded revolutionary—*i.e.*, dictatorial, measures against the enemies of the new order." (Pages 143-144.)

If the Paris Commune had not fallen, but had continued to exist in the midst of a ceaseless struggle, there can be no doubt that it would have been obliged to have recourse to more and more severe measures for the suppression of the counter-revolution. True, Kautsky would not then have had the possibility of contrasting the humane Communards with the inhumane Bolsheviks. But in return, probably, Thiers, would not have had the possibility of inflicting his monstrous bloodletting upon the proletariat of Paris. History, possibly, would not have been the loser.

THE IRRESPONSIBLE CENTRAL COMMITTEE AND THE "DEMOCRATIC" COMMUNE

"On March 19," Kautsky informs us, "in the Central Committee of the National Guard, some demanded a march on Versailles, others an appeal to the electors, and a third party the adoption first of all of revolutionary measures; as if every one of these steps," he proceeds very learnedly to inform us, "were not equally necessary, and as if one excluded the other." (Page 72.) Further on, Kautsky, in connection with these disputes in the Commune, presents us with various warmed-up platitudes as to the mutual relations of reform and revolution. In reality, the following was the situation. If it were decided to march on Versailles, and to do this without losing an hour it was necessary immediately to reorganize the National Guard, to place at its head the best fighting elements of the Paris proletariat, and thereby temporarily to weaken Paris from the revolutionary point of view. But to organize elections in Paris, while at the same time sending out of its walls the flower of the working class, would have been senseless from the point of view of the revolutionary party. Theoretically, a march on Versailles and elections to the Commune, of course, did not exclude each other in the slightest degree, but in practice they did exclude each other: for the success of the elections, it was necessary to postpone the attack; for the attack to succeed, the elections must be put off. Finally, leading the proletariat out to the field and thereby temporarily weakening Paris, it was essential to obtain some guarantee against the possibility of counter-revolutionary attempts in the capital; for Thiers would not have hesitated at any measures to raise a white revolt in the rear of the Communards. It was essential to establish a more military—*i.e.*, a more stringent regime in the capital. "They had to fight," writes Lavrov, "against many internal foes with whom Paris was full, who only yesterday had been rioting around the

Exchange and the Vendome Square, who had their representatives in the administration and in the National Guard, who
possessed their press, and their meetings, who almost openly
maintained contact with the Versaillese, and who became
more determined and more audacious at every piece of carelessness, at every check of the Commune." (Page 87.)

It was necessary, side by side with this, to carry out
revolutionary measures of a financial and generally of an
economic character: first and foremost, for the equipment
of the revolutionary army. All these most necessary measures
of revolutionary dictatorship could with difficulty be reconciled with an extensive electoral campaign. But Kautsky has
not the least idea of what a revolution is in practice. He
thinks that theoretically to reconcile is the same as practically
to accomplish.

The Central Committee appointed March 22 as the day
of elections for the Commune; but, not sure of itself, frightened
at its own illegality, striving to act in unison with more "legal"
institutions, entered into ridiculous and endless negotiations
with a quite helpless assembly of mayors and deputies of
Paris, showing its readiness to divide power with them if
only an agreement could be arrived at. Meanwhile precious
time was slipping by.

Marx, on whom Kautsky, through old habit, tries to rely,
did not under any circumstances propose that, at one and
the same time, the Commune should be elected and the workers
should be led out into the field for the war. In his letter
to Kugelmann, Marx wrote, on April 12, 1871, that the Central
Committee of the National Guard had too soon given up its
power in favor of the Commune. Kautsky, in his own words,
"does not understand" this opinion of Marx. It is quite
simple. Marx at any rate understod that the problem was
not one of chasing legality, but of inflicting a fatal blow upon
the enemy. "If the Central Committee had consisted of
real revolutionaries," says Lavrov, and rightly, "it ought to
have acted differently. It would have been quite unforgivable
for it to have given the enemy ten days' respite before the
election and assembly of the Commune, while the leaders
of the proletariat refused to carry out their duty and did not
recognize that they had the right immediately to *lead* the

proletariat. As it was, the feeble immaturity of the popular parties created a Committee which considered those ten days of inaction incumbent upon it." (Page 78.)

The yearning of the Central Committee to hand over power as soon as possible to a "legal" Government was dictated, not so much by the superstitions of former democracy, of which, by the way, there was no lack, as by fear of responsibility. Under the plea that it was a temporary institution, the Central Committee avoided the taking of the most necessary and absolutely pressing measures, in spite of the fact that all the material apparatus of power was centred in its hands. But the Commune itself did not take over political power in full from the Central Committee, and the latter continued to interfere in all business quite unceremoniously. This created a dual Government, which was extremely dangerous, particularly under military conditions.

On May 3 the Central Committee sent deputies to the Commune demanding that the Ministry for War should be placed under its control. Again there arose, as Lissagaray writes, the question as to whether "the Central Committee should be dissolved, or arrested, or entrusted with the administration of the Ministry for War."

Here was a question, not of the principles of democracy, but of the absence, in the case of both parties, of a clear programme of action, and of the readiness, both of the irresponsible revolutionary organizations in the shape of the Central Committee and of the "democratic" organization of the Commune, to shift the responsibility on to the other's shoulders, while at the same time not entirely renouncing power.

These were political relations which it might seem no one could call worthy of imitation.

"But the Central Committee," Kautsky consoles himself, "never attempted to infringe the principle in virtue of which the supreme power must belong to the delegates elected by universal suffrage. In this respect the "Paris Commune was the direct antithesis of the Soviet Republic." (Page 74.) There was no unity of government, there was no revolutionary decision, there existed a division of power, and, as a result, there came swift and terrible destruction. But to counterbalance this—is it not comforting?—there was no infringement of the "principle" of democracy.

THE DEMOCRATIC COMMUNE AND THE REVOLUTIONARY DICTATORSHIP

Comrade Lenin has already pointed out to Kautsky that attempts to depict the Commune as the expression of formal democracy constitute a piece of absolute theoretical swindling. The Commune, in its tradition and in the conception of its leading political party—the Blanquists—was the expression of *the dictatorship of the revolutionary city over the country.* So it was in the great French Revolution; so it would have been in the revolution of 1871 if the Commune had not fallen in the first days. The fact that in Paris itself a Government was elected on the basis of universal suffrage does not exclude a much more significant fact—namely, that of the military operations carried on by the Commune, one city, against peasant France, that is the whole country. To satisfy the great democrat, Kautsky, the revolutionaries of the Commune ought, as a preliminary, to have consulted, by means of universal suffrage, the whole population of France as to whether it permitted them to carry on a war with Thiers' bands.

Finally, in Paris itself the elections took place after the bourgeoisie, or at least its most active elements, had fled, and after Thiers' troops had been evacuated. The bourgeoisie that remained in Paris, in spite of all its impudence, was still afraid of the revolutionary battalions, and the elections took place under the auspices of that fear, which was the forerunner of what in the future would have been inevitable— namely, of the Red Terror. But to console oneself with the thought that the Central Committee of the National Guard, under the dictatorship of which—unfortunately a very feeble and formalist dictatorship—the elections to the Commune were held, did not infringe the principle of universal suffrage, is truly to brush with the shadow of a broom.

Amusing himself by barren analogies, Kautsky benefits by the circumstance that his reader is not acquainted with the facts. In Petrograd, in November, 1917, we also elected a Commune (Town Council) on the basis of the most "democratic" voting, without limitations for the bourgeoisie. These elections, being boycotted by the bourgeoisie parties, gave us a crushing majority. The "democratically" elected Council voluntarily submitted to the Petrograd Soviet—*i.e.,* placed the fact of the dictatorship of the proletariat higher than the "principle" of universal suffrage, and, after a short time, dissolved itself altogether by its own act, in favor of one of the sections of the Petrograd Soviet. Thus the Petrograd Soviet—that true father of the Soviet regime—has upon itself the seal of a formal "democratic" benediction in no way less than the Paris Commune. *

"At the elections of March 26, eighty members were elected to the Commune. Of these, fifteen were members of the government party (Thiers), and six were bourgeois radicals who were in opposition to the Government, but condemned the rising (of the Paris workers).

"The Soviet Republic," Kautsky teaches us, "would never have allowed such counter-revolutionary elements to stand as candidates, let alone be elected. The Commune, on the other hand, out of respect for democracy, did not place the least obstacle in the way of the election of its bourgeois opponents." (Page 74.)

We have already seen above that here Kautsky completely misses the mark. First of all, at a similar stage of development of the Russian Revolution, there did not take place democratic elections to the Petrograd Commune, in which the Soviet Government placed no obstacle in the way of the bourgeois parties; and if the Cadets, the S.R.s and the Mensheviks, who had their press which was openly calling for

---

* It is not without interest to observe that in the Communal elections of 1871 in Paris there participated 230,000 electors. At the Town elections of November, 1917, in Petrograd, in spite of the boycott of the election on the part of all parties except ourselves and the Left Social Revolutionaries, who had no influence in the capital, there participated 390,000 electors. In Paris, in 1871, the population numbered two millions. In Petrograd, in November, 1917, there were not more than two millions. It must be noticed that our electoral system was infinitely more democratic. The Central Committee of the National Guard carried out the elections on the basis of the electoral law of the empire.

the overthrow of the Soviet Government, boycotted the elections, it was only because at that time they still hoped soon to make an end of us with the help of armed force. Secondly, no democracy expressing all classes was actually to be found in the Paris Commune. The bourgeois deputies—Conservatives, Liberals, Gambettists—found no place in it.

"Nearly all these individuals," says Lavrov, "either immediately or very soon, left the Council of the Commune. They might have been representatives of Paris as a free city under the rule of the bourgeoisie, but were quite out of place in the Council of the Commune, which, willy-nilly, consistently or inconsistently, completely or incompletely, did represent the revolution of the proletariat, and an attempt, feeble though it might be, of building up forms of society corresponding to that revolution." (Pages 111-112.) If the Petrograd bourgeoisie had not boycotted the municipal elections, its representatives would have entered the Petrograd Council. They would have remained there up to the first Social Revolutionary and Cadet rising, after which—with the permission or without the permission of Kautsky—they would probably have been arrested if they did not leave the Council in good time, as at a certain moment did the bourgeois members of the Paris Commune. The course of events would have remained the same: only on their surface would certain episodes have worked out differently.

In supporting the democracy of the Commune, and at the same time accusing it of an insufficiently decisive note in its attitude to Versailles, Kautsky does not understand that the Communal elections, carried out with the ambiguous help of the "lawful" mayors and deputies, reflected the hope of a peaceful agreement with Versailles. This is the whole point. The leaders were anxious for a compromise, not for a struggle. The masses had not yet outlived their illusions. Undeserved revolutionary reputations had not yet had time to be exposed. Everything taken together was called democracy.

"We must rise above our enemies by moral force..." preached Vermorel. "We must not infringe liberty and individual life..." Striving to avoid fratricidal war, Vermorel called upon the liberal bourgeoisie, whom hitherto he had so

mercilessly exposed, to set up "a lawful Government, recognized and respected by the whole population of Paris."
The *Journal Officiel,* published under the editorship of the
Internationalist Longuet, wrote: "The sad misunderstanding,
which in the June days (1848) armed two classes of society
against each other, cannot be renewed.... Class antagonism
has ceased to exist...." (March 30.) And, further: "Now
all conflicts will be appeased, because all are inspired with a
feeling of solidarity, because never yet was there so little
social hatred and social antagonism." (April 3.)

At the session of the Commune of April 25, Jourdé, and
not without foundation, congratulated himself on the fact
that the Commune had "never yet infringed the principle of
private property." By this means they hoped to win over
bourgeois public opinion and find the path to compromise.

"Such a doctrine," says Lavrov, and rightly, "did not
in the least disarm the enemies of the proletariat, who understood excellently with what its sucess threatened them, and
only sapped the proletarian energy and, as it were, deliberately
blinded it in the face of its irreconcilable enemies." (Page
137.) But this enfeebling doctrine was inextricably bound
up with the fiction of democracy. The form of mock legality
it was that allowed them to think that the problem would be
solved without a struggle. "As far as the mass of the population is concerned," writes Arthur Arnould, a member of
the Commune, "it was to a certain extent justified in the
belief in the existence of, at the very least, a hidden agreement with the Government." Unable to attract the bourgeoisie,
the compromisers, as always, deceived the proletariat.

The clearest evidence of all that, in the conditions of the
inevitable and already beginning civil war, democratic parliamentarism expressed only the compromizing helplessness of
the leading groups, was the senseless procedure of the supplementary elections to the Commune of April 6. At this moment,
"it was no longer a question of voting," writes Arthur Arnould. "The situation had become so tragic that there was
not either the time or the calmness necessary for the correct
functioning of the elections.... All persons devoted to the
Commune were on the fortifications, in the forts, in the foremost detachments.... The people attributed no importance

whatever to these supplementary elections. The elections were in reality merely parliamentarism. What was required was not to count voters, but to have soldiers: not to discover whether we had lost or gained in the Commune of Paris, but to defend Paris from the Versaillese." From these words Kautsky might have observed why in practice it is not so simple to combine class war with interclass democracy.

"The Commune is not a Constituent Assembly," wrote in his book, Milliere, one of the best brains of the Commune. "It is a military Council. It must have one aim, victory; one weapon, force; one law, the law of social salvation."

"They could never understand," Lissagaray accuses the leaders, "that the Commune was a barricade, and not an administration."

They began to understand it in the end, when it was too late. Kautsky has not understood it to this day. There is no reason to believe that he will ever understand it.

* * *

The Commune was the living negation of formal democracy, for in its development it signified the dictatorship of working class Paris over the peasant country. It is this fact that dominates all the rest. However much the political doctrinaires, in the midst of the Commune itself, clung to the appearances of democractic legality, every action of the Commune, though insufficient for victory, was sufficient to reveal its illegal nature.

The Commune—that is to say, the Paris City Council— repealed the national law concerning conscription. It called its official organ *The Official Journal of the French Republic.* Though cautiously, it still laid hands on the State Bank. It proclaimed the separation of Church and State, and abolished the Church Budgets. It entered into relations with various embassies. And so on, and so on. It did all this in virtue of the revolutionary dictatorship. But Clemenceau, young democrat as he was then, would not recognize that virtue.

At a conference with the Central Committee, Clemenceau said: "The rising had an unlawful beginning.... Soon the Committee will become ridiculous, and its decrees will be despised. Besides, Paris has not the right to rise against France, and must unconditionally accept the authority of the Assembly."

The problem of the Commune was to dissolve the National Assembly. Unfortunately it did not succeed in doing so. To-day Kautsky seeks to discover for its criminal intentions some mitigating circumstances.

He points out that the Communards had as their opponents in the National Assembly the monarchists, while we in the Constituent Assembly had against us...Socialists, in the persons of the S.R.s, and the Mensheviks. A complete mental eclipse! Kautsky talks about the Mensheviks and the S.R.s, but forgets our sole serious foe—the Cadets. It was they who represented our Russian Thiers party—*i.e.,* a bloc of property owners in the name of property: and Professor Miliukov did his utmost to imitate the "little great man." Very soon indeed—long before the October Revolution— Miliukov began to seek his Galifet in the generals Kornilov, Alexeiev, then Kaledin, Krasnov, in turn. And after Kolchak had thrown aside all political parties, and had dissolved the Constituent Assembly, the Cadet Party, the sole serious bourgeois party, in its essence monarchist through and through, not only did not refuse to support him, but on the contrary devoted more sympathy to him than before.

The Mensheviks and the S.R.s played no independent role amongst us—just like Kautsky's party during the revolutionary events in Germany. They based their whole policy upon a coalition with the Cadets, and thereby put the Cadets in a position to dictate quite irrespective of the balance of political forces. The Socialist-Revolutionary and Menshevik Parties were only an intermediary apparatus for the purpose of collecting, at meetings and elections, the political confidence of the masses awakened by the revolution, and for handing it over for disposal by the counter-revolutionary imperialist party of the Cadets—independently of the issue of the elections.

The purely vassal-like dependence of the S.R.s and Menshevik *majority* on the Cadet *minority* itself represented a very thinly-veiled insult to the idea of "democracy." But this is not all.

86

In all districts of the country where the regime of "democracy" lived too long, it inevitably ended in an open *coup d'etat* of the counter-revolution. So it was in the Ukraine, where the democratic Rada, having sold the Soviet Government to German imperialism, found itself overthrown by the monarchist Skoropadsky. So it was in the Kuban, where the democratic Rada found itself under the heel of Denikin. So it was—and this was the most important experiment of our "democracy"—in Siberia, where the Constituent Assembly, with the formal supremacy of the S.R.s and the Mensheviks, in the absence of the Bolsheviks, and the *de facto* guidance of the Cadets, led in the end to the dictatorship of the Tsarist Admiral Kolchak. So it was, finally, in the north, where the Constituent Assembly government of the Socialist-Revolutionary Chaikovsky became merely a tinsel decoration for the rule of counter-revolutionary generals, Russian and British. So it was, or is, in all the small Border States—in Finland, Esthonia, Latvia, Lithuania, Poland, Georgia, Armenia—where, under the formal banner of "democracy," there is being consolidated the supremacy of the landlords, the capitalists, and the foreign militarists.

THE PARIS WORKER OF 1871 AND THE PETROGRAD
PROLETARIAN OF 1917

One of the most coarse, unfounded, and politically disgraceful comparisons which Kautsky makes between the Commune and Soviet Russia is touching the character of the Paris worker in 1871 and the Russian proletarian of 1917-19. The first Kautsky depicts as a revolutionary enthusiast capable of a high measure of self-sacrifice; the second, as an egoist and a coward, an irresponsible anarchist.

The Parisian worker has behind him too definite a past to need revolutionary recommendations—or protection from the praises of the present Kautsky. None the less, the Petrograd proletarian has not, and cannot have, any reason for avoiding a comparison with his heroic elder brother. The continuous three years' struggle of the Petrograd workers—first for the conquest of power, and then for its maintenance and consolidation—represents an exceptional story of collective heroism and self-sacrifice, amidst unprecedented tortures in the shape of hunger, cold, and constant perils.

Kautsky, as we can discover in another connection, takes for contrast with the flower of the Communards the most sinister elements of the Russian proletariat. In this respect also he is in no way different from the bourgeois sycophants, to whom dead Communards always appear infinitely more attractive than the living.

The Petrograd proletariat seized power four and a half decades after the Parisian. This period has told enormously in our favor. The petty-bourgeois craft character of old and partly of new Paris is quite foreign to Petrograd, the centre of the most concentrated industry in the world. The latter circumstances has extremely facilitated our tasks of agitation and organization, as well as the setting up of the Soviet system.

Our proletariat did not have even a faint measure of the rich revolutionary traditions of the French proletariat. But, instead, there was still very fresh in the memory of the older generation of our workers, at the beginning of the present revolution, the great experiment of 1905, its failure, and the duty of vengeance it had handed down.

The Russian workers had not, like the French, passed through a long school of democracy and parliamentarism, which at a certain epoch represented an important factor in the political education of the proletariat. But, on the other hand, the Russian working class had not had seared into its soul the bitterness of dissolution and the poison of scepticism, which up to a certain, and—let us hope—not very distant moment, still restrain the revolutionary will of the French proletariat.

The Paris Commune suffered a military defeat before economic problems had arisen before it in their full magnitude. In spite of the splendid fighting qualities of the Paris workers, the military fate of the Commune was at once determined as hopeless. Indecision and compromise-mongering above brought about collapse below.

The pay of the National Guard was issued on the basis of the existence of 162,000 rank and file and 6,500 officers; the number of those who actually went into battle, especially after the unsuccessful sortie of April 3, varied between twenty and thirty thousand.

These facts do not in the least compromise the Paris workers, and do not give us the right to consider them cowards and deserters—although, of course, there was no lack of desertion. For a fighting army there must be, first of all, a centralized and accurate apparatus of administration. Of this the Commune had not even a trace.

The War Department of the Commune, was, in the expression of one writer, as it were a dark room, in which all collided. The office of the Ministry was filled with officers and ordinary Guards, who demanded military supplies and food, and complained that they were not relieved. They were sent to the garrison....

"One battalion remained in the trenches for 20 and 30 days, while others were constantly in reserve.... This carelessness soon killed any discipline. Courageous men soon determined to rely only on themselves; others avoided service. In the same way did officers behave. One would leave his post to go to the help of a neighbor who was under fire; others went away to the city..." (Lavrov, page 100.)

Such a regime could not remain unpunished; the Commune was drowned in blood. But in this connection Kautsky has a marvelous solution.

"The waging of war," he says, sagely shaking his head, "is, after all, not a strong side of the proletariat." (Page 76.)

This aphorism, worthy of Pangloss, is fully on a level with the other great remark of Kautsky, namely, that the International is not a suitable weapon to use in wartime, being in its essence an "instrument of peace."

In these two aphorisms, in reality, may be found the present Kautsky, complete, in his entirety— *i. e.*, just a little over a round zero.

The waging of war, do you see, is on the whole, not a strong side of the proletariat, the more that the International itself was not created for wartime. Kautsky's ship was built for lakes and quiet harbors, not at all for the open sea, and not for a period of storms. If that ship has sprung a leak, and has begun to fill, and is now comfortably going to the bottom, we must throw all the blame upon the storm, the unnecessary mass of water, the extraordinary size of the waves, and a series of other unforeseen circumstances for which Kautsky did not build his marvelous instrument.

The international proletariat put before itself as its problem the conquest of power. Independently of whether civil war, "generally," belongs to the inevitable attributes of revolution, "generally," this fact remains unquestioned—that the advance of the proletariat, at any rate in Russia, Germany, and parts of former Austro-Hungary, took the form of an intense civil war not only on internal but also on external fronts. If the waging of war is not the strong side of the proletariat, while the workers' International is suited only for peaceful epochs, then we may as well erect a cross over the revolution and over Socialism; for the waging of war is a fairly *strong* side of the capitalist State, which *without* a war will not admit the workers to supremacy. In that case there remains only to proclaim the so-called "Socialist" democracy to be merely the accompanying feature of capitalist society and bourgeois parliamentarism—*i. e.,* openly to sanction what the Eberts, Schneidermanns, Renaudels, carry out in practice and what Kautsky still, it seems, protests against in words.

The waging of war was not a strong side of the Commune. Quite so; that was why it was crushed. And how mercilessly crushed!

"We have to recall the proscriptions of Sulla, Antony, and Octavius," wrote in his time the very moderate liberal, Fiaux, "to meet such massacres in the history of civilized nations. The religious wars under the last Valois, the night of St. Bartholomew, the Reign of Terror were, in comparison with it, child's play. In the last week of May alone, in Paris, 17,000 corpses of the insurgent Federals were picked up... the killing was still going on about June 15."

"The waging of war, after all, is not the strong side of the proletariat."

It is not true! The Russian workers have shown that they are capable of wielding the "instrument of war" as well. We see here a gigantic step forward in comparison with the Commune. It is not a renunciation of the Commune—for the traditions of the Commune consist not at all in its helplessness—but the continuation of its work. The Commune was weak. To complete its work we have become strong. The Commune was crushed. We are inflicting blow after blow upon the executioners of the Commune. We are taking vengeance for the Commune, and we shall avenge it.

*   *   *

Out of 167,000 National Guards who received pay, only twenty or thirty thousand went into battle. These figures serve as interesting material for conclusions as to the role of formal democracy in a revolutionary epoch. The vote of the Paris Commune was decided, not at the elections, but in the battles with the troops of Thiers. One hundred and sixty-seven thousand National Guards represented the great mass of the electorate. But in reality, in the battles, the fate of the Commune was decided by twenty or thirty thousand persons; the most devoted fighting minority. This minority did not stand alone: it simply expressed, in a more courageous and self-sacrificing manner, the will of the majority. But none the less it *was* a minority. The others who hid at the critical moment were not hostile to the Commune; on the contrary, they actively or passively supported it, but they were less politically conscious, less decisive. On the arena of political democracy, their lower level of political consciousness afforded the possibility of their being deceived by adventurers, swindlers, middle-class cheats, and honest dullards who really deceived themselves. But, at the moment of open class war, they, to a greater or lesser degree, followed the self-sacrificing minority. It was this that found its expression in the organization of the National Guard. If the existence of the Commune had been prolonged, this relationship between the advance guard and the mass of the proletariat would have grown more and more firm.

The organization which would have been formed and consolidated in the process of the open struggle, as the organization of the laboring masses, would have become the organization of their dictatorship—the Council of Deputies of the armed proletariat.

6.

Marx and......Kautsky.

KAUTSKY loftily sweeps aside Marx's views on terror, expressed by him in the *Neue Rheinische Zeitung*—as at that time, do you see, Marx was still very "young," and consequently his views had not yet had time to arrive at that condition of complete enfeeblement which is so clearly to be observed in the case of certain theoreticians in the seventh decade of their life. As a contrast to the green Marx of 1848-49 (the author of the *Communist Manifesto!*) Kautsky quotes the mature Marx of the epoch of the Paris Commune —and the latter, under the pen of Kautsky, loses his great lion's mane, and appears before us as an extremely respectable reasoner, bowing before the holy places of democracy, declaiming on the sacredness of human life, and filled with all due reverence for the political charms of Schneidermann, Vandervelde, and particularly of his own physical grandson, Jean Longuet. In a word, Marx, instructed by the experience of life, proves to be a well-behaved Kautskian.

From the deathless *Civil War in France*, the pages of which have been filled with a new and intense life in our own epoch, Kautsky has quoted only those lines in which the mighty theoretician of the social revolution contrasted the generosity of the Communards with the bourgeois ferocity of the Versaillese. Kautsky has devastated these lines and made them commonplace. Marx, as the preacher of detached humanity, as the apostle of general love of mankind! Just as if we were talking about Buddha or Leo Tolstoy... It is more than natural that, against the international campaign which represented the Communards as *souteneurs* and the women of the Commune as prostitutes, against the vile slanders which attributed to the conquered fighters ferocious features drawn from the degenerate imagination of the victorious bourgeoisie, Marx should emphasize and underline those features of tenderness and nobility which not infrequently were merely the reverse side of indecision. Marx was Marx. He was neither an empty pedant, nor, all the more, the legal defender of the revolution: he combined a scientific analysis of the Commune with its revolutionary apology. He not only explained and criticised—he defended and struggled. But, emphasizing the mildness of the Commune which failed, Marx left no doubt possible concerning the measures which the Commune ought to have taken in order not to fail.

The author of the *Civil War* accuses the Central Committee—*i.e.,* the then Council of National Guards' Deputies, of having too soon given up its place to the elective Commune. Kautsky "does not understand" the reason for such a reproach. This conscientious non-understanding is one of the symptoms of Kautsky's mental decline in connection with questions of the revolution generally. The first place, according to Marx, ought to have been filled by a purely fighting organ, a centre of the insurrection and of military operations against Versailles, and not the organized self-government of the labor democracy. For the latter the turn would come later.

Marx accuses the Commune of not having at once begun an attack against the Versailles, and of having entered upon the defensive, which always appears "more humane," and gives more possibilities of appealing to moral law and the sacredness of human life, but in conditions of civil war never leads to victory. Marx, on the other hand, first and foremost wanted a revolutionary victory. Nowhere, by one word, does he put forward the principle of democracy as something standing above the class struggle. On the contrary, with the concentrated contempt of the revolutionary and the Communist, Marx—not the young editor of the *Rhine Paper*, but the mature author of *Capital*: our genuine Marx with the mighty leonine mane, not as yet fallen under the hands of the hairdressers of the Kautsky school— with what concentrated contempt he speaks about the "artificial atmosphere of parliamentarism" in which physical and spiritual dwarfs like

Thiers seem giants! The *Civil War*, after the barren and
pedantic pamhlet of Kautsky, acts like a storm that clears the
air.

In spite of Kautsky's slanders, Marx had nothing in common with the view of democracy as the last, absolute, supreme
product of history. The development of bourgeois society
itself, out of which contemporary democracy grew up, in no
way represents that process of gradual democratization which
figured before the war in the dreams of the greatest Socialist
illusionist of democracy—Jean Jaurès—and now in those of
the most learned of pedants, Karl Kautsky. In the empire
of Napoleon III, Marx sees "the only possible form of government in the epoch in which the bourgeoisie has already
lost the possibility of governing the people, while the working class has not yet acquired it." In this way, not democracy,
but Bonapartism, appears in Marx's eyes as the final form of
bourgeois power. Learned men may say that Marx was mistaken, as the Bonapartist empire gave way for half a century
to the "Democratic Republic." But Marx was not mistaken.
In essence he was right. The Third Republic has been the
period of the complete decay of democracy. Bonapartism
has found in the Stock Exchange Republic of Poincaré-
Clémenceau, a more finished expression than in the Second
Empire. True, the Third Republic was not crowned by the
imperial diadem; but in return there loomed over it the
shadow of the Russian Tsar.

In his estimate of the Commune, Marx carefully avoids
using the worn currency of democratic terminology. "The
Commune was," he writes, "not a parliament, but a working
institution, and united in itself both executive and legislative
power." In the first place, Marx puts forward, not the
particular democratic form of the Commune, but its class essence. The Commune, as is known, abolished the regular
army and the police, and decreed the confiscation of Church
property. It did this in the right of the revolutionary dictatorship of Paris, without the permission of the general democracy of the State, which at that moment formally had found
a much more "lawful" expression in the National Assembly
of Thiers. But a revolution is not decided by votes. "The
National Assembly," says Marx, "was nothing more nor less

than one of the episodes of that revolution, the true embodiment of which was, nevertheless, armed Paris." How far this is from formal democracy!

"It only required that the Communal order of things," says Marx, "should be set up in Paris and in the secondary centres, and the old central government would in the provinces also have yielded to the *self-government of the producers*." Marx, consequently, sees the problem of revolutionary Paris, not in appealing from its victory to the frail will of the Constituent Assembly, but in covering the whole of France with a centralized organization of Communes, built up not on the external principles of democracy but on the genuine self-government of the producers.

Kautsky has cited as an argument against the Soviet Constitution the indirectness of elections, which contradicts the fixed laws of bourgeois democracy. Marx characterizes the proposed structure of labor France in the following words :—"The management of the general affairs of the village communes of every district was to devolve on the Assembly of plenipotentiary delegates meeting in the chief town of the district; while the district assemblies were in turn to send delegates to the National Assembly sitting in Paris."

Marx, as we can see, was not in the least degree disturbed by the many degrees of indirect election, in so far as it was a question of the State organization of the proletariat itself. In the framework of bourgeois democracy, indirectness of election confuses the demarcation line of parties and classes; but in the "self-government of the producers"—*i.e.*, in the class proletarian State, indirectness of election is a question not of politics, but of the technical requirements of self-government, and within certain limits may present the same advantages as in the realm of trade union organization.

The Philistines of democracy are indignant at the inequality in representation of the workers and peasants which, in the Soviet Constitution, reflects the difference in the revolutionary roles of the town and the country. Marx writes: "The Commune desired to bring the rural producers under the intellectual leadership of the central towns of their districts, and there to secure to them, in the workmen of the towns, the natural guardians of their interests." The question was not one of making the peasant equal to the worker on paper, but of spiritually raising the peasant to the level of the worker. All questions of the proletarian State Marx decides according to the revolutionary dynamics of living forces, and not according to the play of shadows upon the marketplace screen of parliamentarism.

In order to reach the last confines of mental collapse, Kautsky denies the universal authority of the Workers' Councils on the ground that there is no legal boundary between the proletariat and the bourgeoisie. In the indeterminate nature of the social divisions Kautsky sees the source of the arbitrary authority of the Soviet dictatorship. Marx sees directly the contrary. "The Commune was an extremely elastic form of the State, while all former forms of government had suffered from narrowness. Its secret consists in this, that in its very essence it was the government of the working class, the result of the struggle between the class of producers and the class of appropriators, the political form, long sought, under which there could be accomplished the economic emancipation of labor." The secret of the Commune consisted in the fact that by its very essence it was a government of the working class. This secret, explained by Marx, has remained, for Kautsky, even to this day, a mystery sealed with seven seals.

The Pharisees of democracy speak with indignation of the repressive measures of the Soviet Government, of the closing of newspapers, of arrests and shooting. Marx replies to "the vile abuse of the lackeys of the Press" and to the reproaches of the "well-intentioned bourgeois doctrinaries," in connection with the repressive measures of the Commune in the following words:—"Not satisfied with their open waging of a most bloodthirsty war against Paris, the Versaillese strove secretly to gain an entry by corruption and conspiracy. Could the Commune at such a time *without shamefully betraying its trust,* have observed the customary forms of liberalism, just as if profound peace reigned around it? Had the government of the Commune been akin in spirit to that of Thiers, there would have been no more occasion to suppress newspapers of the party of order in Paris than there was to suppress newspapers of the Commune at Versailles." In this way, what Kautsky demands in the name of the sacred foundations of democracy Marx brands as a shameful betrayal of trust.

Concerning the destruction of which the Commune is accused, and of which now the Soviet Government is accused, Marx speaks as of "an inevitable and comparatively insignificant episode in the titanic struggle of the new-born order with the old in its collapse." Destruction and cruelty are inevitable in any war. Only sycophants can consider them a crime "in the war of the slaves against their oppressors, *the only just war in history.*" (Marx.) Yet our dread accuser Kautsky, in his whole book, does not breathe a word of the fact that we are in a condition of perpetual revolutionary self-defence, that we are waging an intensive war against the oppressors of the world, the "only just war in history."

Kautsky yet again tears his hair because the Soviet Government, during the Civil War, has made use of the severe method of taking hostages. He once again brings forward pointless and dishonest comparisons between the fierce Soviet Government and the humane Commune. Clear and definite in this connection sounds the opinion of Marx. "When Thiers, from the very beginning of the conflict, had enforced the humane practice of shooting down captured Communards, the Commune, to protect the lives of those prisoners, *had nothing left for it* but to resort to the Prussian custom of taking hostages. The lives of the hostages had been forfeited over and over again by the continued shooting of the prisoners on the part of the Versaillese. *How could their lives be spared any longer* after the blood-bath with which MacMahon's Pretorians celebrated their entry into Paris?" How otherwise, we shall ask together with Marx, can one act in conditions of civil war, when the counter-revolution, occupying a considerable portion of the national territory, seizes wherever it can the unarmed workers, their wives, their mothers, and shoots or hangs them: how otherwise can one act than to seize as hostages the beloved or the trusted of the bourgeoisie, thus placing the whole bourgeois class under the Damocles' sword of mutual responsibility?

It would not be difficult to show, day by day through the history of the civil war, that all the severe measures of the

Soviet Government were forced upon it as measures of revolutionary self-defense. We shall not here enter into details. But, to give though it be but a partial criterion for valuing the conditions of the struggle, let us remind the reader that, at the moment when the White Guards, in company with their Anglo-French allies, shoot every Communist without exception who falls into their hands, the Red Army spares all prisoners without exception, including even officers of high rank.

"Fully grasping its historical task, filled with the heroic decision to remain equal to that task," Marx wrote, "the working class may reply with a smile of calm contempt to the vile abuse of the lackeys of the Press and to the learned patronage of well-intentioned bourgeois doctrinaires, who utter their ignorant stereotyped commonplaces, their characteristic nonsense, with the profound tone of oracles of scientific immaculateness."

If the well-intentioned bourgeois doctrinaires sometimes appear in the guise of retired theoreticians of the Second International, this in no way deprives their characteristic nonsense of the right of remaining nonsense.

7

THE WORKING CLASS AND ITS SOVIET POLICY

THE RUSSIAN PROLETARIAT

THE initiative in the social revolution proved, by the force of events, to be imposed, not upon the old proletariat of Western Europe, with its mighty economic and political organization, with its ponderous traditions of parliamentarism and trade unionism, but upon the young working-class of a backward country. History, as always, moved along the line of least resistance. The revolutionary epoch burst upon us through the least barricaded door. Those extraordinary, truly superhuman, difficulties which were thus flung upon the Russian proletariat have prepared, hastened, and to a considerable extent assisted the revolutionary work of the West European proletariat which still lies before us.

Instead of examining the Russian Revolution in the light of the revolutionary epoch that has arrived throughout the world, Kautsky discusses the theme of whether or no the Russian proletariat has taken power into its hands too soon.

"For Socialism," he explains, "there is necessary a high development of the people, a high morale amongst the masses, strongly-developed social instincts, sentiments of solidarity, etc. Such a form of morale," Kautsky further informs us, "was very highly developed amongst the proletariat of the Paris Commune. It is absent amongst the masses which at the present time set the tone amongst the Bolshevik proletariat." (Page 177.)

For Kautsky's purpose, it is not sufficient to fling mud at the Bolsheviks as a political party before the eyes of his readers. Knowing that Bolshevism has become amalgamated with the Russian proletariat, Kautsky makes an attempt to fling mud at the Russian proletariat as a whole, representing it as an ignorant, greedy mass, without any ideals, which is guided only by the instincts and impulses of the moment.

Throughout his booklet Kautsky returns many times to the question of the intellectual and moral level of the Russian workers, and every time only to deepen his characterization of them as ignorant, stupid and barbarous. To bring about the most striking contrasts, Kautsky adduces the example of how a workshop committee in *one* of the war industries during the Commune decided upon compulsory night duty in the works for *one* worker so that it might be possible to distribute repaired arms by night. "As under present circumstances it is absolutely necessary to be extremely economical with the resources of the Commune," the regulation read, "the night duty will be rendered without payment...." "Truly," Kautsky concludes, "these working men did not regard the period of their dictatorship as an opportune moment for the satisfaction of their personal interests." (Page 90.) Quite otherwise is the case with the Russian working class. That class has no intelligence, no stability, no ideals, no steadfastness, no readiness for self-sacrifice, and so on. "It is just as little capable of choosing suitable plenipotentiary leaders for itself," Kautsky jeers, "as Munchausen was able to drag himself from the swamp by means of his own hair." This comparison of the Russian proletariat with the impostor Munchausen dragging himself from the swamp is a striking example of the brazen tone in which Kautsky speaks of the Russian working class.

He brings extracts from various speeches and articles of ours in which undesirable phenomena amongst the working class are shown up, and attempts to represent matters in such a way as if the life of the Russian proletariat between 1917-20 —*i.e.*, in the greatest of revolutionary epochs—is fully described by passivity, ignorance, and egotism.

Kautsky, forsooth, does not know, has never heard, cannot guess, may not imagine, that during the civil war the Russian proletariat had more than one occasion of freely giving its labor, and even of establishing "unpaid" guard duties—not of *one* worker for the space of *one* night, but of tens of thousands of workers for the space of a long series of disturbed nights. In the days and weeks of Yudenich's advance on Petrograd, one telephonogram of the Soviet was sufficient to ensure that many thousands of workers should spring to their posts in all the factories, in all the wards of the city. And this not in the first days of the Petrograd Commune, but after a two years' struggle in cold and hunger.

Two or three times a year our party mobilizes a high proportion of its numbers for the front. Scattered over a distance of 8,000 versts, they die and teach others to die. And when, in hungry and cold Moscow, which has given the flower of its workers to the front, a Party Week is proclaimed, there pour into our ranks from the proletarian masses, in the space of seven days, 15,000 persons. And at what moment? At the moment when the danger of the destruction of the Soviet Government had reached its most acute point. At the moment when Orel had been taken, and Denikin was approaching Tula and Moscow, when Yudenich was threatening Petrograd. At that most painful moment, the Moscow proletariat, in the course of a week, gave to the ranks of our party 15,000 men, who only waited a new mobilization for the front. And it can be said with certainty that never yet, with the exception of the week of the November rising in 1917, was the Moscow proletariat so single-minded in its revolutionary enthusiasm, and in its readiness for devoted struggle, as in those most difficult days of peril and self-sacrifice.

When our party proclaimed the watchword of Subbotniks and Voskresniks (Communist Saturdays and Sundays), the revolutionary idealism of the proletariat found for itself a striking expression in the shape of voluntary labor. At first tens and hundreds, later thousands, and now tens and hundreds of thousands of workers every week give up several hours of their labor without reward, for the sake of the economic reconstruction of the country. And this is done by half-starved people, in torn boots, in dirty linen—because the country has neither boots nor soap. Such, in reality, is that Bolshevik proletariat to whom Kautsky recommends a course of self-sacrifice. The facts of the situation, and their relative importance, will appear still more vividly before us if we recall that all the egoist, bourgeois, coarsely selfish elements of the proletariat—all those who avoid service at the front and in the Subbotniks, who engage in speculation and in weeks of starvation incite the workers to strikes—all of them vote at the Soviet elections for the Mensheviks; that is, for the Russian Kautskies.

Kautsky quotes our words to the effect that, even before the November Revolution, we clearly realized the defects in education of the Russian proletariat, but, recognizing the inevitability of the transference of power to the working class, we considered ourselves justified in hoping that during the struggle itself, during its experience, and with the ever-increasing support of the proletariat of other countries, we should deal adequately with our difficulties, and be able to guarantee the transition of Russia to the Socialist order. In this connection, Kautsky asks: "Would Trotsky undertake to get on a locomotive and set it going, in the conviction that he would during the journey have time to learn and to arrange everything? One must preliminarily have acquired the qualities necessary to drive a locomotive before deciding to set it going. Similarly the proletariat ought beforehand to have acquired those necessary qualities which make it capable of administering industry, once it had to take it over." (Page 173.)

This instructive comparison would have done honor to any village clergyman. None the less, it is stupid. With infinitely more foundation one could say: "Will Kautsky dare to mount a horse before he has learned to sit firmly in the saddle, and to guide the animal in all its steps?" We have foundations for believing that Kautsky would not make up his mind to such a dangerous purely Bolshevik experiment. On the other hand, we fear that, through not risking to mount the horse, Kautsky would have considerable difficulty in learning the secrets of riding on horse-back. For the fundamental Bolshevik prejudice is precisely this: that one learns to ride on horse-back only when sitting on the horse.

Concerning the driving of the locomotive, this principle is at first sight not so evident; but none the less it is there. No one yet has learned to drive a locomotive sitting in his study. One has to get up on to the engine, to take one's stand in the tender, to take into one's hands the regulator, and to turn it. True, the engine allows training manœuvres only under the guidance of an old driver. The horse allows of instructions in the riding school only under the guidance of experienced trainers. But in the sphere of State administration such artificial conditions cannot be created. The bourgeoisie does not build for the proletariat academies of State administration, and does not place at its disposal, for preliminary practice, the helm of the State. And besides, the workers and peasants learn even to ride on horse-back not in the riding school, and without the assistance of trainers.

To this we must add another consideration, perhaps the most important. No one gives the proletariat the opportunity of choosing whether it will or will not mount the horse, whether it will take power immediately or postpone the moment. Under certain conditions the working class is bound to take power, under the threat of political self-annihilation for a whole historical period.

Once having taken power, it is impossible to accept one set of consequences at will and refuse to accept others. If the capitalist bourgeoisie consciously and malignantly transforms the disorganization of production into a method of political struggle, with the object of restoring power to itself, the proletariat is *obliged* to resort to Socialization, independently of whether this is beneficial or otherwise at the *given moment.*

And, once having taken over production, the proletariat is obliged, under the pressure of iron necessity, to learn by its own experience a most difficult art—that of organizing Socialist economy. Having mounted the saddle, the rider is obliged to guide the horse—on the peril of breaking his neck.

* * *

To give his high-souled supporters, male and female, a complete picture of the moral level of the Russian proletariat, Kautsky adduces, on page 172 of his book, the following mandate, issued, it is alleged, by the Murzilovka Soviet: "The Soviet hereby empowers Comrade Gregory Sareiev, in accordance with his choice and instructions, to requisition and lead to the barracks, for the use of the Artillery Division stationed in Murzilovka, Briansk County, sixty women and girls from the bourgeois and speculating class, September 16, 1918." (*What are the Bolshevists doing?* Published by Dr. Nath. Wintch-Malejeff. Lausanne, 1919. Page 10.)

Without having the least doubt of the forged character of this document and the lying nature of the whole communication, I gave instructions, however, that careful inquiry should be made, in order to discover what facts.and episodes lay at the root of this invention. A carefully carried out investigation showed the following:—

(1) In the Briansk County there is absolutely no village by the name of Murzilovka. There is no such village in the neighboring counties either. The most similar in name is the village of Muraviovka, Briansk County; but no artillery division has ever been stationed there, and altogether nothing ever took place which might be in any way connected with the above "document."

(2) The investigation was also carried on along the line of the artillery units. Absolutely nowhere were we able to discover even an indirect allusion to a fact similar to that adduced by Kautsky from the words of his inspirer.

(3) Finally the investigation dealt with the question of whether there had been any rumors of this kind on the spot. Here, too, absolutely nothing was discovered; and no wonder. The very contents of the forgery are in too brutal a contrast with the morals and public opinion of the foremost workers and peasants who direct the work of the Soviets, even in the most backward regions.

In this way, the document must be described as a pitiful forgery, which might be circulated only by the most malignant sycophants in the most yellow of the gutter press.

While the investigation described above was going on, Comrade Zinovieff showed me a number of a Swedish paper (*Svenska Dagbladet*) of November 9, 1919, in which was printed the facsimile of a mandate running as follows:—

"*Mandate.* The bearer of this, Comrade Karaseiev, has the right of socializing in the town of Ekaterinodar (obliterated) girls aged from 16 to 36 at his pleasure.—GLAVKOM IVASH-CHEFF."

This document is even more stupid and impudent that
that quoted by Kautsky. The town of Ekaterinodar—the
centre of the Kuban—was, as is well known, for only a very
short time in the hands of the Soviet Government. Apparently
the author of the forgery, not very well up in his revolutionary
chronology, rubbed out the date on this document, lest by
some chance it should appear that "Glavkom Ivashcheff"
socialized the Ekaterinodar women during the reign of Denikin's militarism there. That the document might lead into
error the thick-witted Swedish bourgeois is not at all amazing.
But for the Russian reader it is only too clear that the document is not merely a forgery, but drawn up by a *foreigner,
dictionary in hand*. It is extremely curious that the names of
both the socializers of women, "Gregory Sareiev" and "Karaseiev" sound absolutely non-Russia. The ending "eiev" in
Russian names is found rarely, and only in definite combinations. But the accuser of the Bolsheviks himself, the author
of the English pamphlet on whom Kautsky bases his evidence,
has a name that does actually end in "eiev." It seems obvious
that this Anglo-Bulgarian police agent, sitting in Lausanne,
creates socializers of women, in the fullest sense of the word,
after his own likeness and image.

Kautsky, at any rate, has original inspirers and assistants!

SOVIETS, TRADE UNIONS, AND THE PARTY

The Soviets, as a form of the organization of the working
class, represents for Kautsky, "in relation to the party and
professional organizations of more developed countries, not a
higher form of organization, but first and foremost a substitute
(Notbehelf), arising out of the absence of political organizations." (Page 68.)

Let us grant that this is true in connection with Russia.
But then, why have Soviets sprung up in Germany? Ought
one not absolutely to repudiate them in the Ebert Republic?
We note, however, that Hilferding, the nearest sympathizer
of Kautsky, proposes to include the Soviets in the Constitution.
Kautsky is silent.

The estimate of Soviets as a "primitive" organization is
true to the extent that the open revolutionary struggle is

"more primitive" than parliamentarism. But the artificial complexity of the latter embraces only the upper strata, insignificant in their size. On the other hand, revolution is only possible where the masses have their vital interests at stake. The November Revolution raised on to their feet such deep layers as the pre-revolutionary social democracy could not even dream of. However wide were the organizations of the party and the trade unions in Germany, the revolution immediately proved incomparably wider than they. The revolutionary masses found their direct representation in the most simple and generally comprehensive delegate organization—in the Soviet. One may admit that the Council of Deputies falls behind both the party and the trade union in the sense of the clearness of its programme, or the exactness of its organization. But it is far and away in front of the party and the trade unions in the size of the masses drawn by it into the organized struggle; and this superiority in quality gives the Soviet undeniable revolutionary preponderance.

The Soviet embraces workers of all undertakings, of all professions, of all stages of cultural development, all stages of political consciousness—and thereby objectively is forced to formulate the *general* interests of the proletariat.

The *Communist Manifesto* viewed the problem of the Communist just in this sense—namely, the formulating of the general historical interests of the working class as a whole.

"The Communists are only distinguished from other proletarian parties," in the words of the *Manifesto*, "by this: that in the different national struggles of the proletariat they point out, and bring to the fore, the common interests of the proletariat, independently of nationality; and again that, in the different stages of evolution through which the struggle between the proletariat and bourgeoisie passes, they constantly represent the interests of the movement taken as a whole."

In the form of the all-embracing class organization of the Soviets, the movement takes itself "as a whole." Hence it is clear why the Communists could and had to become the guiding party in the Soviets. But hence also is seen all the narrowness of the estimate of Soviets as "substitutes for the party" (Kautsky), and all the stupidity of the attempt to include the Soviets, in the form of an auxiliary lever, in the mechanism of bourgeois democracy. (Hilferding.)

The Soviets are the organization of the proletarian revolution, and have purpose either as an organ of the struggle for power or as the apparatus of power of the working class.

Unable to grasp the revolutionary role of the Soviets, Kautsky sees their root defects in that which constitutes their greatest merit. "The demarcation of the bourgeois from the worker," he writes, "can never be actually drawn. There will always be something arbitrary in such demarcation, which fact transforms the Soviet idea into a particularly suitable foundation for dictatorial and arbitrary rule, but renders it unfitted for the creation of a clear, systematically built-up constitution." (Page 170.)

Class dictatorship, according to Kautsky, cannot create for itself institutions answering to its nature, because there do not exist lines of demarcation between the classes. But in that case, what happens to the class struggle altogether? Surely it was just, in the existence of numerous transitional stages between the bourgeoisie and the proletariat, that the lower middle-class theoreticians always found their principal argument against the "principle" of the class struggle? For Kautsky, however, doubts as to principle begin just at the point where the proletariat, having overcome the shapelessness and unsteadiness of the intermediate class, having brought one part of them over to its side and thrown the remainder into the camp of the bourgeoisie, has actually organized its dictatorship in the Soviet Constitution.

The very reason why the Soviets are absolutely irreplaceable apparatus in the proletarian State is that their framework is elastic and yielding, with the result that not only social but political changes in the relationship of classes and sections can immediately find their expression in the Soviet apparatus. Beginning with the largest factories and works, the Soviets then draw into their organization the workers of private workshops and shop-assistants, proceed to enter the village, organize the peasants against the landowners, and finally the lower and middle-class sections of the peasantry against the richest.

The Labor State collects numerous staffs of employees, to a considerable extent from the ranks of the bourgeoisie and the bourgeois educated classes. To the extent that they become disciplined under the Soviet regime, they find representation in the Soviet system. Expanding—and at certain moments contracting—in harmony with the expansion and contraction of the social positions conquered by the proletariat, the Soviet system remains the State apparatus of the social revolution, in its internal dynamics, its ebbs and flows, its mistakes and successes. With the final triumph of the social revolution, the Soviet system will expand and include the whole population, in order thereby to lose the characteristics of a form of State, and melt away into a mighty system of producing and consuming co-operation.

If the party and the trade unions were organizations of preparation for the revolution, the Soviets are the weapon of the revolution itself. After its victory, the Soviets become the organs of power. The role of the party and the unions, without decreasing is nevertheless essentially altered.

In the hands of the party is concentrated the general control. It does not immediately administer, since its apparatus is not adapted for this purpose. But it has the final word in all fundamental questions. Further, our practice has led to the result that, in all moot questions, generally—conflicts between departments and personal conflicts within departments—the last word belongs to the Central Committee of the party. This affords extreme economy of time and energy, and in the most difficult and complicated circumstances gives a guarantee for the necessary unity of action. Such a regime is possible only in the presence of the unquestioned authority of the party, and the faultlessness of its discipline. Happily for the revolution, our party does possess in an equal measure both of these qualities. Whether in other countries which have not received from their past a strong revolutionary organization, with a great hardening in conflict, there will be created just as authoritative a Communist Party by the time of the proletarian revolution, it is difficult to foretell; but it is quite obvious that on this question, to a very large extent, depends the progress of the Socialist revolution in each country.

The exclusive role of the Communist Party under the conditions of a victorious proletarian revolution is quite comprehensible. The question is of the dictatorship of a class. In the composition of that class there enter various elements, heterogeneous moods, different levels of development. Yet the dictatorship pre-supposes unity of will, unity of direction, unity of action. By what other path then can it be attained? The revolutionary supremacy of the proletariat pre-supposes within the proletariat itself the political supremacy of a party, with a clear programme of action and a faultless internal discipline.

The policy of coalitions contradicts internally the regime of the revolutionary dictatorship. We have in view, not coalitions with bourgeois parties, of which of course there can be no talk, but a coalition of Communists with other "Socialist" organizations, representing different stages of backwardness and prejudice of the laboring masses.

The revolution swiftly reveals all that is unstable, wears out all that is artificial; the contradictions glozed over in a coalition are swiftly revealed under the pressure of revolutionary events. We have had an example of this in Hungary, where the dictatorship of the proletariat assumed the political form of the coalition of the Communists with disguised Opportunists. The coalition soon broke up. The Communist Party paid heavily for the revolutionary instability and the political treachery of its companions. It is quite obvious that for the Hungarian Communists it would have been more profitable to have come to power later, after having afforded to the Left Opportunists the possibility of compromising themselves once and for all. It is quite another question as to how far this was possible. In any case, a coalition with the Opportunists, only temporarily hiding the relative weakness of the Hungarian Communists, at the same time prevented them from growing stronger at the expense of the Opportunists; and brought them to disaster.

The same idea is sufficiently illustrated by the example of the Russian revolution. The coalition of the Bolsheviks with the Left Socialist Revolutionists, which lasted for several months, ended with a bloody conflict. True, the reckoning for the coalition had to be paid, not so much by us Communists as by our disloyal companions. Apparently, such a coalition, in which we were the stronger side and, therefore,

were not taking too many risks in the attempt, at one definite
stage in history, to make use of the extreme Left-wing of
the bourgeois democracy, tactically must be completely justified. But, none the less, the Left S.R. episode quite clearly
shows that the regime of compromises, agreements, mutual
concessions—for that is the meaning of the regime of coalition—cannot last long in an epoch in which situations alter
with extreme rapidity, and in which supreme unity in point
cf view is necessary in order to render possible unity of
action.

We have more than once been accused of having sub-
stituted for the dictatorship of the Soviets the dictatorship
cf our party. Yet it can be said with complete justice that
the dictatorship of the Soviets became possible only by means
of the dictatorship of the party. It is thanks to the clarity
of its theoretical vision and its strong revolutionary organization that the party has afforded to the Soviets the possibility
of becoming transformed from shapeless parliaments of labor
into the apparatus of the supremacy of labor. In this "substitution" of the power of the party for the power of the
working class there is nothing accidental, and in reality there
is no substitution at all. The Communists express the fundamental interests of the working class. It is quite natural that,
in the period in which history brings up those interests, in
all their magnitude, on to the order of the day, the Communists have become the recognized representatives of the
working class as a whole.

But where is your guarantee, certain wise men ask us,
that it is just your party that expresses the interests of
historical development? Destroying or driving underground
the other parties, you have thereby prevented their political
competition with you, and consequently you have deprived
yourselves of the possibility of testing your line of action.

This idea is dictated by a purely liberal conception of
the course of the revolution. In a period in which all antagonisms assume an open character, and the political struggle
swiftly passes into a civil war, the ruling party has sufficient
material standard by which to test its line of action, without
the possible circulation of Menshevik papers. Noske crushes
the Communists, but they grow. We have suppressed the

Mensheviks and the S.R.s—and they have disappeared. This criterion is sufficient for us. At all events, our problem is not at every given moment statistically to measure the grouping of tendencies; but to render victory for our tendency secure. For that tendency is the tendency of the revolutionary dictatorship; and in the course of the latter, in its internal friction, we must find a sufficient criterion for self-examination.

The continuous "independence" of the trade union movement, in the period of the proletarian revolution, is just as much an impossibility as the policy of coalition. The trade unions become the most important economic organs of the proletariat in power. Thereby they fall under the leadership of the Communist Party. Not only questions of principle in the trade union movement, but serious conflicts of organization within it, are decided by the Central Committee of our party.

The Kautskians attack the Soviet Government as the dictatorship of a "section" of the working class. "If only," they say, "the dictatorship was carried out by the *whole* class!" It is not easy to understand what actually they imagine when they say this. The dictatorship of the proletariat, in its very essence, signifies the immediate supremacy of the revolutionary vanguard, which relies upon the heavy masses, and, where necessary, obliges the backward tail to dress by the head. This refers also to the trade unions. After the conquest of power by the proletariat, they acquire a compulsory character. They must include all industrial workers. The party, on the cther hand, as before, includes in its ranks only the most class-conscious and devoted; and only in a process of careful selection does it widen its ranks. Hence follows the guiding role of the Communist minority in the trade unions, which answers to the supremacy of the Communist Party in the Soviets, and represents the political expression of the dictatorship of the proletariat.

The trade unions become the direct organizers of social production. They express not only the interests of the industrial workers, but the interests of industry itself. During the first period, the old currents in trade unionism more than once raised their head, urging the unions to haggle with the Soviet State, lay down conditions for it, and demand from it guarantees. The further we go, however, the more do the unions recognize that they are organs of production of the Soviet State, and assume responsibility for its fortunes—not opposing themselves to it, but identifying themselves with it. The unions become the organizers of labor discipline. They demand from the workers intensive labor under the most difficult conditions, to the extent that the Labor State is not yet able to alter those conditions.

The unions become the apparatus of revolutionary repression against undisciplined, anarchical, parasitic elements in the working class. From the old policy of trade unionism, which at a certain stage is inseparable from the industrial movement within the framework of capitalist society, the unions pass along the whole line on to the new path of the policy of revolutionary Communism.

THE PEASANT POLICY

The Bolsheviks "hoped," Kautsky thunders, "to overcome the substantial peasants in the villages by granting political rights exclusively to the poorest peasants. They then again granted representation to the substantial peasantry." (Page 216.)

Kautsky enumerates the external "contradictions" of our peasant policy, not dreaming to inquire into its general direction, and into the internal contradictions visible in the economic and political situation of the country.

In the Russian peasantry as it entered the Soviet order there were three elements: the poor, living to a considerable extent by the sale of their labor-power, and forced to buy additional food for their requirements; the middle peasants, whose requirements were covered by the products of their farms, and who were able to a limited extent to sell their surplus; and the upper layer—*i.e.*, the rich peasants, the vulture (kulak) class, which systematically bought labor-power and sold their agricultural produce on a large scale. It is quite unnecessary to point out that these groups are not distinguished by definite symptoms or by homogeneousness throughout the country.

Still, on the whole, and generally speaking, the peasant

poor represented the natural and undeniable allies of the town proletariat, whilst the vulture class represented its just as undeniable and irreconcilable enemies. The most hesitation was principally to be observed amongst the widest, the *middle* section of the peasantry.

Had not the country been so exhausted, and if the proletariat had had the possibility of offering to the peasant masses the necessary quantity of commodities and cultural requirements, the adaptation of the toiling majority of the peasantry to the new regime would have taken place much less painfully. But the economic disorder of the country, which was not the result of our land or food policy, but was generated by the causes which preceded the appearance of that policy, robbed the town for a prolonged period of any possibility of giving the village the products of the textile and metal-working industries, imported goods, and so on. At the same time, industry could not entirely cease drawing from the village all, albeit the smallest quantity, of its food resources. The proletariat demanded of the peasantry the granting of food credits, economic subsidies in respect of values which it is only now about to create. The symbol of those future values was the credit symbol, now finally deprived of all value. But the peasant mass is not very capable of historical detachment. Bound up with the Soviet Government by the abolition of landlordism, and seeing in it a guarantee against the restoration of Tsarism, the peasantry at the same time not infrequently opposes the collection of corn, considering it a bad bargain so long as it does not itself receive printed calico, nails, and kerosine.

The Soviet Government naturally strove to impose the chief weight of the food tax upon the upper strata of the village. But, in the unformed social conditions of the village, the influential peasantry, accustomed to lead the middle peasants in its train, found scores of methods of passing on the food tax from itself to the wide masses of the peasantry, thereby placing them in a position of hostility and opposition to the Soviet power. It was necessary to awaken in the lower ranks of the peasantry suspicion and hostility towards the speculating upper strata. This purpose was served by the Committees of Poverty. They were built up of the rank and file, of elements who in the last epoch were oppressed, driven into a dark corner, deprived of their rights. Of course, in their midst there turned out to be a certain number of semi-parasitic elements. This served as the chief text for the demagogues amongst the populist "Socialists," whose speeches found a grateful echo in the hearts of the village vultures. But the mere fact of the transference of power to the village poor had an immeasurable revolutionary significance. For the guidance of the village semi-proletarians, there were despatched from the towns parties from amongst the foremost workers, who accomplished invaluable work in the villages. The Committees of Poverty became shock battalions against the vulture class. Enjoying the support of the State, they thereby obliged the middle section of the peasantry to choose, not only between the Soviet power and the power of the landlords, but between the dictatorship of the proletariat and the semi-proletarian elements of the village on the one hand, and the yoke of the rich speculators on the other. By a series of lessons, some of which were very severe, the middle peasantry was obliged to become convinced that the Soviet regime, which had driven away the landlords and bailiffs, in its turn imposes new duties upon the peasantry, and demands sacrifices from them. The political education of tens of millions of the middle peasantry did not take place as easily and smoothly as in the school-room, and it did not give immediate and unquestionable results. There were risings of the middle peasants, uniting with the speculators, and always in such cases falling under the leadership of White Guard landlords; there were abuses committed by local agents of the Soviet Government, particularly by those of the Committees of Poverty. But the fundamental political end was attained. The powerful class of rich peasantry, if it was not finally annihilated, proved to be shaken to its foundations, with its self-reliance undermined. The middle peasantry, remaining politically shapeless, just as it is economically shapeless, began to learn to find its representative in the foremost worker, as before it found it in the noisy village speculator. Once this fundamental result was achieved, the Committees of Poverty, as temporary institutions, as a sharp wedge driven into the village masses, had to yield their place to the Soviets, in which the village poor are represented side by side with the middle peasantry.

The Committees of Poverty existed about six months, from June to December, 1918. In their institution, as in their abolition, Kautsky sees nothing but the "waverings" of Soviet policy. Yet at the same time he himself has not even a suspicion of any practical lessons to be drawn. And after all, how should he think of them? Experience such as we are acquiring in this respect knows no precedent; and questions and problems such as the Soviet Government is now solving in practice have no solution in books. What Kautsky calls contradictions in policy are, in reality, the *active manoeuvring* of the proletariat in the spongy, undivided, peasant mass. The sailing ship has to manœuvre before the wind; yet no one will see contradictions in the manœuvres which finally bring the ship to harbor.

In questions as to agricultural communes and Soviet farms, there could also be found not a few "contradictions," in which, side by side with individual mistakes, there are expressed various stages of the revolution. What quantity of land shall the Soviet State leave for itself in the Ukraine, and what quantity shall it hand over to the peasants; what policy shall it lay down for the agricultural communes; in what form shall it give them support, so as not to make them the nursery for parasitism; in what form is control to be organized over them—all these are absolutely new problems of Socialist economic construction, which have been settled beforehand neither theoretically nor practically, and in the settling of which the general principles of our programme have even yet to find their actual application and their testing in practice, by means of inevitable temporary deviations to right or left.

But even the very fact that the Russian proletariat has found support in the peasantry Kautsky turns against us. "This has introduced into the Soviet regime an economically reactionary element which was spared (!) the Paris Commune, as its dictatorship did not rely on peasant Soviets."

As if in reality we could accept the heritage of the feudal and bourgeois order with the possibility of excluding from it at will "an economically reactionary element"! Nor is this all. Having poisoned the Soviet regime by its "reactionary element," the peasantry has deprived us of its support. To-day it "hates" the Bolsheviks. All this Kautsky knows very certainly from the radios of Clémenceau and the squibs of the Mensheviks.

In reality, what is true is that wide masses of the peasantry are suffering from the absence of the essential products of industry. But it is just as true that every other regime— and there were not a few of them, in various parts of Russia, during the last three years—proved infinitely more oppressive for the shoulders of the peasantry. Neither monarchical nor democratic governments were able to increase their stores of manufactured goods. Both of them found themselves in need of the peasant's corn and the peasant's horses. To carry out their policy, the bourgeois governments—including the Kautskian-Menshevik variety—made use of a purely bureaucratic apparatus, which reckons with the requirements of the peasant's farm to an infinitely less degree than the Soviet apparatus, which consists of workers and peasants. As a result, the middle peasant, in spite of his waverings, his dissatisfaction, and even his risings, ultimately always comes to the conclusion that, however difficult it is for him at present under the Bolsheviks, under every other regime it would be infinitely more difficult for him. It is quite true that the Commune was "spared" peasant support. But in return the Commune was not spared annihilation by the peasant armies of Thiers! Whereas our army, four-fifths of whom are peasants, is fighting with enthusiasm and with success for the Soviet Republic. And this one fact, controverting Kautsky and those inspiring him, gives the best possible verdict on the peasant policy of the Soviet Government.

THE SOVIET GOVERNMENT AND THE EXPERTS

"The Bolsheviks at first thought they could manage without the intelligentsia, without the experts," Kautsky narrates to us. (Page 191.) But then, becoming convinced of the necessity of the intelligentsia, they abandoned their severe repressions, and attempted to attract them to work by all sorts of measures, incidentally by giving them extremely high salaries. "In this way," Kautsky says ironically," "the true path, the true method of attracting experts consists in first of all giving them a thorough good hiding." (Page 192.) Quite so. With all due respect to all philistines, the dictatorship of the proletariat does just consist in "giving a hiding" to the classes that were previously supreme, before forcing them to recognize the new order and to submit to it.

The professional intelligentsia, brought up with a prejudice about the omnipotence of the bourgeoisie, long would not, could not, and did not believe that the working class is really capable of governing the country; that it seized power not by accident; and that the dictatorship of the proletariat is an insurmountable fact. Consequently, the bourgeois intelligentsia treated its duties to the Labor State extremely lightly, even when it entered its service; and it considered that to receive money from Wilson, Clémenceau or Mirbach for anti-Soviet agitation, or to hand over military secrets and technical resources to White Guards and foreign imperialists, is a quite natural and obvious course under the regime of the proletariat. It became necessary to show it in practice, and to show it severely, that the proletariat had not seized power in order to allow such jokes to be played off at its expense.

In the severe penalties adopted in the case of the intelligentsia, our bourgeois idealist sees the "consequence of a policy which strove to attract the educated classes, not by means of persuasion, but by means of kicks from before and behind." (Page 193.) In this way, Kautsky seriously imagines that it is possible to attract the bourgeois intelligentsia to the work of Socialist construction by means of mere persuasion—and this in conditions when, in all other countries, there is still supreme the bourgeoisie which hesitates at no methods of terrifying, flattering, or buying over the Russian intelligentsia and making it a weapon for the transformation of Russia into a colony of slaves.

Instead of analyzing the course of the struggle, Kautsky, when dealing with the intelligentsia, gives once again merely academical recipes. It is absolutely false that our party had the idea of managing without the intelligentsia, not realizing to the full its importance for the economic and cultural work that lay before us. On the contrary. When the struggle for the conquest and consolidation of power was in full blast, and the majority of the intelligentsia was playing the part cf a shock battalion of the bourgeoisie, fighting against us openly or sabotaging our institutions, the Soviet power fought mercilessly with the experts, precisely because it knew their enormous importance from the point of view of organization so long as they do not attempt to carry on an independent "democratic" policy and execute the orders of one of the fundamental classes of society. Only after the opposition of the intelligentsia had been broken by a severe struggle did the possibility open before us of enlisting the assistance of the experts. We immediately entered that path. It proved not as simple as it might have seemed at first. The relations which existed under capitalist conditions between the working man and the director, the clerk and the manager, the soldier and the officer, left behind a very deep class distrust of the experts; and that distrust had become still more acute during the first period of the civil war, when the intelligentsia did its utmost to break the labor revolution by hunger and cold. It was not easy to outlive this frame of mind, and to pass from the first violent antagonism to peaceful collaboration. The laboring masses had gradually to become accustomed to see in the engineer, the agricultural expert, the officer, not the oppressor of yesterday but the useful worker of to-day—a necessary expert, entirely under the orders of the Workers' and Peasants' Government.

We have already said that Kautsky is wrong when he attributes to the Soviet Government the desire to replace experts by proletarians. But that such a desire was bound to spring up in wide circles of the proletariat cannot be denied. A young class which had proved to its own satisfaction that it was capable of overcoming the greatest obstacles in its path, which had torn to pieces the veil of mystery which had hitherto surrounded the power of the propertied classes, which had realized that all good things on the earth were not the direct gift of heaven—that a revolutionary class was naturally inclined, in the person of the less mature of its elements, at first to over-estimate its capacity for solving each and every problem, without having recourse to the aid of experts educated by the bourgeoisie.

It was not merely yesterday that we began the struggle with such tendencies, in so far as they assumed a definite character. "To-day, when the power of the Soviets has been set on a firm footing," we said at the Moscow City Conference cn March 28, 1918, "the struggle with sabotage must express itself in the form of transforming the saboteurs of yesterday into the servants, executive officials, technical guides, of the new regime, wherever it requires them. If we do not grapple with this, if we do not attract all the forces necessary to us and enlist them in the Soviet service, our struggle of yesterday with sabotage would thereby be condemned as an absolutely vain and fruitless struggle.

"Just as in dead machines, so into those technical experts, engineers, doctors, teachers, former officers, there is sunk a certain portion of our national capital, which we are obliged to exploit and utilize if we want to solve the root problems standing before us.

"Democratization does not at all consist — as every Marxist learns in his A B C—in abolishing the meaning of skilled forces, the meaning of persons possessing special knowledge, and in replacing them everywhere and anywhere by elective boards.

"Elective boards, consisting of the best representatives of the working class, but not equipped with the necessary technical knowledge, cannot replace one expert who has passed through the technical school, and who knows how to carry out the given technical work. That flood-tide of the collegiate principle which is at present to be observed in all spheres is the quite natural reaction of a young, revolutionary, only yesterday oppressed class, which is throwing out the one-man principle of its rulers of yesterday—the landlords and the generals—and everywhere is appointing its elected representatives. This, I say, is quite a natural and, in its origin, quite a healthy revolutionary reaction; but it is not the last word in the economic constructive work of the proletatarian class.

"The next step must consist in the self-limitation of the collegiate principle, in a healthy and necessary act of self-limitation by the working class, which knows where the decisive word can be spoken by the elected representatives of the workers themselves, and where it is necessary to give way to a technical specialist, who is equipped wtih certain knowledge, on whom a great measure of responsibility must be laid, and who must be kept under careful political control. But it is necessary to allow the expert freedom to act, freedom to create; because no expert, be he ever so little gifted or capable, can work in his department when subordinate in his own technical work to a board of men who do not know that department. Political, collegiate and Soviet control everywhere and anywhere; but for the executive functions, we must appoint technical experts, put them in responsible positions, and impose responsibility upon them.

"Those who fear this are quite unconsciously adopting an attitude of profound internal distrust towards the Soviet regime. Those who think that the enlisting of the saboteurs of yesterday in the administration of technically expert posts threatens the very foundations of the Soviet regime, do not realize that it is not through the work of some engineer or of some general of yesterday that the Soviet regime may stumble —in the political, in the revolutionary, in the military sense, the Soviet regime is unconquerable. But it *may* stumble through its own incapacity to grapple with the problems of creative organization. The Soviet regime is bound to draw from the old institutions all that was vital and valuable in them, and harness it on to the new work. If, comrades, we do not accomplish this, we shall not deal successfully with our principal problems; for it would be absolutely impossible for us to bring forth from our masses, in the shortest possible time, all the necessary experts, and throw aside all that was accumulated in the past.

"As a matter of fact, it would be just the same as if we said that all the machines which hitherto had served to exploit the workers were now to be thrown aside. It would be madness. The enlisting of scientific experts is for us just as essential as the administration of the resources of production and transport, and all the wealth of the country generally. We must, and in addition we must immediately, bring under our control all the technical experts we possess, and introduce in practice for them the principle of compulsory labor; at the same time leaving them a wide margin of activity, and maintaining over them careful political control." *

The question of experts was particularly acute, from the very beginning, in the War Department. Here, under the pressure of iron necessity, it was solved first.

In the sphere of administration of industry and transport, the necessary forms of organization are very far from being attained, even to this day. We must seek the reason in the fact that during the first two years we were obliged to sacrifice the interests of industry and transport to the requirements of military defence. The extremely changeable course of the civil war, in its turn, threw obstacles in the way of the establishment of regular relations with the experts. Qualified technicians of industry and transport, doctors, teachers, professors, either went away with the retreating armies of Kolchak and Denikin, or were compulsorily evacuated by them.

Only now, when the civil war is approaching its conclusion, is the intelligentsia in its mass making its peace with the Soviet Government, or bowing before it. Economic problems have acquired first-class importance. One of the most important amongst them is the problem of the scientific organization of production. Before the experts there opens a boundless field of activity. They are being accorded the independence necessary for creative work. The general control of industry on a national scale is concentrated in the hands of the Party of the proletariat.

THE INTERNAL POLICY OF THE SOVIET GOVERNMENT

"The Bolsheviks," Kautsky mediates, "acquired the force necessary for the seizure of political power through the fact that, amongst the political parties in Russia, they were the most energetic in their demaids for peace—peace at any price,

---

* **Labor, Discipline, and Order will save the Socialist Soviet Republic** (Moscow, 1918). Kautsky knows this pamphlet, as he quotes from it several times. This, however, does not prevent him passing over the passage quoted above, which makes clear the attitude of the Soviet Government to the intelligentsia.

a separate peace—without interesting themselves as to the influence this would have on the general international situation, as to whether this would assist the victory and world domination of the German military monarchy, under the protection of which they remained for a long time, just like Indian or Irish rebels or Italian anarchists." (Page 53.)

Of the reasons for our victory, Kautsky knows only the one that we stood for peace. He does not explain the Soviet Government has continued to exist now that it has again mobilized a most important proportion of the soldiers of the imperial army, in order for two years successfully to combat its political enemies.

The watchword of peace undoubtedly played an enormous part in our struggle; but precisely because it was directed against the *imperialist* war. The idea of peace was supported most strongly of all, not by the tired soldiers, but by the foremost workers, for whom it had the import, not for a rest, but of a pitiless struggle against the exploiters. It was those same workers who, under the watchword of peace, later laid down their lives on the Soviet fronts.

The affirmation that we demanded peace without reckoning on the effect it would have on the international situation is a belated echo of Cadet and Menshevik slanders. The comparison of us with the Germanophil nationalists of India and Ireland seeks its justification in the fact that German imperialism did actually *attempt* to make use of us as it did the Indians and the Irish. But the chauvinists of France spared no efforts to make use of Liebknecht and Luxemburg—even of Kautsky and Bernstein—in their own interests. The whole question is, did we allow ourselves to be utilized? Did we, by our conduct, give the European workers even the shadow of a ground to place us in the same category as German imperialism? It is sufficient to remember the course of the Brest negotiations, their breakdown, and the German advance of February, 1918, to reveal all the cynicism of Kautsky's accusation. In reality, there was no peace for a single day between ourselves and German imperialism. On the Ukrainian and Caucasian fronts, we, in the measure of our then extremely feeble energies, continued to wage war without openly calling it such. We were too weak to organize war along the whole Russo-German front. We maintained persistently the fiction of peace, utilizing the fact that the chief German forces were drawn away to the west. If German imperialism did prove sufficiently powerful, in 1917-18, to impose upon us the Brest Peace, after all our efforts to tear that noose from our necks, one of the principal reasons was the disgraceful behavior of the German Social-Democratic Party, of which Kautsky remained an integral and essential part. The Brest Peace was pre-determined on August 4, 1914. At that moment, Kautsky not only did not declare war against German militarism, as he later demanded from the Soviet Government, which was in 1918 still powerless from a military point of view; Kautsky actually proposed voting for the War Credits, "under certain conditions"; and generally behaved in such a way that for months it was impossible to discover whether he stood for the War or against it. And this political coward, who at the decisive moment gave up the principal positions of Socialism, dares to accuse us of having found ourselves obliged, at a certain moment, to retreat—not in principle, but materially. And why? Because we were betrayed by the German Social Democracy, corrupted by Kautskianism—*i.e.*, by political prostitution disguised by theories.

We did concern ourselves with the international situation! In reality, we had a much more profound criterion by which to judge the international situation; and it did not deceive us. Already before the February Revolution the Russian Army no longer existed as a fighting force. Its final collapse was pre-determined. If the February Revolution had not taken place, Tsarism would have come to an agreement with the German monarchy. But the February Revolution which prevented that finally destroyed the army built on a monarchist basis, precisely because it was a revolution. A month sooner or later the army was bound to fall to pieces. The military policy of Kerensky was the policy of an ostrich. He closed his eyes to the decomposition of the army, talked sounding phrases, and uttered verbal threats against German imperialism.

In such conditions, we had only one way out: to take our stand on the platform of peace, as the inevitable conclusion from the military powerlessness of the revolution, and to transform that watchword into the weapon of revolutionary influence on all the peoples of Europe. That is, instead of, together with Kerensky, peacefully awaiting the final military catastrophe—which might bury the revolution in its ruins— we proposed to take possession of the watchword of peace and to lead after it the proletariat of Europe—and first and foremost the workers of Austro-Germany. It was in the light of this view that we carried on our peace negotiations with the Central Empires, and it was in the light of this that we drew up our Notes to the governments of the Entente. We drew out the negotiations as long as we could, in order to give the European working masses the possibility of realizing the meaning of the Soviet Government and its policy. The January strike of 1918 in Germany and Austria showed that out efforts had not been in vain. That strike was the first serious premonition of the German Revolution. The German imperialists understood then that it was just we who represented for them a deadly danger. This is very strikingly shown in Lundendorff's book. True, they could not risk any longer coming out against us in an open crusade. But wherever they could fight against us secretly deceiving the German workers with the help of the German Social-Democracy, they did so; in the Ukraine, on the Don, in the Caucasus. In Central Russia, in Moscow, Count Mirbach from the very first day of his arrival stood as the centre of counter-revolutionary plots against the Soviet Government—just as Comrade Yoffe in Berlin was in the closest possible touch with the revolution. The Extreme Left group of the German revolutionary movement, the party of Karl Liebknecht and Rosa Luxemburg, all the time went hand in hand with us. The German revolution at once took on the form of Soviets, and the German proletariat, in spite of the Brest Peace, did not for a moment entertain any doubts as to whether we were with Liebknecht or Ludendorff. In his evidence before the Reichstag Commission in November, 1919, Ludendorff explained how "the High Command demanded the creation of an institution with the object of disclosing the connection of revolutionary tendencies in Germany with Russia. Yoffe arrived in Berlin, and in various towns there were set up Russian consulates. This had the most painful consequences in the army and navy." Kautsky, however, has the audacity to write that "if matters did come to a German revolution, truly it is not the Bolsheviks who are responsible for it. (Page 162.)

Even if we had had the possibility in 1917-18, by means of revolutionary abstention, of supporting the old Imperial Army instead of hastening its destruction, we should have merely been assisting the Entente, and would have covered up by our aid its brigands' peace with Germany, Austria, and all the countries of the world generally. With such a policy we should at the decisive moment have proved absolutely disarmed in the face of the Entente—still more disarmed than Germany is to-day. Whereas, thanks to the November Revolution and the Brest Peace we are to-day the only country which opposes the Entente rifle in hand. By our international policy, we not only did not assist the Hohenzollern to assume a position of world domination; on the contrary, by our November Revolution we did more than anyone else to prepare his overthrow. At the same time, we gained a military breathing-space, in the course of which we created a large and strong army, the first army of the proletariat in history, with which to-day not all the unleashed hounds of the Entente can cope.

The most critical moment in our international situation arose in the autumn of 1918, after the destruction of the German armies. In the place of two mighty camps, more or less neutralizing each other, there stood before us the victorious Entente, at the summit of its world power, and there lay broken Germany, whose Junker blackguards would have considered it a happiness and an honor to spring at the throat of the Russian proletariat for a bone from the kitchen of Clemenceau. We proposed peace to the Entente, and were again ready—for we were obliged—to sign the most painful conditions. But Clemenceau, in whose imperialist rapacity there have remained in their full force all the characteristics of lower-middle-class thick-headedness, refused the Junkers their bone, and at the same time decided at all costs to decorate the Invalides with the scalps of the leaders of the Soviet Republic. By this policy Clemenceau did us not a small service. We defended ourselves successfully, and held out.

What, then, was the guiding principle of our external

policy, once the first months of existence of the Soviet Government had made clear the considerable vitality as yet of the capitalist governments of Europe? Just that which Kautsky accepts to-day uncomprehendingly as an accidental result— *to hold out!*

We realized too clearly that the very fact of the existence of the Soviet Government is an event of the greatest revolutionary importance; and this realization dictated to us our concessions and our temporary retirements—not in principle but in practical conclusions from a sober estimate of our own forces. We retreated like an army which gives up to the enemy a town, and even a fortress, in order, having retreated, to concentrate its forces not only for defence but for an advance. We retreated like strikers amongst whom to-day energies and resources have been exhausted, but who, clenching their teeth, are preparing for a new struggle. If we were not filled with an unconquerable belief in the world significance of the Soviet dictatorship, we should not have accepted the most painful sacrifices at Brest-Litovsk. If our faith had proved to be contradicted by the actual course of events, the Brest Peace would have gone down to history as the futile capitulation of a doomed regime. That is how the situation was judged *then,* not only by the Kühlmanns, but also by the Kautskies of all countries. But we proved right in our estimate, as of our weakness then, so of our strength in the future. The existence of the Ebert Republic, with its universal suffrage, its parliamentary swindling, its "freedom" of the Press, and its murder of labor leaders, is merely a necessary link in the historical chain of slavery and scoundrelism. The existence of the Soviet Government is a fact of immeasurable revolutionary significance. It was necessary to retain it, utilizing the conflict of the capitalist nations, the as yet unfinished imperialist war, the self-confident enffrontery of the Hohenzollern bands, the thick-wittedness of the world-bourgeoisie as far as the fundamental questions of the revolution were concerned, the antagonism of America and Europe, the complication of relations within the Entente. We had to lead our yet unfinished Soviet ship over the stormy waves, amid rocks and reefs, completing its building and armament en route.

Kautsky has the audacity to repeat the accusation that we did not, at the beginning of 1918, hurl ourselves unarmed against our mighty foe. Had we done this we would have been crushed.* The first great attempt of the proletariat to seize power would have suffered defeat. The revolutionary wing of the European proletariat would have been dealt the severest possible blow. The Entente would have made peace with the Hohenzollern over the corpse of the Russian Revolution, and the world capitalist reaction would have received a respite for a number of years. When Kautsky says that, concluding the Brest Peace, we did not think of its influence on the fate of the German Revolution, he is uttering a disgraceful slander. We considered the question from all sides, and our *sole criterion* was the interests of the international revolution.

We came to the conclusion that those interests demanded that the only Soviet Government in the world should be preserved. And we proved right. Whereas Kautsky awaited our fall, if not with impatience, at least with certainty; and on this expected fall built up his whole international policy.

The minutes of the session of the Coalition Government of November 19, 1918, published by the Bauer Ministry, run:—"First, a continuation of the discussion as to the relations of Germany and the Soviet Republic. Haase advises a policy of procrastination. Kautsky agrees with Haase: *decision must be postponed. The Soviet Government will not last long. It will inevitably fall in the course of a few weeks...*"

In this way, at the time when the situation of the Soviet

* The Vienna **Arbeiterzeitung** opposes, as is fitting, the wise Russian Communists to the foolish Austrians. "Did not Trotsky," the paper writes, "with a clear view and understanding of possibilities, sign the Brest-Litovsk peace of violence, notwithstanding that it served for the consolidation of German imperialism? The Brest Peace was just as harsh and shameful as is the Versailles Peace. But does this mean that Trotsky had to be rash enough to continue the war against Germany? Would not the fate of the Russian Revolution long ago have been sealed? Trotsky bowed before the unalterable necessity of signing the shameful treaty in anticipation of the German revolution." The honor of having foreseen all the consequences of the Brest Peace belongs to Lenin. But this, of course, alters nothing in the argument of the organ of the Vienniese Kautskians.

Government was really extremely difficult—for the destruction of German militarism had given the Entente, it seemed,
the full possibility of finishing with us "in the course of a few
weeks"—at that moment Kautsky not only does not hasten to
our aid, and even does not merely wash his hands of the
whole affair; he participates in active treachery against revolutionary Russia. To aid Scheidemann in his role of *watch-
dog* of the bourgeoisie, instead of the "programme" role assigned to him of its *"grave-digger,"* Kautsky himself hastens
to become the grave-digger of the Soviet Government. But
the Soviet Government is alive. It will outlive all its grave-
diggers.

8

PROBLEMS OF THE ORGANIZATION OF LABOR

THE SOVIET GOVERNMENT AND INDUSTRY

I F, in the first period of the Soviet revolution, the principal accusation of the bourgeois world was directed against our savagery and blood-thirstiness, later, when that argument, from frequent use, had become blunted, and had lost its force, we were made responsible chiefly for the economic disorganization of the country. In harmony with his present mission, Kautsky methodically translates into the language of pseudo-Marxism all the bourgeois charges against the Soviet Government of destroying the industrial life of Russia. The Bolsheviks began socialization without a plan. They socialized what was not ready for socialization. The Russian working class, altogether, is not yet prepared for the administration of industry; and so on, and so on.

Repeating and combining these accusations, Kautsky, with dull obstinacy, hides the real cause for our economic disorganization: the imperialist slaughter, the civil war, and the blockade.

Soviet Russia, from the first months of its existence, found itself deprived of coal, oil, metal, and cotton. First the Austro-German and then the Entente imperialisms, with the assistance of the Russian White Guards, tore away from Soviet Russia the Donetz coal and metal working region, the oil districts of the Caucasus, Turkestan with its cotton, Ural with its richest deposits of metals, Siberia with its bread and meat. The Donetz area had usually supplied our industry with 94 per cent. of its coal and 74 per cent. of its crude ore. The Ural supplied the remaining 20 per cent. of the ore and 4 per cent. of the coal. Both these regions, during the civil war, were cut off from us. We were deprived of half a milliard poods of coal imported from abroad. Simultaneously, we were left without oil: the oilfields, one and all, passed into the hands of our enemies. One needs to have a truly brazen forehead to speak, in face of these facts, of the destructive influence of "premature," "barbarous," etc., socialization. An industry which is completely deprived of fuel and raw materials—whether that industry belongs to a capitalist trust or to the Labor State, whether its factories be socialized or not—its chimneys will not smoke in either case without coal or oil. Something might be learned about this, say, in Austria; and for that matter in Germany itself. A weaving factory administered according to the best Kautskian methods—if we admit that anything at all can be administered by Kautskian methods, except one's own inkstand—will not produce prints if it is not supplied with cotton. And we were simultaneously deprived both of Turkestan and American cotton. In addition, as has been pointed out, we had no fuel.

Of course, the blockade and the civil war came as the result of the proletarian revolution in Russia. But it does not at all follow from this that the terrible devastation caused by the Anglo-American-French blockade and the robber campaigns of Kolchak and Denikin have to be put down to the discredit of the Soviet methods of economic organization.

The imperialist war that preceded the revolution, with its all-devouring material and technical demands, imposed a much greater strain on our young industry than on the industry of more powerful capitalist countries. Our transport suffered particularly severely. The exploitation of the railways increased considerably; the wear and tear correspondingly; while repairs were reduced to a strict minimum. The inevitable hour of Nemesis was brought nearer by the fuel crisis. Our almost simultaneous loss of the Donetz coal, foreign coal, and the oil of the Caucasus, obliged us in the sphere of transport to have recourse to wood. And, as the supplies of wood fuel were not in the least calculated with a view to this, we had to stoke our boilers with recently stored raw wood, which has an extremely destructive effect on the mechanism of locomotives that are already worn out. We see, in consequence, that the chief reasons for the collapse of transport preceded

November, 1917. But even those reasons which are directly or indirectly bound up with the November Revolution fall under the heading of political consequences of the revolution; and in no circumstances do they affect Socialist economic methods.

The influence of political disturbances in the economic sphere was not limited only to questions of transport and fuel. If world industry, during the last decade, was more and more becoming a single organism, the more directly does this apply to national industry. On the other hand, the war and the revolution were mechanically breaking up and tearing asunder Russian industry in every direction. The industrial ruin of Poland, the Baltic fringe, and later of Petrograd, began under Tsarism and continued under Kerensky, embracing ever new and newer regions. Endless evacuations simultaneous with the destruction of industry, of necessity meant the destruction of transport also. During the civil war, with its changing fronts, evacuations assumed a more feverish and consequently a still more destructive character. Each side temporarily or permanently evacuated this or that industrial centre, and took all possible steps to ensure that the most important industrial enterprises could not be utilized by the enemy: all valuable machines were carried off, or at any rate their most delicate parts, together with the technical and best workers. The evacuation was followed by a re-evacuation, which not infrequently completed the destruction both of the property transferred and of the railways. Some most important industrial areas—especially in the Ukraine and in the Urals —changed hands several times.

To this it must be added that, at the time when the destruction of techniacl equipment was being accomplished on an unprecedented scale, the supply of machines from abroad, which hitherto played a decisive part in our industry, had completely ceased.

But not only did the dead elements of production—buildings, machines, rails, fuel, and raw material—suffer terrible losses under the combined blows of the war and the revolution. Not less, if not more, did the chief factor of industry, its living creative force—the proletariat—suffer. The proletariat was consolidating the November revolution, building and defending the apparatus of Soviet power, and carrying on a ceaseless struggle with the White Guards. The skilled workers are, as a rule, at the same time the most advanced. The civil war tore away many tens of thousands of the best workers for a long time from productive labor, swallowing up many thousands of them for ever. The Socialist revolution placed the chief burden of its sacrifices upon the proletarian vanguard, and consequently on industry.

All the attention of the Soviet State has been directed, for the two and a half years of its existence, to the problem of military defence. The best forces and its principal resources were given to the front.

In any case, the class struggle inflicts blows upon industry. That accusation, long before Kautsky, was levelled at it by all the philosophers of the social harmony. During simple economic strikes the workers consume, and do not produce. Still more powerful, therefore, are the blows inflicted upon economic life by the class struggle in its severest form—in the form of armed conflicts. But it is quite clear that the civil war cannot be classified under the heading of Socialist economic methods.

The reasons enumerated above are more than sufficient to explain the difficult economic situation of Soviet Russia. There is no fuel, there is no metal, there is no cotton, transport is destroyed, technical equipment is in disorder, living labor-power is scattered over the face of the country, and a high percentage of it has been lost to the front—is there any need to seek supplementary reasons in the economic Utopianism of the Bolsheviks in order to explain the fall of our industry? On the contrary, each of the reasons quoted alone is sufficient to evoke the question: how is it possible at all that, under such conditions, factories and workshops should continue to function?

And yet they do continue principally in the shape of war industry, which is at present living at the expense of the rest. The Soviet Government was obliged to re-create it, just like the army, out of fragments. War industry, set up again under these conditions of unprecedented difficulty, has fulfilled and is fulfilling its duty: the Red Army is clothed, shod, equipped with its rifle, its machine gun, its cannon, its bullet, its shell, its aeroplane, and all else that it requires.

As soon as the dawn of peace made its appearance—after the destruction of Kolchak, Yudenich, and Denikin—we placed before ourselves the problem of economic organization in the fullest possible way. And already, in the course of three or four months of intensive work in this sphere, it has become clear beyond all possibility of doubt that, thanks to its most intimate connection with the popular masses, the elasticity of its apparatus, and its own revolutionary initiative, the Soviet Government disposes of such resources and methods for economic reconstruction as no other government ever had or has to-day.

True, before us there arose quite new questions and new difficulties in the sphere of the organization of labor. Socialist theory had no answers to these questions, and could not have them. We had to find the solution in practice, and test it in practice. Kautskianism is a whole epoch behind the gigantic economic problems being solved at present by the Soviet Government. In the form of Menshevism, it constantly throws obstacles in our way, opposing the practical measures of our economic reconstruction by bourgeois prejudices and bureaucratic-intellectual scepticism.

To introduce the reader to the very essence of the questions of the organization of labor, as they stand at present before us, we quote below the report of the author of this book at the Third All-Russian Congress of Trade Unions. With the object of the fullest possible elucidation of the question, the text of the speech is supplemented by considerable extracts from the author's reports at the All-Russian Congress of Economic Councils and at the Ninth Congress of the Communist Party.

REPORT ON THE ORGANIZATION OF LABOR

Comrades, the internal civil war is coming to an end. On the western front, the situation remains undecided. It is possible that the Polish bourgeoisie will hurl a challenge at its fate.... But even in this case—we do not seek it—the war will not demand of us that all-devouring concentration of forces which the simultaneous struggle on four fronts imposed upon us. The frightful pressure of the war is becoming weaker. Economic requirements and problems are more and more coming to the fore. History is bringing us, along the whole line, to our fundamental problem—the organization of labor on new social foundations. The organization of labor is in its essence the organization of the new society: every historical form of society is in its foundation a form of organization of labor. While every previous form of society was an organization of labor in the interests of a minority, which organized its State apparatus for the oppression of the overwhelming majority of the workers, we are making the first attempt in world-history to organize labor in the interests of the laboring majority itself. This, however, does not exclude the element of compulsion in all its forms, both the most gentle and the extremely severe. The element of State compulsion not only does not disappear from the historical arena, but on the contrary will still play, for a considerable period, an extremely prominent part.

As a general rule, man strives to avoid labor. Love for work is not at all an inborn characteristic: it is created by economic pressure and social education. One may even say that man is a fairly lazy animal. It is on this quality, in reality, that is founded to a considerable extent all human progress; because if man did not strive to expend his energy economically, did not seek to receive the largest possible quantity of products in return for a small quantity of energy, there would have been no technical development or social culture. It would appear, then, from this point of view that human laziness is a progressive force, Old Antonio Labriola, the Italian Marxist, even used to picture the man of the future as a "happy and lazy genius." We must not, however, draw the conclusion from this that the party and the trade unions must propagate this quality in their agitation as a moral duty. No, no! We have sufficient of it as it is. The problem before the social organization is just to bring "laziness" within a definite framework, to discipline it, and to pull mankind together with the help of methods and measures invented by mankind itself.

The key to economic organization is labor-power, skilled, elementarily trained, semi-trained, untrained, or unskilled. To work out methods for its accurate registration, mobilization, distribution, productive application, means practically to solve the problem of economic construction. This is a problem for a whole epoch—a gigantic problem. Its difficulty is intensified by the fact that we have to reconstruct labor on Socialist foundations in conditions of hitherto unknown poverty and terrifying misery.

The more our machine equipment is worn out, the more disordered our railways grow, the less hope there is for us of receiving machines to any significant extent from abroad in the near future, the greater is the importance acquired by the question of living labor-power. At first sight it would seem that there is plenty of it. But how are we to get at it? How are we to apply it? How are we productively to organize it? Even with the cleaning of snow drifts from the railway tracks, we were brought face to face with very big difficulties. It was absolutely impossible to meet those difficulties by means of buying labor-power on the market, with the present insignificant purchasing power of money, and in the most complete absence of manufactured products. Our fuel requirements cannot be satisfied, even partially, without a mass application, on a scale hitherto unknown, of labor-power to work on wood, fuel, peat, and combustible slate. The civil war has played havoc with our railways, our bridges, our buildings, our stations. We require at once tens and hundreds of thousands of hands to restore order to all this. For production on a large scale in our timber, peat, and other enterprises, we require housing for our workers, if they be only temporary huts. Hence, again, the necessity of devoting a considerable amount of labor-power to building work. Many workers are required to organize river navigation; and so on, and so forth....

Capitalist industry utilizes auxiliary labor-power on a large scale, in the shape of peasants employed on industry for only part of the year. The village, throttled by the grip of landlessness, always threw a certain surplus of labor-power on to the market. The State obliged it to do this by its demand for taxes. The market offered the peasant manufactured goods. To-day, we have none of this. The village has acquired more land; there is not sufficient agricultural machinery; workers are required for the land; industry can at present give practically nothing to the village; and the market no longer has an attractive influence on labor-power.

Yet labor-power is required—required more than at any time before. Not only the worker, but the peasant also, must give to the Soviet State his energy, in order to ensure that laboring Russia, and with it the laboring masses, should not be crushed. The only way to attract the labor-power necessary for our economic problems is to introduce *compulsory labor service.*

The very principle of compulsory labor service is for the Communist quite unquestionable. "He who works not, neither shall he eat." And as all must eat, all are obliged to work. Compulsory labor service is sketched in our Constitution and in our Labor Code. But hitherto it has always remained a mere principle. Its application has always had an accidental, impartial, episodic character. Only now, when along the whole line we have reached the question of the economic re-birth of the country, have problems of compulsory labor service arisen before us in the most concrete way possible. The only solution of economic difficulties that is correct from the point of view both of principle and of practice is to treat the population of the whole country as the reservoir of the necessary labor power—an almost inexhaustible reservoir— and to introduce strict order into the work ofits registration, mobilization, and utilization.

How are we practically to begin the utilization of labor-power on the basis of compulsory military service?

Hitherto only the War Department has had any experience in the sphere of the registration, mobilization, formation, and transference from one place to another of large masses. These technical methods and principles were inherited by our War Department, to a considerable extent, from the past.

In the economic sphere there is no such heritage; since in that sphere there existed the principle of private property, and labor-power entered each factory separately from the market. It is consequently natural that we should be obliged, at any rate during the first period, to make use of the apparatus of the War Department on a large scale for labor mobilizations.

We have set up special organizations for the application of the principle of compulsory labor service in the centre and in the districts: in the provinces, the counties, and the rural districts, we have already compulsory labor committees at work. They rely for the most part on the central and local organs of the War Department. Our economic centres—the Supreme Economic Council, the People's Commissariat for Agriculture, the People's Commissariat for Ways and Communications, the People's Commissariat for Food—work out estimates of the labor-power they require. The Chief Committee for Compulsory Labor Service receives these estimates, co-ordinates them, brings them into agreement with the local resources of labor-power, gives corresponding directions to its local organs, and through them carries out labor mobilizations. Within the boundaries of regions, provinces, and counties, the local bodies carry out this work independently, with the object of satisfying local economic requirements.

All this organization is at present only in the embryo stage. It is still very imperfect. But the course we have adopted is unquestionably the right one.

If the organization of the new society can be reduced fundamentally to the reorganization of labor, the organization of labor signifies in its turn the correct introduction of general labor service. This problem is in no way met by measures of a purely departamental and administrative character. It touches the very foundations of economic life and the social structure. It finds itself in conflict with the most powerful psychological habits and prejudices. The introduction of compulsory labor service pre-supposes, on the one hand, a colossal work of education, and, on the other, the greatest possible care in the practical method adopted.

The utilization of labor-power must be to the last degree economical. In our labor mobilizations we have to reckon with the economic and social conditions of every region, and with the requirements of the principal occupation of the local population—i.e., of agriculture. We have, if possible, to make use of the previous auxiliary occupations and part-time industries of the local population. We have to see that the transference of mobilized labor-power should take place over the shortest possible distances—*i.e.,* to the nearest sectors of the labor front. We must see that the number of workers mobilized correspond to the breadth of our economic problem. We must see that the workers mobilized be supplied in good time with the necessary implements of production, and with food. We must see that at their head be placed experienced and business-like instructors. We must see that the workers mobilized become convinced on the spot that their labor-power is being made use of cautiously and economically and is not being expended haphazard. Wherever it is possible, direct mobilization must be replaced by the labor task—*i.e.,* by the imposition on the rural district of an obligation to supply, for example, in such a time such a number of cubic sazhens of wood, or to bring up by carting to such a station so many poods of cast-iron, etc. In this sphere, it is essential to study experience as it accumulates with particular care, to allow a great measure of elasticity to the economic apparatus, to show more attention to local interests and social peculiarities of tradition. In a word, we have to complete, ameliorate, perfect, the system, methods, and organs for the mobilization of labor-power. But at the same time it is necessary once for all to make clear to ourselves that the principle itself of compulsory labor service has just so radically and permanently replaced the principle of free hiring as the socialization of the means of production has replaced capitalist property.

THE MILITARIZATION OF LABOR

The introduction of compulsory labor service is unthinkable without the application, to a greater or less degree, of the methods of militarization of labor. This term at once brings us into the region of the greatest possible superstitions and outcries from the opposition.

To understand what militarization of labor in the Workers' State means, and what its methods are, one has to make clear to oneself in what way the army itself was militarized—for, as we all know, in its first days the army did not at all possess the necessary "military" qualities. During these two years we mobilized for the Red Army nearly as many soldiers as there are members in our trade unions. But the members of the trade unions are workers, while in the army the workers constitute about 15 per cent., the remainder being a peasant mass. And, none the less, we can have no doubt that the true builder and "militarizer" of the Red Army has been the foremost worker, pushed forward by the party and the trade union organization. Whenever the situation at the front was difficult, whenever the recently-mobilized peasant mass did not display sufficient stability, we turned on the one hand to the Central Committee of the Communist Party, and on the other to the All-Russian Council of Trade Unions. From both these sources the foremost workers were sent to the front, and there built the Red Army after their own likeness and image—educating, hardening, and militarizing the peasant mass.

This fact must be kept in mind to-day with all possible clearness because it throws the best possible light on the meaning of militarization in the workers' and peasants' State. The militarization of labor has more than once been put forward as a watchword and realized in separate branches of economic life in the bourgeois countries, both in the West and in Russia under Tsarism. But our militarization is distinguished from those experiments by its aims and methods, just as much as the class-conscious proletariat organized for emancipation is distinguished from the class-conscious bourgeoisie organized for exploitation.

From the confusion, semi-unconscious and semi-deliberate, of two different historical forms of militarization—the proletarian or Socialist and the bourgeois—there spring the greater part of the prejudices, mistakes, protests, and outcries on this subject. It is on such a confusion of meanings that the whole position of the Mensheviks, our Russian Kautskies, is founded, as it was expressed in their theoretical resolution moved at the present Congress of Trade Unions.

The Mensheviks attacked not only the militarization of labor, but general labor service also. They reject these methods as "compulsory." They preach that general labor service means a low productivity of labor, while militarization means senseless scattering of labor-power.

"Compulsory labor always is unproductive labor,"—such

is the exact phrase in the Menshevik resolution. This affirmation brings us right up to the very essence of the question. For, as we see, the question is not at all whether it is wise or unwise to proclaim this or that factory militarized, or whether it is helpful or otherwise to give the military revolutionary tribunal powers to punish corrupt workers who steal materials and instruments, so precious to us, or who sabotage their work. No, the Mensheviks have gone much further into the question. Affirming that compulsory labor is *always* unproductive, they thereby attempt to cut the ground from under the feet of our economic reconstruction in the present tarnsitional epoch. For it is beyond question that to step from bourgeois anarchy to Socialist economy without a revolutionary dictatorship, and without compulsory forms of economic organization, is impossible.

In the first paragraph of the Menshevik resolution we are told that we are living in the period of transition from the capitalist method of production to the Socialist. What does this mean? And, first of all, whence does this come? Since what time has this been admitted by our Kautskians? They accused us—and this formed the foundation of our differences—of Socialist Utopianism; they declared—and this constituted the essence of their political teaching—that there can be no talk about the transition to Socialism in our epoch, and that our revolution is a bourgeois revolution, and that we Communists are only destroying capitalist economy, and that we are not leading the country forward but are throwing it back. This was the root difference—the most profound, the most irreconcilable—from which all the others followed. Now the Mensheviks tell us incidentally, in the introductory paragraph of their resolution, as something that does not require proof, that we are in the period of transition from capitalism to Socialism. And this quite unexpected admission, which, one might think, is extremely like a complete capitulation, is made the more lightly and carelessly that, as the whole resolution shows, it imposes no revolutionary obligations on the Mensheviks. They remain entirely captive to the bourgeois ideology. After recognizing that we are on the road to Socialism, the Mensheviks with all the greater ferocity attack those methods without which, in the harsh and difficult conditions of the present day, the transition to Socialism **cannot** be acomplished.

Compulsory labor, we are told, is always unproductive. We ask what does compulsory labor mean here, that is, to what kind of labor is it opposed? Obviously, to free labor. What are we to understand, in that case, by free labor? That phrase was formulated by the progressive philosophers of the bourgeoisie, in the struggle against unfree, *i.e.*, against the serf labor of peasants, and against the standardized and regulated labor of the craft guilds. Free labor meant labor which might be "freely" bought in the market; freedom was reduced to a legal fiction, on the basis of freely-hired slavery. We know of no other form of free labor in history. Let the very few representatives of the Mensheviks at this Congress explain to us what they mean by free, non-compulsory labor, if not the market of labor-power.

History has known slave labor. History has known serf labor. History has known the regulated labor of the mediæval craft guilds. Throughout the world there now prevails hired labor, which the yellow journalists of all countries oppose, as the highest possible form of liberty, to Soviet "slavery." We, on the other hand, oppose capitalist slavery by socially-regulated labor on the basis of an economic plan, obligatory for the whole people and consequently compulsory for each worker in the country. Without this we cannot even dream of a transition to Socialism. The element of material, physical, compulsion may be greater or less; that depends on many conditions—on the degree of wealth or poverty of the country, on the heritage of the past, on the general level of culture, on the condition of transport, on the administrative aparatus, etc., etc. But obligation, and, consequently, compulsion, are essential conditions in order to bind down the bourgeois anarchy, to secure socialization of the means of production and labor, and to reconstruct economic life on the basis of a single plan.

For the Liberal, freedom in the long run means the market. Can or cannot the capitalist buy labor-power at a moderate price—that is for him the sole measure of the freedom of labor. That measure is false, not only in relation to the future but also in connection with the past.

It would be absurd to imagine that, during the time of bondage-right, work was carried entirely under the stick of physical compulsion, as if an overseer stood with a whip behind the back of every peasant. Mediæval forms of economic life grew up out of definite conditions of production, and created definite forms of social life, with which the peasant grew accustomed, and which he at certain periods considered just, or at any rate unalterable. Whenever he, under the influence of a change in material conditions, displayed hostility, the State descended upon him with its material force, thereby displaying the compulsory character of the organization of labor.

The foundations of the militarization of labor are those forms of State compulsion without which the replacement of capitalist economy by the Socialist will for ever remain an empty sound. Why do we speak of *militarization?* Of course, this is only an analogy—but an analogy very rich in content. No social organization except the army has ever considered itself justified in subordinating citizens to itself in such a measure, and to control them by its will on all sides to such a degree, as the State of the proletarian dictatorship considers itself justified in doing, and does. Only the army—just because in its way it used to decide questions of the life or death of nations, States, and ruling classes—was endowed with powers of demanding from each and all complete submission to its problems, aims, regulations, and orders. And it achieved this to the greater degree, the more the problems of military organization coincided with the requirements of social development.

The question of the life or death of Soviet Russian is at present being settled on the labor front; our economic, and together with them our professional and productive organizations, have the right to demand from their members all that devotion, discipline, and executive thoroughness, which hitherto only the army required.

On the other hand, the relation of the capitalist to the worker is not at all founded merely on the "free" contract, but includes the very powerful elements of State regulation and material compulsion.

The competition of capitalist with capitalist imparted a

certain very limited reality to the fiction of freedom of labor; but this competition, reduced to a minimum by trusts and syndicates, we have finally eliminated by destroying private property in the means of production. The transition to Socialism, verbally acknowledged by the Mensheviks, means the transition from anarchical distribution of labor-power—by means of the game of buying and selling, the movement of market prices and wages—to systematic distribution of the workers by the economic organizations of the county, the province, and the whole country. Such a form of planned distribution pre-supposes the subordination of those distributed to the economic plan of the State. And this is the essence of *compulsory labor service,* which inevitably enters into the programme of the Socialist organization of labor, as its fundamental element.

If organized economic life is unthinkable without compulsory labor service, the latter is not to be realized without the abolition of fiction of the freedom of labor, and without the substitution for it of the obligatory principle, which is supplemented by real compulsion.

That free labor is more productive than compulsory labor is quite true when it refers to the period of transition from feudal society to bourgeois society. But one needs to be a Liberal or—at the present day—a Kautskian, to make that truth permanent, and to transfer its application to the period of transition from the bourgeois to the Socialist order. If it were true that compulsory labor is unproductive always and under every condition, as the Menshevik resolution says, all our constructive work would be doomed to failure. For we can have no way to Socialism except by the authoritative regulation of the economic forces and resources of the country, and the centralized distribution of labor-power in harmony with the general State plan. The Labor State considers itself empowered to send every worker to the place where his work is necessary. And not one serious Socialist will begin to deny to the Labor State the right to lay its hand upon the worker who refuses to execute his labor duty. But the whole point is that the Menshevik path of transition to "Socialism" is a milky way, without the bread monopoly, without the abolition of the market, without the revolutionary dictatorship, and without the militarization of labor.

Without general labor service, without the right to order and demand fulfilment of orders, the trade unions will be transformed into a mere form without a reality; for the young Socialist State requires trade unions, not for a struggle for better conditions of labor—that is the task of the social and State organizations as a whole—but to organize the working class for the ends of production, to educate, discipline, distribute, group, retain certain categories and certain workers at their posts for fixed periods—in a word, hand in hand with the State to exercise their authority in order to lead the workers into the framework of a single economic plan. To defend, under such conditions, the "freedom" of labor means to defend fruitless, helpless, absolutely unregulated searches for better conditions, unsystematic, chaotic changes from factory to factory, in a hungry country, in conditions of terrible disorganization of the transport and food apparatus... What except the complete collapse of the working-class and complete economic anarchy could be the result of the stupid attempt to reconcile bourgeois freedom of labor with proletarian socialization of the means of production?

Consequently, comrades, militarization of labor, in the root sense indicated by me, is not the invention of invidual politicians or an invention of our War Department, but represents the inevitable method of organization and disciplining of labor-power during the period of transition from capitalism to Socialism. And if the compulsory distribution of labor-power, its brief or prolonged retention at particular industries and factories, its regulation within the framework of the general State economic plan—if these forms of compulsion lead always and everywhere, as the Menshevik resolution states, to the lowering of productivity, then you can erect a monument over the grave of Socialism. For we cannot build Socialism on decreased production. Every social organization is in its foundation an organization of labor, and if our new organization of labor leads to a lowering of its productivity, it thereby most fatally leads to the destruction of the Socialist society we are building, whichever way we twist and turn, whatever measures of salvation we invent.

That is why I stated at the very beginning that the Menshevik argument against militarization leads us to the root question of general labor service and its influence on the productivity of labor. It is true that compulsory labor is always unproductive? We have to reply that that is the most pitiful and worthless Liberal prejudice. The whole question is: who applies the principle of compulsion, over whom, and for what purpose? What State, what class, in what conditions, by what methods? Even the serf organization was in certain conditions a step forward, and led to the increase in the productivity of labor. Production has grown extremely under capitalism, that is, in the epoch of the free buying and selling of labor-power on the market. But free labor, together with the whole of capitalism, entered the stage of imperialism and blew itself up in the imperialist war. The whole economic life of the world entered a period of bloody anarchy, monstrous perturbations, the impoverishment, dying out, and destruction of masses of the people. Can we, under such conditions, talk about the productivity of free labor, when the fruits of that labor are destroyed ten times more quickly than they are created? The imperialistic war, and that which followed it, displayed the impossibility of society existing any longer on the foundation of free labor. Or perhaps someone possesses the secret of how to separate free labor from the delirium tremens of imperialism, that is, of turning back the clock of social development half a century or a century?

If it were to turn out that the planned, and consequently compulsory, organization of labor which is arising to replace imperialism led to the lowering of economic life, it would mean the destruction of all our culture, and a retrograde movement of humanity back to barbarism and savagery.

Happily, not only for Soviet Russia but for the whole of humanity, the philosophy of the low productivity of compulsory labor—"everywhere and under all conditions"—is only a belated echo of ancient Liberal melodies. The productivity of labor is the total productive meaning of the most complex combination of social conditions, and is not in the least measured or pre-determined by the legal form of labor.

The whole of human history is the history of the organization and education of collective man for labor, with the object of attaining a higher level of productivity. Man, as I have already permitted myself to point out, is lazy; that is, he instinctively strives to receive the largest possible quantity of products for the least possible expenditure of energy. Without such a striving, there would have been no economic development. The growth of civilization is measured by the productivity of human labor, and each new form of social relations must pass through a test on such lines.

"Free," that is, freely-hired labor, did not appear all at once upon the world, with all the attributes of productivity. It acquired a high level of productivity only gradually, as a result of a prolonged application of methods of labor organization and labor education. Into that education there entered the most varying methods and practices, which in addition changed from one epoch to another. First of all the bourgeoisie drove the peasant from the village to the high road with its club, having preliminarily robbed him of his land, and when he would not work in the factory it branded his forehead with red-hot irons, hung him, sent him to the gallows; and in the long run it taught the tramp who had been shaken out of his village to stand at the lathe in the factory. At this stage, as we see, "free" labor is little different as yet from convict labor, both in its material conditions and in its legal aspect.

At different times the bourgeoisie combined the red-hot irons of repression in different proportions with methods of moral influence, and, first of all, the teaching of the priest. As early as the sixteenth century, it reformed the old religion of Catholicism, which defended the feudal order, and adapted for itself a new religion in the form of the Reformation, which combined the free soul with free trade and free labor. It found for itself new priests, who became the spiritual shop-assistants, pious counter-jumpers of the bourgeoisie. The school, the press, the market place, and parliament were adapted by the bourgeoisie for the moral fashioning of the working-class. Different forms of wages—day-wages, piece wages, contract and collective bargaining—all these are merely changing methods in the hands of the bourgeoisie for the labor mobilization of the proletariat. To this there are added all sorts of forms for encouraging labor and exciting ambition. Finally, the bourgeoisie learned how to gain possession even of the trade unions—*i.e.*, the organizations of the working class itself; and it made use of them on a large scale, particularly in Great Britain, to discipline the workers. It domesticated the leaders, and with their help inoculated the workers with the fiction of the necessity for peaceful organic labor, for a faultless attitude to their duties, and for a strict execution of the laws of the bourgeois State. The crown of all this work is Taylorism, in which the elements of the scientific organization of the process of production are combined with the most concentrated methods of the system of sweating.

From all that has been said above, it is clear that the productivity of freely-hired labor is not something that appeared all at once, perfected, presented by history on a salver. No, it was the result of a long and stubborn policy of repression, education, organization, and encouragement, applied by the bourgeoisie in its relations with the working class. Step by step it learned to squeeze out of the workers ever more and more of the products of labor; and one of the most powerful weapons in its hand turned out to be the proclamation of free hiring as the sole free, normal, healthy, productive, and saving form of labor.

A legal form of labor which would of its own virtue guarantee its productivity has not been known in history, and cannot be known. The legal superstructure of labor corresponds to the relations and current ideas of the epoch. The productivity of labor is developed, on the basis of the development of technical forces, by labor education, by the gradual adaptation of the workers to the changed methods of production and the new form of social relations.

The creation of Socialist society means the organization of the workers on new foundations, their adaptation to those foundations, and their labor re-education, with the one unchanging end of the increase in the productivity of labor. The working class, under the leadership of its vanguard, must itself re-educate itself on the foundations of Socialism. Whoever has not understood this is ignorant of the A B C of Socialist construction.

What methods have we, then, for the re-education of the workers? Infinitely wider than the bourgeoisie has—and, in addition, honest, direct, open methods, infected neither by hypocrisy nor by lies. The bourgeoisie had to have recourse to deception, representing its labor as free, when in reality it was not merely socially-imposed, but actually slave labor. For it was the labor of the majority in the interests of the minority. We, on the other hand, organize labor in the interests of the workers themselves, and therefore we can have no motives for hiding or masking the socially compulsory character of our labor organization. We need the fairy stories neither of the priests, nor of the Liberals, nor of the Kautskians. We say directly and openly to the masses that they can save, rebuild, and bring to a flourishing condition a Socialist country only by means of hard work, unquestioning discipline and exactness in execution on the part of every worker.

The chief of our resources is moral influence—propaganda not only in word but in deed. General labor service has an obligatory character; but this does not mean at all that it represents violence done to the working class. If compulsory labor came up against the opposition of the majority of the workers it would turn out a broken reed, and with it the whole of the Soviet order. The militarization of labor, when the workers are opposed to it, is the State slavery of Arakeheyev. The militarization of labor by the will of the workers themselves is the Socialist dictatorship. That compulsory labor service and the militarization of labor do not force the will of the workers, as "free" labor used to do, is best shown by the flourishing, unprecedented in the history of humanity, of labor voluntarism in the form of "Subbotniks" (Communist Saturdays). Such a phenomenon there never was before, anywhere or at any time. By their own voluntary labor, freely given—once a week and oftener—the workers clearly demonstrate not only their readiness to bear the yoke of "compulsory" labor but their eagerness to give the State besides that a certain quantity of additional labor. The "Subbotniks" are not only a splendid demonstration of Communist solidarity, but also the best possible guarantee for the successful introduction of general labor service. Such truly Communist tendencies must be shown up in their true light, extended, and developed with the help of propaganda.

The chief spiritual weapon of the bourgeoisie is religion; ours is the open explanation to the masses of the exact position of things, the extension of scientific and technical knowledge, and the initiation of the masses into the general economic plan of the State, on the basis of which there must be brought to bear all the labor-power at the disposal of the Soviet regime.

Political economy provided us with the principal substance of our agitation in the period we have just left: the capitalist social order was a riddle, and we explained that riddle to the masses. To-day, social riddles are explained to the masses by the very mechanism of the Soviet order, which draws the masses into all branches of administration. Political economy will more and more pass into the realms of history. There move forward into the foreground the sciences which study nature and the methods of subordinating it to man.

The trade unions must organize scientific and technical educational work on the widest possible scale, so that every worker in his own branch of industry shoud find the impulses for theoretical work of the brain, while the latter should again return him to labor, perfecting it and making him more productive. The press as a whole must fall into line with the economic problems of the country—not in that sense alone in which this is being done at present—*i.e.*, not in the sense of a mere general agitation in favor of a revival of labor—but in the sense of the discussion and the weighing of concrete economic problems and plans, ways and means of their solution, and, most important of all, the testing and criticism of results already achieved. The newspapers must from day to day follow the production of the most important factories and other enterprises, registering their successes and failures encouraging some and pillorying others....

Russian capitalism, in consequence of its lateness, its lack of independence, and its resulting parasitic features, has had much less time than European capitalism technically to educate the laboring masses, to train and discipline them for production. That problem is now in its entirety imposed upon the industrial organizations of the proletariat. A good engineer, a good mechanic, and a good carpenter, must have in the

Soviet Republic the same publicity and fame as hitherto was enjoyed by prominent agitators, revolutionary fighters, and, in the most recent period, the most courageous and capable commanders and commissaries. Greater and lesser leaders of technical development must occupy the central position in the public eye. Bad workers must be made ashamed of doing their work badly.

We still retain, and for a long time will retain, the system of wages. The further we go, the more will its importance become simply to guarantee to all members of society all the necessaries of life; and thereby it will cease to be a system of wages. But at present we are not sufficiently rich for this. Our main problem is to raise the quantity of products turned out, and to this problem all the remainder must be subordinated. In the present difficult period the system of wages is for us, first and foremost, not a method for guaranteeing the personal existence of any separate worker, but a method of estimating what that individual worker brings by his labor to the Labor Republic.

Consequently, wages, in the form both of money and of goods, must be brought into the closest possible touch with the productivity of individual labor. Under capitalism, the system of piece-work and of grading, the application of the Taylor system, etc., have as their object to increase the exploitation of the workers by the squeezing-out of surplus value. Under Socialist production, piece-work, bonuses, etc., have as their problem to increase the volume of social product, and consequently to raise the general well-being. Those workers who do more for the general interest than others receive the right to a greater quantity of the social product than the lazy, the careless, and the disorganizers.

Finally, when it rewards some, the Labor State cannot but punish others—those who are clearly infringing labor solidarity, undermining the common work, and seriously impairing the Socialist renaissance of the country. Repression for the attainment of economic ends is a necessary weapon of the Socialist dictatorship.

All the measures enumerated above—and together with them a number of others—must assist the development of rivalry in the sphere of production. Without this we shall never rise above the average, which is a very unsatisfactory level. At the bottom of rivalry lies the vital instinct—the struggle for existence—which in the bourgeois order assumes the character of competition. Rivalry will not disappear even in the developed Socialist society; but with the growing guarantee of the necessary requirements of life rivalry will acquire an ever less selfish and purely idealist character. It will express itself in a striving to perform the greatest possible service for one's village, county, town, or the whole of society, and to receive in return renown, gratitude, sympathy, or, finally, just internal satisfaction from the consciousness of work well done. But in the difficult period of transition, in conditions of the extreme shortage of material goods, and the as yet insufficiently developed state of social solidarity, rivalry must inevitably be to a greater or less degree bound up with a striving to guarantee for oneself one's own requirements.

This, comrades, is the sum of resources at the disposal of the Labor State in order to raise the productivity of labor. As we see, there is no ready-made solution here. We shall find it written in no book. For there could not be such a book. We are now only beginning, together with you, to write that book in the sweat and the blood of the workers. We say: working men and women, you have crossed to the path of regulated labor. Only along that road will you build the Socialist society. Before you there lies a problem which no one will settle for you: the problem of increasing production on new social foundations. Unless you solve that problem, you will perish. If you solve it, you will raise humanity by a whole head.

LABOR ARMIES

The question of the application of armies to labor purposes, which has acquired amongst us an enormous importance from the point of view of principle, was approached by us by the path of practice, not at all on the foundations of theoretical consideration. On certain borders of Soviet Russia, circumstances had arisen which had left considerable military forces free for an indefinite period. To transfer them to other

active fronts, especially in the winter, was difficult in consequence of the disorder of railway transport. Such, for
example, proved the position of the Third Army, distributed
over the provinces of the Ural and the Ural area. The
leading workers of that army, understanding that as yet it
could not be demobilized, themselves raised the question of its
transference to labor work. They sent to the centre a more
or less worked-out draft decree for a labor army.

The problem was novel and difficult. Would the Red
soldiers work? Would their work be sufficiently productive?
Would it pay for itself? In this connection there were doubts
even in our own ranks. Needless to say, the Mensheviks
struck up a chorus of opposition. The same Abramovich, at
the Congress of Economic Councils called in January or the
beginning of February—that is to say, when the whole affair
was still in draft stage—foretold that we should suffer an inevitable failure, for the whole undertaking was senseless, an
Arakcheyev Utopia, etc., etc. We considered the matter
otherwise. Of course the difficulties were great, but they were
not distinguishable in principle from many other difficulties
of Soviet constructive work.

Let us consider in fact what was the organism of the
Third Army. Taken all in all, one rifle division and one
cavalry division—a total of fifteen regiments—and, in addition,
special units. The remaining military formations had already
been transformed to other armies and fronts. But the apparatus of military administration had remained untouched as
yet, and we considered it probable that in the spring we
should have to transfer it along the Volga to the Caucasus
front, against Denikin, if by that time he were not finally
broken. On the whole, in the Third Army there remained
about 120,000 Red soldiers in administrative posts, institutions, military units, hospitals, etc. In this general mass,
mainly peasant in its composition, there were reckoned about
16,000 Communists and members of the organization of sympathizers—to a considerable extent workers of the Ural. In
this way, in its composition and structure, the Third Army
represented a peasant mass bound together into a military
organization under the leadership of the foremost workers.
In the army there worked a considerable number of military

specialists, who carried out important military functions while remaining under the general control of the Communists. If we consider the Third Army from this general point of view, we shall see that it represents in miniature the whole of Soviet Russia. Whether we take the Red Army as a whole, or the organization of the Soviet regime in the county, province, or the whole Republic, including the economic organs, we shall find everywhere the same scheme of organization: millions of peasants drawn into new forms of political, economic, and social life by the organized workers, who occupy a controlling position in all spheres of Soviet construction. To posts requiring special knowledge, we send experts of the bourgeois school. They are given the necessary independence, but control over their work remains in the hands of the working class, in the person of its Communist Party. The introduction of general labor service is again only conceivable for us as the mobilization of mainly peasant labor-power under the guidance of the most advanced workers. In this way there were not, and could not, be any obstacles in principle in the way of application of the army to labor. In other words, the opposition in principle to labor armies, on the part of those same Mensheviks, was in reality opposition to "compulsory" labor generally, and consequently against general labor service and against Soviet methods of economic reconstruction as a whole. This opposition did not trouble us a great deal.

Naturally, the military apparatus as such is not adapted directly to the process of labor. But we had no illusions about that. Control had to remain in the hands of the appropriate economic organs; the army supplied the necessary labor power in the form of organized, compact units, suitable in the mass for the execution of the simplest homogeneous types of work: the freeing of roads from snow, the storage of fuel, building work, organization of cartage, etc., etc.

To-day we have already had considerable experience in the work of the labor application of the army, and can give not merely a preliminary or hypothetical estimate. What are the conclusions to be drawn from that experience? The Mensheviks have hastened to draw them. The same Abramovich, again, announced at the Miners' Congress that we had become bankrupt, that the labor armies represent parasitic formations, in which there are 100 officials for every ten workers. Is this true? No. This is the irresponsible and malignant criticism of men who stand on one side, do not know the facts ,collect only fragments and rubbish, and are concerned in any way and every way either to declare our bankruptcy or to prophecy it. In reality, the labor armies have not only not gone bankrupt, but, on the contrary, have had important successes, have displayed their fidelity, are developing and are becoming stronger and stronger. Just those prophets have gone bankrupt who foretold that nothing would come of the whole plan, that nobody would begin to work, and that the Red soldiers would not go to the labor front but would simply scatter to their homes.

These criticisms were dictated by a philistine scepticism, lack of faith in the masses, lack of faith in bold initiative, and organization. But did we not hear exactly the same criticism, at bottom, when we had recourse to extensive mobilizations for military problems? Then too we were frightened, we were terrified by stories of mass desertion, which was absolutely inevitable, it was alleged, after the imperialist war. Naturally, desertion there was, but considered by the test of experience it proved not at all on such a mass scale as was foretold; it did not destroy the army; the bond of morale and organization—Communist voluntarism and State compulsion combined—allowed us to carry out mobilizations of millions to carry through numerous formations and redistributions, and to solve the most difficult military problems. In the long run, the army was victorious. In relation to labor problems, on the foundation of our military experience, we awaited the same results; and we were not mistaken. The Red soldiers did not scatter when they were transformed from military to labor service, as the sceptics prophesied. Thanks to our splendidly-organized agitation, the transference itself took place amidst great enthusiasm. True, a certain portion of the soldiers tried to leave the army, but this always happens when a large military formation is transferred from one front to another, or is sent from the rear to the front—in general when it is shaken up—and when potential desertion becomes active. But immediately the political sections, the press, the organs of struggle with desertion, etc., entered into their rights; and to-day the percentage of deserters from our labor armies is in no way higher than in our armies on active service.

The statement that the armies, in view of their internal structure, can produce only a small percentage of workers, is true only to a certain extent. As far as the Third Army is concerned, I have already pointed out that it retained its complete apparatus of administration side by side with an extremely insignificant number of military units. While we—owing to military and not economic considerations—retained untouched the staff of the army and its administrative apparatus, the percentage of workers produced by the army was actually extremely low. From the general number of 120,000 Red soldiers, 21% proved to be employed in administrative and economic work; 16% were engaged in daily detail work (guards, etc.) in connection with the large number of army institutions and stores; the number of sick, mainly typhus cases, together with the medico-sanitary personnel, was about 13%; about 25% were not available for various reasons (detachment, leave, absence without leave, etc.). In this way, the total personnel available for work constitutes no more than 23%; this is the maximum of what can be drawn for labor from the given army. Actually, at first, there worked only about 14%, mainly drawn from the two divisions, rifle and cavalry, which still remained with the army.

But as soon as it was clear that Denikin had been crushed, and that we should not have to send the Third Army down the Volga in the spring to assist the forces on the Caucasus front, we immediately entered upon the disbanding of the clumsy army apparatus and a more regular adaptation of the army institutions to problems of labor. Although this work is not yet complete, it has already had time to give some very significant results. At the present moment (March, 1920), the former Third Army gives about 38% of its total composition as workers. As for the military units of the Ural military area working side by side with it, they already provide 49% of their number as workers. This result is not so bad, if we compare it with the amount of work done in factories and workshops, amongst which in the case of many quite recently, in the case of some even to-day, absence from work for legal and illegal reasons reached 50% and over.* To this one must add that workers in factories and workshops are not infrequently assisted by the adult members of their family, while the Red soldiers have no auxiliary force but themselves.

If we take the case of the 19-year-olds, who have been mobilized in the Ural with the help of the military apparatus— principally for wood fuel work—we shall find that, out of their general number of over 30,000, over 75% attend work. This is already a very great step forward. It shows that, using the military apparatus for mobilization and formation, we can introduce such alterations in the construction of purely labor units as guarantee an enormous increase in the percentage of those who participate directly in the material process of production.

Finally, in connection with the productivity of military labor, we can also now judge on the basis of experience. During the first days, the productivity of labor in the principal departments of work, in spite of the great moral enthusiasm, was in reality very low, and might seem completely discouraging when one read the first labor communiqués. Thus, for the preparation of a cubic sazhen of wood, at first, one had to reckon thirteen to fifteen labor days; whereas the standard— true, rarely attained at the present day—is reckoned at three days. One must add, in addition, that artistes in this sphere are capable, under favorable conditions, of producing one cubic sazhen per day per man. What happened in reality? The military units were quartered far from the forest to be felled. In many cases it was necessary to march to and from work 6 to 8 versts, which swallowed up a considerable portion of the working day. There were not sufficient axes and saws on the spot. Many Red soldiers, born in the plains, did not know the forests, had never felled trees, had never chopped or sawed them up. The provincial and county Timber Committees were very far from knowing at first how to use the military units, how to direct them where they were required, how to equip them as they should be equipped. It is not

---

* Since that time this percentage has been considerably lowered (June, 1920).

156

wonderful that all this had as its result an extremely low level of productivity. But after the most crying defects in organization were eliminated, results were achieved that were much more satisfactory. Thus, acocrding to the most recent data, in that same First Labor Army, four and a half working days are now devoted to one sazhen of wood, which is not so far from the present standard. What is most comforting, however, is the fact that the productivity of labor systematically increases, in the measure of the improvement of its conditions.

While as to what can be achieved in this respect, we have a brief but very rich experience in the Moscow Engineer Regiment. The Chief Board of Military Engineers, which controlled this experiment, began with fixing the standard of production as three working days for a cubic sazhen of wood. This standard soon proved to be surpassed. In January there were spent on a cubic sazhen of wood two and one-third working days; in February, 2.1; in March, 1.5; which represents an exclusively high level of productivity. This result was achieved by moral influence, by the exact registration of the individual work of each man, by the awakening of labor pride, by the distribution of bonuses to the workers who produced more than the average result—or, to speak in the language of the trade unions, by a sliding scale adaptable to all individual changes in the productivity of labor. This experiment, carried out almost under laboratory conditions, clearly indicates the path along which we have to go in future.

At present we have functioning a series of labor armies—the First, the Petrograd, the Ukrainian, the Caucasian, the South Volga, the Reserve. The latter, as is known, assisted considerably to raise the traffic capacity of the Kazan-Ekaterinburg Railway; and, wherever the experiment of the adaptation of military units for labor problems was carried out with any intelligence at all, the results showed that this method is unquestionably live and correct.

The prejudice concerning the inevitably parasitic nature of military organization—under each and every condition—proves to be shattered. The Soviet Army reproduces within itself the tendencies of the Soviet social order. We must not think in the petrifying terms of the last epoch: "militarism," "military organization," "the unproductiveness of compulsory labor." We must approach the phenomena of the new epoch without any prejudices, and with eyes wide open; and we must remember that Saturday exists for man, and not vice versa; that all forms of organization, including the military, are only weapons in the hands of the working class in power, which has both the right and the possibility of adapting, altering, refashioning, those weapons, until it has achieved the requisite result.

THE SINGLE ECONOMIC PLAN

The widest possible application of the principle of general labor service, together with measures for the militarization of labor, can play a decisive part only in case they are applied on the basis of a single economic plan covering the whole country and all branches of productive activity. This plan must be drawn up for a number of years, for the whole epoch that lies before us. It is naturally broken up into separate periods or stages, corresponding to the inevitable stages in the economic rebirth of the country. We shall have to begin with the most simple and at the same time most fundamental problems.

We have first of all to afford the working class the very possibility of living—though it be in the most difficult conditions—and thereby to preserve our industrial centres and save the towns. This is the point of departure. If we do not wish to melt the town into agriculture, and transform the whole country into a peasant State, we must support our transport, even at the minimum level, and secure bread for the towns, fuel and raw materials for industry, fodder for the cattle. Without this we shall not make one step forward. Consequently, the first part of the plan comprises the improvement of transport, or, in any case, the prevention of its further deterioration and the preparation of the most necessary supplies of food, raw materials, and fuel. The whole of the next period will be in its entirety filled with the concentration and straining of labor-power to solve these root problems; and only in this way shall we lay the foundations for all that is to come. It was such a problem, incidentally, that we put before our labor armies. Whether the first or the following periods will be measured by months or by years, it is fruitless at present to guess. This depends on many reasons, beginning with the international situation and ending with the degree of single-mindedness and steadfastness of the working class.

The second period is the period of machine-building in the interests of transport and the storage of raw material and fuel. Here the core is in the locomotive.

At the present time the repairing of locomotives is carried on in too haphazard a fashion, swallowing up energies and resources beyond all measure. We must reorganize the repairing of our rolling-stock, on the basis of the mass production of spare parts. To-day, when the whole network of the railways and the factories is in the hands of one master, the Labor State, we can and must fix single types of locomotives and trucks for the whole country, standardize their constituent parts, draw all the necessary factories into the work of the mass production of spare parts, reduce repairing to the simple replacing of worn-out parts by new, and thereby make it possible to build new locomotives on a mass scale out of spare parts.

Now that the sources of fuel and raw material are again open to us, we must concentrate our exclusive attention on the building of locomotives.

The third period will be one of machine-building in the interests of the production of articles of primary necessity.

Finally, the fourth period, reposing on the conquests of the first three, will allow us to begin the production of articles of personal or secondary significance on the widest possible scale.

This plan has great significance, not only as a general guide for the practical work of our economic organs, but also as a line along which propaganda amongst the laboring masses in connection with our economic problems is to proceed. Our labor mobilization will not enter into real life, will not take root, if we do not excite the living interest of all that is honest, class-conscious, and inspired in the working class. We must explain to the masses the whole truth as to our situation and as to our views for the future; we must tell them openly that our economic plan, with the maximum of exertion on the part of the workers, will neither to-morrow nor the day after give us a land flowing with milk and honey: for during the first period our chief work will consist in preparing the conditions for the production of the means of production. Only after we have secured, though on the smallest possible scale, the possibility of rebuilding the means of transport and production, shall we pass on to the production of articles for general consumption. In this way the fruit of their labor, which is the direct object of the workers, in the shape of articles for personal consumption, will arrive only in the last, the fourth, stage of our economic plan; and only then shall we have a serious improvement in our life. The masses, who for a prolonged period will still bear all the weight of labor and of privation, must realize to the full the inevitable internal logic of this economic plan if they are to prove capable of carrying it out.

The sequence of the four economic periods outlined above must not be understood too absolutely. We do not, of course, propose to bring completely to a standstill our textile industry: we could not do this for military considerations alone. But in order that our attention and our forces should not be distracted under the pressure of requirements and needs crying to us from all quarters, it is essential to make use of the economic plan as the fundamental criterion, and separate the important and the fundamental from the auxiliary and secondary. Needless to say, under no circumstances are we striving for a narrow "national" Communism: the raising of the blockade, and the European revolution all the more, would introduce the most radical alterations in our economic plan, cutting down the stages of its development and bringing them together. But we do not know when these events will take place; and we must act in such a way that we can hold out and become stronger under the most unfavorable circumstances—that is to say, in face of the slowest conceivable development of the European and the world revolution. In case we are able actually to establish trading relations with the capitalist countries, we shall again be guided by the economic plan sketched above. We shall exchange part of our raw material for locomotives or for necessary machines, but under no circumstances for clothing, boots, or colonial products: our first item is not articles of consumption, but the implements of transport and production.

We should be short-sighted sceptics, and the most typical bourgeois curmudgeons, if we imagined that the rebirth of our economic life will take the form of a gradual transition from the present economic collapse to the conditions that preceded that collapse, *i.e.*, that we shall reascend the same steps by which we descended, and only after a certain, quite prolonged, period will be able to raise our Socialist economy to the level at which it stood on the eve of the imperialist war. Such a conception would not only be not consoling, but absolutely incorrect. Economic collapse, which destroyed and broke up in its path an incalculable quantity of values, also destroyed a great deal that was poor and rotten, that was absolutely senseless; and thereby it cleared the path for a new method of reconstruction, corresponding to that technical equipment which world economy now possesses.

If Russian capitalism developed not from stage to stage, but leaping over a series of stages, and instituted American factories in the midst of primitive steppes, the more is such a forced march possible for Socialist economy. After we have conquered our terrible misery, have accumulated small supplies of raw material and food, and have improved our transport, we shall be able to leap over a whole series of intermediate stages, benefiting by the fact that we are not bound by the chains of private property, and that therefore we are able to subordinate all undertakings and all the elements of economic life to a single State plan.

Thus, for example, we shall undoubtedly be able to enter the period of elecrification, in all the chief branches of industry and in the sphere of personal consumption, without passing through "the age of steam." The programme of electrification is already drawn up in a series of logically consequent stages, corresponding to the fundamental stages of the general economic plan.

A new war may slow down the realization of our economic intentions; our energy and persistence can and must hasten the process of our economic rebirth. But, whatever be the rate at which economic events unfold themselves in the future, it is clear that at the foundation of all our work—

labor mobilization, militarization of labor, Subbotniks, and other forms of Communist labor voluntarism—there must lie the *single economic plan.* And the period that is upon us requires from us the complete concentration of all our energies on the first elementary problems: food, fuel, raw material, transport. *Not to allow our attention to be distracted, not to dissipate our forces, not to waste our energies.* Such is the sole road to salvation.

COLLEGIATE AND ONE-MAN MANAGEMENT

The Mensheviks attempt to dwell on yet another question which seems favorable to their desire once again to ally themselves with the working class. This is the question of the method of administration of industrial enterprises—the question of the collegiate (board) or the one-man principle. We are told that the transference of factories to single directors instead of to a board is a crime against the working class and the Socialist revolution. It is remarkable that the most zealous defenders of the Socialist revolution against the principle of one-man management are those same Mensheviks who quite recently still considered that the idea of a Socialist revolution was an insult to history and a crime against the working class.

The first who must plead guilty in the face of the Socialist revolution is our Party Congress, which expressed itself in favor of the principle of one-man management in the administration of industry, and above all in the lowest grades, in the factories and plants. It would be the greatest possible mistake, however, to consider this decision as a blow to the independence of the working class. The independence of the workers is determined and measured not by whether three workers or one are placed at the head of a factory, but by factors and phenomena of a such more profound character— the construction of the economic organs with the active assistance of the trade unions; the building up of all Soviet organs by means of the Soviet congresses, representing tens of millions of workers; the attraction into the work of administration, or control of administration, of those who are administered. It is in such things that the independence of the working class can be expressed. And if the working class, on the foundation of its existence, comes though its congresses, Soviet party and trade union, to the conclusion that it is better to place one person at the head of a factory, and not a board, it is making a decision dictated by the independence of the working class. It may be correct or incorrect from the point of view of the technique of administration, but it is not imposed upon the proletariat, it is dictated by its own will and pleasure. It would consequently be a most crying error to confuse the question as to the supremacy of the proletariat with the question of boards of workers at the head of factories. The dictatorship of the proletariat is expressed in the abolition of private property in the means of production, in the supremacy over the whole Soviet mechanism of the collective will of the workers, and not at all in the form in which individual economic enterprises are administered.

Here it is necessary to reply to another accusation directed against the defenders of the one-man principle. Our opponents say: "This is the attempt of the Soviet militarists to transfer their experience in the military sphere to the sphere of economics. Possibly in the army the one-man principle is satisfactory, but it does not suit economical work." Such a criticism is incorrect in every way. It is untrue that in the army we began with the one-man principle: even now we are far from having completely adopted it. It is also untrue that in defence of one-man forms of administration of our economic enterprises with the attraction of experts, we took our stand only on the foundation of our military experience. In reality, in this question we took our stand, and continue to do so on purely Marxist views of the revolutionary problems and creative duties of the proletariat when it has taken power into its own hands. The necessity of making use of technical knowledge and methods accumulated in the past, the necessity of attracting experts and of making use of them on a wide scale, in such a way that our technique should go not backwards but forwards—all this was understood and recognized by us, not only from the very beginning of the revolution, but even long before October. I consider that if the civil war had not plundered our economic organs of all that was strongest, most independent, most endowed with initiative, we should undoubtedly have entered the path of one-man management in the sphere of economic administration much sooner, and much less painfully.

Some comrades look on the apparatus of industrial administration first and foremost as on a school. This is, of course, absolutely erroneous. The task of administration is to administer. If a man desires and is able to learn admistration, let him go to school, to the special courses of instruction: let him go as an assistant, watching and acquiring experience: but a man who is appointed to control a factory is not going to school, but to a responsible post of economic administration. And, even if we look at this question in the limited, and therefore incorrect light of a "school," I will say that when the one-man principle prevails the school is ten times better: because just as you cannot replace one good worker by three immature workers, similarly, having placed a board of three immature workers in a responsible post, you deprive them of the possibility of realizing their own defects. Each looks to the others when decisions are being made, and blames the others when success is not forthcoming.

That this is not a question of principle for the opponents of the one-man principle is shown best of all by their not demanding the collegiate principle for the actual workshops, jobs, and pits. They even say with indignation that only a madman can demand that a board of three or five should manage a workshop. There must be one manager, and one only. Why? If collegiate administration is a "school," why do we not require an elementary school? Why should we not introduce boards into the workshops? And, if the collegiate principle is not a sacred gospel for the workshops, why is it compulsory for the factories?

Abramovich said here that, as we have few experts—thanks to the Bolsheviks, he repeats after Kautsky—we shall replace them by boards of workers. That is nonsense. No board of persons who do not know the given business can replace one man who knows it. A board of lawyers will not replace one switchman. A board of patients will not replace the doctor. The very idea is incorrect. A board in itself does not give knowledge to the ignorant. It can only hide the ignorance of the ignorant. If a person is appointed to a responsible administrative post, he is under the watch, not only of others but of himself, and sees clearly what he knows and what he does not know. But there is nothing worse than a board of ignorant, badly-prepared workers appointed to a purely practical post, demanding expert knowledge. The members of the board are in a state of perpetual panic and mutual dissatisfaction, and by their helplessness introduce hesitation and chaos into all their work. The working class is very deeply interested in raising its capacity for administration, that is, in being educated; but this is attained in the sphere of industry by the periodical report of the administrative body of a factory before the whole factory, and the discussion of the economic plan for the year or for the current month. All the workers who display serious interest in the work of industrial organization are registered by the directors of the undertaking, or by special commissions; are taken through appropriate courses closely bound up with the practical work of the factory itself; and are then appointed, first to less responsible, and then to more responsible posts. In such a way we shall embrace many thousands, and, in the future, tens .of thousands. But the question of "threes" and "fives" interests, not the laboring masses, but the more backward, weaker, less fitted for independent work, section of the Soviet labor bureaucracy. The foremost, intelligent, determined administrator naturally strives to take the factory into his hands as a whole, and to show both to himself and to others that he can carry out his work. While if that administrator is a weakling, who does not stand very steadily on his feet, he attempts to associate another with himself, for in the company of another his own weakness will be unnoticed. In such a collegiate principle there is a very dangerous foundation—the extinction of personal responsibility. If a worker is capable but not experienced, he naturally requires a guide: under his control he will learn, and to-morrow we shall appoint him the foreman of a little factory. That is the way by which he will go forward. In an accidental board, in which the strength and the weakness of each are not clear, the feeling of responsibility inevitably disappears.

Our resolution speaks of a systematic *approach* to the one-man principle—naturally, not by one stroke of the pen.

Variants and combinations are possible here. Where the worker can manage alone, let us put him in charge of the factory and give him an expert as an assistant. Where there is a good expert, let us put him in charge and give him as assistants two or three of the workers. Finally, where a "board" has in practice shown its capacity for work, let us preserve it. This is the sole serious attitude to take up, and only in such a way shall we reach the correct organization of production.

There is another consideration of a social and educational character which seems to me most important. Our guiding layer of the working class is too thin. That layer which knew underground work, which long carried on the revolutionary struggle, which was abroad, which read much in prisons and in exile, which had political experience and a broad outlook, is the most precious section of the working class. Then there is a younger generation which has consciously been making the revolution, beginning with 1917. This is a very valuable section of the working class. Wherever we cast our eye—on Soviet construction, on the trade unions, on the front of the civil war—everywhere we find the principal part being played by this upper layer of the proletariat. The chief work of the Soviet Government during these two and a half years consisted in manœuvring and throwing the foremost section of the workers from one front to another. The deeper layers of the working class, which emerged from the peasant mass, are revolutionarily inclined, but are still too poor in initiative. The disease of our Russian peasant is the herd instinct, the absence of personality: in other words, the same quality that used to be extolled by our reactionary Populists, and that Leo Tolstoy extolled in the character of Platon Karatayev: the peasant melting into his village community, subjecting himself to the land. It is quite clear that Socialist economy is founded not on Platon Karatayev, but on the thinking worker endowed with initiative. That personal initiative it is necessary to develop in the worker. The personal basis under the bourgeoisie meant selfish individualism and competition. The personal basis under the working class is in contradiction neither to solidarity nor to brotherly co-operation. Socialist solidarity can rely neither on absence of personality nor on the herd instinct. And it is just absence of personality that is frequently hidden behind the collegiate principle.

In the working class there are many forces, gifts, and talents. They must be brought out and displayed in rivalry. The one-man principle in the administrative and technical sphere assists this. That is why it is higher and more fruitful than the collegiate principle.

CONCLUSION OF THE REPORT

Comrades, the arguments of the Menshevik orators, particularly of Abramovich, reflect first of all their complete detachment from life and its problems. An observer stands on the bank of a river which he has to swim over, and deliberates on the qualities of the water and on the strength of the current. He has to swim over: that is his task! But our Kautskian stands first on one foot and then on the other. "We do not deny," he says, "the necessity of swimming over, but at the same time, as realists, we see the danger—and not only one, but several: the current is swift, there are submerged stones, people are tired, etc., etc. But when they tell you that we deny the very necessity of swimming over, that is not true— no, not under any circumstances. Twenty-three years ago we did not deny the necessity of swimming over...."

And on this is built all, from beginning to end. First, say the Mensheviks, we do not deny, and never did deny, the necessity of self-defence: consequently we do not repudiate the army. Secondly, we do not repudiate in principle general labor service. But, after all, where is there anyone in the world, with the exception of small religious sects, who denies self-defence "in principle"! Nevertheless, the matter does not move one step forward as a result of your abstract admission. When it came to a real struggle, and to the creation of a real army against the real enemies of the working class, what did you do then? You opposed, you sabotaged—while not repudiating self-defence in principle. You said and wrote in your papers: "Down with the civil war!" at the time when we were surrounded by White Guards, and the knife was at our throat. Now you, approving our victorious self-defence after the event, transfer your critical gaze to new problems, and attempt to teach us. "In general, we do not repudiate the principle of general labor service," you say, "but...without legal compulsion." Yet in these very words there is a monstrous internal contradiction! The idea of "obligatory service" itself includes the element of compulsion. A man is *obliged*, he is bound to do something. If he does not do it, obviously he will suffer compulsion, a penalty. Here we approach the question of what penalty. Abramovich says: "Economic pressure, yes; but not legal compulsion." Comrade Holtzman, the representative of the Metal Workers' Union, excellently demonstrated all the scholasticism of this idea. Even under the capitalism, that is to say under the regime of "free" labor, economic pressure is inseparable from legal compulsion. Still more so now.

In my report I attempted to explain that the adaptation of the workers on new social foundations to new forms of labor, and the attainment of a higher level of productivity of labor, are possible only by means of the simultaneous application of various methods—economic interest, legal compulsion, the influence of an internally co-ordinated economic organization, the power of repression, and, first and last, moral influence, agitation, propaganda, and the general raising of the cultural level.

Only by the combination of all these methods can we attain a high level of Socialist economy.

If even under capitalism economic interest is inevitably combined with legal compulsion, behind which stands the material force of the State, in the Soviet State—that is, the State of transition to Socialism—we can draw no watertight compartment at all between economic and legal compulsion. All our most important industries are in the hands of the State. When we say to the turner Ivanov, "You are bound at once to work at the Sormovo factory; if you refuse, you will not receive your ration," what are we to call it? Economic pressure or legal compulsion? He cannot go to another factory, for all factories are in the hands of the State, which will not allow such a change. Consequently, economic pressure melts here into the pressure of State compulsion. Abramovich apparently would like us, as regulators of the distribution of labor power, to make use only of such means as the raising of wages, bonuses, etc., in order to attract the necessary workers to our most important factories. Apparently that comprises all his thoughts on the subject. But if we put the question in this way, every serious worker in the trade union movement will understand it is pure utopia. We cannot hope for a free influx of labor power from the market, for to achieve this the State would need to have in its hands sufficiently extensive "reserves of manœuvre," in the form of food, housing, and transport, i.e., precisely those conditions which we have yet only to create. Without systematically-organized transference of labor power on a mass scale, according to the demands of the economic organization, we shall achieve nothing. Here the moment of compulsion arises before us in all its force of economic necessity. I read you a telegram from Ekaterinburg dealing with the work of the First Labor Army. It says that there have passed through the Ural Committee for Labor Service over 4,000 workers. Whence have they appeared? Mainly from the former Third Army. They were not allowed to go to their homes, but were sent where they were required. From the army they were handed over to the Committee for Labor Service, which distributed them according to their categories and sent them to the factories. This, from the Liberal point of view, is "violence" to the freedom of the individual. Yet an overwhelming majority of the workers went willingly to the labor front, as hitherto to the military, realizing that the common interest demanded this. Part went against their will. These were compelled.

Naturally, it is quite clear that the State must, by means of the bonus system, give the better workers better conditions of existence. But this not only does not exclude, but on the contrary pre-supposes, that the State and the trade unions—without which the Soviet State will not build up industry—acquire new rights of some kind over the worker. The worker does not merely bargain with the Soviet State: no, he is subordinated to the Soviet State, under its orders in every direction—for it is *his* State.

"If," Abramovich says, "we were simply told that it is a question of industrial discipline, there would be nothing to quarrel about; but why introduce militarization?" Of course, to a considerable extent, the question is one of the discipline of the trade unions; but of the new discipline of new, *Productional,* trade unions. We live in a Soviet country, where the working class is in power—a fact which our Kautskians do not understand. When the Menshevik Rubtzov said that there remained only the fragment of the trade union movement in my report, there was a certain amount of truth in it. Of the trade unions, as he understands them—that is to say, trade unions of the old craft type—there in reality has remained very little; but the industrial productional organization of the working class, in the conditions of Soviet Russia, has the very greatest tasks before it. What tasks? Of course, not the tasks involved in a struggle with the State, in the name of the interests of labor; but tasks involved in the construction, side by side with the State, of Socialist economy. Such a form of union is in principle a new organization, which is distinct, not only from the trade unions, but also from the revolutionary industrial unions in bourgeois society, just as the supremacy of the proletariat is distinct from the supremacy of the bourgeoisie. The productional union of the ruling working class no longer has the problems, the methods, the discipline, of the union for struggle of an oppressed class. All our workers are *obliged* to enter the unions. The Mensheviks are against this. This is quite comprehensible, because in reality they are against the *dictatorship of the proletariat.* It is to this, in the long run, that the whole question is reduced. The Kautskians are against the dictatorship of the proletariat, and are thereby against all its consequences. Both economic and political compulsion are only forms of the expression of the dictatorship of the working class in two closely connected regions. True, Abramovich demonstrated to us most learnedly that under Socialism there will be no compulsion, that the principle of compulsion contradicts Socialism, that under Socialism we shall be moved by the feeling of duty, the habit of working, the attractiveness of labor, etc., etc. This is unquestionable. Only this unquestionable truth must be a little extended. In point of fact, under Socialism there will not exist the apparatus of compulsion itself, namely, the State: for it will have melted away entirely into a producing and consuming commune. None the less, the road to Socialism lies through a period of the highest possible intensification of the principle of the State. And you and I are just passing through that period. Just as a lamp, before going out, shoots up in a brilliant flame, so the State, before disappearing, assumes the form of the dictatorship of the proletariat, *i.e.*, the most ruthless form of State, which embraces the life of the citizens authoritatively in every direction. Now just that insignificant little fact—that historical step of the State dictatorship—Abramovich, and in his person the whole of Menshevism, did not notice; and consequently, he has fallen over it.

No organization except the army has ever controlled man with such severe compulsion as does the State organization of the working class in the most difficult period of transition. It is just for this reason that we speak of the militarization of labor. The fate of the Mensheviks is to drag along at the tail of events, and to recognize those parts of the revolutionary programme which have already had time to lose all practical significance. To-day the Mensheviks, albeit with reservations, do not deny the lawfulness of stern measures with the White Guards and with deserters from the Red Army: they have been forced to recognize this after their own lamentable experiments with "democracy." They have to all appearances understood—very late in the day—that, when one is face to face with the counter-revolutionary bands, one cannot live by phrases about the great truth that under Socialism we shall need no Red Terror. But in the economic sphere, the Mensheviks still attempt to refer us to our sons, and particularly to our grandsons. None the less, we have to rebuild our economic life to-day, without waiting, under circumstances of a very painful heritage from bourgeois society and a yet unfinished civil war.

Menshevism, like all Kautskianism generally, is drowned in democratic analogies and Socialist abstractions. Again and again it has been shown that for it there do not exist the problems of the transitional period, *i.e.*, of the proletarian revolution. Hence the lifelessness of its criticism, its advice, its plans, and its recipes. The question is not what is going to happen in twenty or thirty years' time—at that date, of course, things will be much better—but of how to-day to struggle out of our ruins, how immediately to distribute labor-power, how to-day to raise the productivity of labor, and how, in particular, to act in the case of those 4,000 skilled workers whom we combed out of the army in the Ural. To dismiss them to the four corners of the earth, saying "seek for better conditions where you can find them, comrades"? No, we could not act in this way. We put them into military echelones, and distributed them amongst the factories and the works.

"Wherein, then, does your Socialism," Abramovich cries, "differ from Egyptian slavery? It was just by similar methods that the Pharaohs built the pyramids, forcing the masses to labor." Truly an inimitable analogy for a "Socialist"! Once again the little insignificant fact has been forgotten— the class nature of the government! Abramovich sees no difference between the Egyptian regime and our own. He has forgotten that in Egypt there were Pharaohs, there were slave-owners and slaves. It was not the Egyptian peasants who decided through their Soviets to build the pyramids; there existed a social order based upon hierarchial caste; and the workers were obliged to toil by a class that was hostile to them. Our compulsion is applied by a workers' and peasants' government, in the name of the interests of the laboring masses. That is what Abramovich has not observed. We learn in the school of Socialism that all social evolution is founded on classes and their struggle, and all the course of human life is determined by the fact of what class stands at the head of affairs, and in the name of what caste is applying its policy. That is what Abramovich has not grasped. Perhaps he is well acquainted with the Old Testament, but Socialism is for him a book sealed with seven seals.

Going along the path of shallow Liberal analogies, which do not reckon with the class nature of the State, Abramovich might (and in the past the Mensheviks did more than once) identify the Red and the White Armies. Both here and there went on mobilizations, principally of the peasant,masses. Both here and there the element of compulsion has its place. Both here and there there were not a few officers who had passed through one and the same school of Tsarism. The same rifles, the same cartridges in both camps. Where is the difference? There is a difference, gentlemen, and it is defined by a fundamental test: who is in power? The working class or the land-lord class, Pharoahs or peasants, White Guards or the Petro-grad proletariat? There is a difference, and evidence on the subject is furnished by the fate of Yudenich, Kolchak, and Denikin. Our peasants were mobilized by the workers; in Kolchak's camp, by the White Guard officer class. Our army has pulled itself together, and has grown strong; the White Army has fallen asunder in dust. Yes, there is a difference between the Soviet regime and the regime of the Pharoahs. And it is not in vain that the Petrograd proletarians began their revolution by shooting the Pharaohs on the steeples of Petrograd.*

One of the Menshevik orators attempted incidentally to represent me as a defender of militarism in general. Accord-ing to his information, it appears, do you see, that I am de-fending nothing more or less than German militarism. I proved, you must understand, that the German N.C.O. was a marvel of nature, and all that he does is above criticism. What did I say in reality? Only that militarism, in which all the fea-tures of social evolution find their most finished, sharp, and clear expression, could be examined from two points of view. First from the political or Socialist—and here it depends en-tirely on the question of what class is in power; and secondly, from the point of veiw of organization, as a system of the strict distribution of duties, exact mutual relations, unques-tioning responsibility, and harsh insistence on execution. The bourgeois army is the apparatus of savage oppression and re-pression of the workers; the Socialist army is a weapon for the liberation and defence of the workers. But the unques-tioning subordination of the parts to the whole is a character-istic common to every army. A severe internal regime is in-separable from the military organization. In war every piece of slackness, every lack of thoroughness, and even a simple mistake, not infrequently bring in their train the most heavy sacrifices. Hence the striving of the military organization to bring clearness, definiteness, exactness of relations and res-

---

* This was the name given to the imperial police, whom the Minister for Home Affairs, Protopopoff, distributed at the end of February, 1917, over the roofs of houses and in the belfries.

ponsibilities, to the highest degree of development. "Military" qualities in this connection are valued in every sphere. It was in this sense that I said that every class prefers to have in its service those of its members who, other things being equal, have passed through the military school. The German peasant, for example, who has passed out of the barracks in the capacity of an N.C.O. was for the German monarchy, and remains for the Ebert Republic, much dearer and more valuable than the same peasant who has not passed through military training. The apparatus of the German railways was splendidly organized, thanks to a considerable degree to the employment of N.C.O.'s and officers in administrative posts in the transport department. In this sense we also have something to learn from militarism. Comrade Tsiperovich, one of our foremost trade union leaders, admitted here that the trade union worker who has passed through military training—who has, for example, occupied the responsible post of regimental commissary for a year—does not become worse from the point of view of trade union work as a result. He is returned to the union the same proletarian from head to foot, for he was fighting for the proletariat; but he has returned a veteran—hardened, more independent, more decisive—for he has been in very responsible positions. He had occasions to control several thousands of Red soldiers of different degrees of class-consciousness—most of them peasants. Together with them he has lived through victories and reverses, he has advanced and retreated. There were cases of treachery on the part of the command personnel, of peasant risings, of panic—but he remained at his post, he held together the less class-conscious mass, directed it, inspired it with his example, punished traitors and cowards. This experience is a great and valuable experience. And when a former regimental commissary returns to his trade union, he becomes not a bad organizer.

On the question of the *collegiate principle*, the arguments of Abramovich are just as lifeless as on all other questions—the arguments of a detached observer standing on the bank of a river.

Abramovich explained to us that a good board is better than a bad manager, that into a good board there must enter a good expert. All this is splendid—only why do not the **Men-sheviks** offer us several hundred boards? I think that the Supreme Economic Council will find sufficient use for them. But we—not observers, but workers—must build from the material at our disposal. We have specialists, we have experts, of whom, shall we say, one-third are conscientious and educated, another third only half-conscientious and half-educated, and the last third are no use at all. In the working class there are many talented, devoted, and energetic people. Some—unfortunately few—have already the necessary knowledge and experience. Some have character and capacity, but have not knowledge or experience. Others have neither one nor the other. Out of this material we have to create our factory and other administrative bodies; and here we cannot be satisfied with general phrases. First of all, we must select all the workers who have already in experience shown that they can direct enterprises, and give such men the possibility of standing on their own feet. Such men themselves ask for one-man management, because the work of controlling a factory is not a school for the backward. A worker who knows his business thoroughly desires to *control*. If he has decided and ordered, his decision must be accomplished. He may be replaced— that is another matter; but while he is the master —the Soviet, proletarian master—he controls the undertaking entirely and completely. If he has to be included in a board of weaker men, who interfere in the administration, nothing will come of it. Such a working-class administrator must be given an expert assistant, one or two according to the enterprise. If there is no suitable working-class administrator, but there is a conscientious and trained expert, we shall put him at the head of an enterprise, and attach to him two or three prominent workers in the capacity of assistants, in such a way that every decision of the expert should be known to the assistants, but that they should not have the right to reverse that decision. They will, step by step, follow the specialist in his work, will learn something, and in six months or a year will thus be able to occupy independent posts.

Abramovich quoted from my own speech the example of the hairdresser who has commanded a division and an army. True! But what, however, Abramovich does not know is that, if our Communist comrades have begun to command regiments, divisions, and armies, it is because previously they were commissaries attached to expert commanders. The responsibility fell on the expert, who knew that, if he made a mistake, he would bear the full brunt, and would not be able to say that he was only an "adviser" or a "member of the board." To-day in our army the majority of the posts of command, particularly in the lower—*i.e.,* politically the most important—grades, are filled by workers and foremost peasants. But with what did we begin? We put officers in the posts of command, and attached to them workers as commissaries; and they learned, and learned with success, and learned to beat the enemy.

Comrades, we stand face to face with a very difficult period, perhaps the most difficult of all. To difficult periods in the life of peoples and classes there correspond harsh measures. The further we go the easier things will become, the freer every citizen will feel, the more imperceptible will become the compelling force of the proletarian State. Perhaps we shall then even allow the Mensheviks to have papers, if only the Mensheviks remain in existence until that time. But to-day we are living in the period of dictatorship, political and economic. And the Mensheviks continue to undermine that dictatorship. When we are fighting on the civil front, preserving the revolution from its enemies, and the Menshevik paper writes: "Down with the civil war," we cannot permit this. A dictatorship is a dictatorship, and war is war. And now that we have crossed to the path of the greatest concentration of forces on the field of the economic rebirth of the country, the Russian Kautskies, the Mensheviks, remain true to their counter-revolutionary calling. Their voice, as hitherto, sounds as the voice of doubt and decomposition, of disorganization and undermining, of distrust and collapse.

Is it not monstrous and grotesque that, at this Congress, at which 1,500 representatives of the Russian working class are present, where the Mensheviks constitute less than 5%, and the Communists about 90%, Abramovich should say to us: "Do not be attracted by methods which result in a little band taking the place of the people." "All through the people," says the representative of the Mensheviks, "no guardians of the laboring masses! All through the laboring masses, through their independent activity!" And, further, "It is impossible to convince a class by arguments." Yet look at this very hall: here is that class! The working class is here before you, and with us; and it is just you, an insignificant band of Mensheviks, who are attempting to convince it by bourgeois arguments! It is you who wish to be the guardians of that class. And yet it has its own high degree of independence, and that independence, it has displayed, incidentally, in having overthrown you and gone forward along its own path!

9

KARL KAUTSKY, HIS SCHOOL AND HIS BOOK.

THE Austro-Marxian school (Bauer, Renner, Hilferding, Max Adler, Friedrich Adler) in the past more than once was contrasted with the school of Kautsky, as veiled opportunism might be contrasted with true Marxism. This has proved to be a pure historical misunderstanding, which deceived some for a long time, some for a lesser period, but which in the end was revealed with all possible clearness. Kautsky is the founder and the most perfect representative of the Austrian forgery of Marxism. While the real teaching of Marx is the theoretical formula of action, of attack, of the development of revolutionary energy, and of the carrying of the class blow to its logical conclusion, the Austrian school was transformed into an academy of passivity and evasiveness, because of a vulgar historical and conservative school, and reduced its work to explaining and justifying, not guiding and overthrowing. It lowered itself to the position of a handmaid to the current demands of parliamentarism and opportunism, replaced dialectic by swindling sophistries, and, in the end, in spite of its great play with ritual revolutionary phraseology, became transformed into the most secure buttress of the capitalist State, together with the altar and throne that rose above it. If the latter was engulfed in the abyss, no blame for this can be laid upon the Austro-Marxian school.

What characterizes Austro-Marxism is repulsion and fear in the face of revolutionary action. The Austro-Marxist is capable of displaying a perfect gulf of profundity in the explanation of yesterday, and considerable daring in prophesying concerning to-morrow—but for to-day he never has a great thought or capacity for great action. To-day for him always disappears before the wave of little opportunist worries, which later are explained as the most inevitable link between the past and the future.

The Austro-Marxist is inexaustible when it is a question of discovering reasons to prevent initiative and render difficult revolutionary action. Austro-Marxism is a learned and boastful theory of passivity and capitulation. Naturally, it is not by accident that it was just in Austria, in that Babylon torn by fruitless national antagonisms, in that State which represented the personified impossibility to exist and develop, that there arose and was consolidated the pseudo-Marxian philosophy of the impossibility of revolutionary action.

The foremost Austrian Marxists represent, each in his own way, a certain "individuality." On various questions they more than once did not see eye to eye. They even had political differences. But in general they are fingers of the same hand.

Karl Renner is the most pompous, solid, and conceited representative of this type. The gift of literary imitation, or, more simply, of stylist forgery, is granted to him to an exceptional extent. His May-Day article represented a charming combination of the most revolutionary words. And, as both words and their combinations live, within certain limits, with their own independent life, Renner's articles awakened in the hearts of many workers a revolutionary fire which their author apparently never knew. The tinsel of Austro-Viennese culture, the chase of the external, of title of rank, was more characteristic of Renner than of his other colleagues. In essence he always remained merely an imperial and royal officer, who commanded Marxist phraseology to perfection.

The transformation of the author of the jubilee article on Karl Marx, famous for its revolutionary pathos, into a comic-opera-Chancellor, who expresses his feelings of respect and thanks to the Scandinavian monarchs, is in reality one of the most instructive paradoxes of history.

Otto Bauer is more learned and prosaic, more serious and more boring, than Renner. He cannot be denied the capacity to read books, collect facts, and draw conclusions adapted to the tasks imposed upon him by practical politics, which in turn are guided by others. Bauer has no political will. His

chief art is to reply to all acute practical questions by commonplaces. His political thought always lives a parallel life
to his will—it is deprived of all courage. His words are
always merely the scientific compilation of the talented stu-
dent of a University seminar. The most disgraceful actions
of Austrian opportunism the meanest servility before the
power of the possessing classes on the part of the Austro-
German Social Democracy, found in Bauer their grave eluci-
dator, who sometimes expressed himself with dignity against
the form, but always agreed in the essence. If it ever occured
to Bauer to display anything like temperament and political
energy, it was exclusively in the struggle against the revolutionary wing—in the accumulation of arguments, facts, quota-
tions, *against* revolutionary action. His highest period was
that (after 1907) in which, being as yet too young to be a
deputy, he played the part of secretary of the Social-Democratic group, supplied it with materials, figures, substitutes for
ideas, instructed it, drew up memoranda, and appeared almost
to be the inspirer of great actions, when in reality he was only
supplying substitutes, and adulterated substitutes, for the parliamentary opportunists.

Max Adler represents a fairly ingenuous variety of the
Austro-Marxian type. He is a lyric poet, a philosopher, a
mystic—a philosophical lyric poet of passivity, as Renner is
its publicist and legal expert, as Hilferding is its economist,
as Bauer is its sociologist. Max Adler is cramped in a world
of three dimensions, although he had found a very comfortable place for himself with the framework of Viennese bourgeois Socialism and the Hapsburg State. The combination
of the petty business activity of an attorney and of political
humiliation, together with barren philosophical efforts and the
cheap tinsel flowers of idealism, have imbued that variety
which Max Adler represented with a sickening and repulsive
quality.

Rudolf Hilferding, a Viennese like the rest, entered the
German Social-Democractic Party almost as a mutineer, but
as a mutineer of the Austrian stamp, *i.e.,* always ready to
capitulate without a fight. Hilferding took the external mobili-
ty and bustle of the Austrian policy which brought him up
for revolutionary initiative; and for a round dozen of months

he demanded—true, in the most moderate terms—a more intelligent policy on the part of the leaders of the German Social-Democracy. But the Austro-Viennese bustle swiftly disappeared from his own nature. He soon became subjected to the mechanical rhythm of Berlin and the automatic spiritual life of the German Social-Democracy. He devoted his intellectual energy to the purely theoretical sphere, where he did not say a great deal, true—no Austro-Marxist has ever said a great deal in any sphere—but in which he did, at any rate, write a serious book. With this book on his back, like a porter with a heavy load, he entered the revolutionary epoch. But the most scientific book cannot replace the absence of will, of initiative, of revolutionary instinct and political decision, without which action is inconceivable. A doctor by training, Hilferding is inclined to sobriety, and, in spite of his theoretical education, he represents the most primitive type of empiricist in questions of policy. The chief problem of to-day is for him not to leave the lines laid down for him by yesterday, and to find for this conservative and bourgeois apathy a scientific, economic explanation.

Friedrich Adler is the most balanced representative of the Austro-Marxian type. He has inherited from his father the latter's political temperament. In the petty exhausting struggle with the disorder of Austrian conditions, Friedrich Adler allowed his ironical scepticism finally to destroy the revolutionary foundations of his world outlook. The temperament inherited from his father more than once drove him into opposition to the school created by his father. At certain moments Friedrich Adler might seem the very revolutionary negation of the Austrian school. In reality, he was and remains its necessary coping-stone. His explosive revolutionism foreshadowed acute attacks of despair amidst Austrian opportunism, which from time to time became terrified at its own insignificance.

Friedrich Adler is a sceptic from head to foot: he does not believe in the masses, or in their capacity for action. At the time when Karl Liebknecht, in the hour of supreme triumph of German militarism, went out to the Potsdamerplatz to call the oppressed masses to the open struggle, Friedrich Adler went into a bourgeois restaurant to assassinate there the

Austrian Premier. By his solitary shot, Friedrich Adler
vainly attempted to put an end to his own scepticism. After
that hysterical strain, he fell into still more complete prostration.

The black-and-yellow crew of social-patriotism (Auster-
litz, Leitner, etc.) hurled at Adler the terrorist all the abuse
of which the cowardly sentiments were capable.

But when the acute period was passed, and the prodigal
son returned from his convict prison into his father's house
with the halo of a martyr, he proved to be doubly and trebly
valuable in that form for the Austrian Social-Democracy. The
golden halo of the terrorist was transformed by the experienced
counterfeiters of the party into the sounding coin of the
demagogue. Friedrich Adler became a trusted surety for the
Austerlitzes and Renners in face of the masses. Happily,
the Austrian workers are coming less and less to distinguish
the sentimental lyrical prostration of Friedrich Adler from
the pompous shallowness of Renner, the erudite impotence of
Max Adler, or the analytical self-satisfaction of Otto Bauer.

The cowardice in thought of the theoreticians of the
Austro-Marxian school has completely and wholly been revealed when faced with the great problems of a revolutionary
epoch. In his immortal attempt to include the Soviet system in
the Ebert-Noske Constitution, Hilferding gave voice not only to
his own spirit but to the spirit of the whole Austro-Marxian
school, which, with the approach of the revolutionary epoch,
made an attempt to become exactly as much more Left than
Kautsky as before the revolution it was more Right. From
this point of view, Max Adler's view of the Soviet system
is extremely instructive.

The Viennese eclectic philosopher admits the significance
of the Soviets. His courage goes so far that he adopts them.
He even proclaims them the apparatus of the Social Revolution. Max Adler, of course, is for a social revolution. But
not for a stormy, barricaded, terrorist, bloody revolution, but
for a sane, economically balanced, legally canonized, and
philosophically approved revolution.

Max Adler is not even terrified by the fact that the Soviets
infringe the "principle" of the constitutional separation of
powers (in the Austrian Social-Democracy there are many

fools who see in such an infringement a great defect of the Soviet System!). On the contrary, Max Adler, the trade union lawyer and legal adviser of the social revolution, sees in the concentration of powers even an advantage, which allows the direct expression of the proletarian will. Max Adler is in favor of the direct expression of the proletarian will; but only not by means of the direct seizure of power through the Soviets. He proposes a more solid method. In each town, borough, and ward, the Workers' Councils must "control" the police and other officials, imposing upon them the "proletarian will." What, however, will be the "constitutional" position of the Soviets in the republic of Zeiz, Renner and company? To this our philosopher replies: "The Workers' Councils in the long run will receive as much constitutional power as they acquire by means of their own activity." (*Arbeiterzeitung*, No. 179, July 1, 1919.)

The proletarian Soviets must gradually *grow up* into the political power of the proletariat, just as previously, in the theories of reformism, all the proletarian organizations had to grow up into Socialism; which consummation, however, was a little hindered by the unforeseen misunderstandings, lasting four years, between the Central Powers and the Entente —and all that followed. It was found necessary to reject the economical programme of a gradual development into Socialism without a social revolution. But, as a reward, there opened the perspective of the gradual development of the Soviets into the social revolution, without an armed rising and a seizure of power.

In order that the Soviets should not sink entirely under the burden of borough and ward problems, our daring legal adviser proposes the propaganda of social-democratic ideas! Political power remains as before in the hands of the bourgeoisie and its assistants. But in the wards and the boroughs the Soviets control the policemen and their assistants. And, to console the working class and at the same time to centralize its thought and will, Max Adler on Sunday afternoons will read lectures on the constitutional position of the Soviets, as in the past he read lectures on the constitutional position of the trade unions.

"In this way," Max Adler promises, "the constitutional

regulation of the position of the Workers Councils, and their power and importance, would be guaranteed along the whole line of public and social life; and—without the dictatorship of the Soviets—the Soviet system would acquire as large an influence as it could possibly have even in a Soviet republic. At the same time we should not have to pay for that influence by political storms and economic destruction" (idem). As we see, in addition to all his other qualities, Max Adler remains still in agreement with the Austrian tradition: to make a revolution without quarrelling with his Excellency the Public Prosecutor.

* * *

The founder of this school, and its highest authority, is Kautsky. Carefully protecting, particularly after the Dresden party congress and the first Russian Revolution, his reputation as the keeper of the shrine of Marxist orthodoxy, Kautsky from time to time would shake his head in disapproval of the more compromising outbursts of his Austrian school. And, following the example of the late Victor Adler, Bauer, Renner, Hilferding—altogether and each separately—considered Kautsky too pedantic, too inert, but a very reverend and a very useful father and teacher of the church of quietism.

Kautsky began to cause serious mistrust in his own school during the period of his revolutionary culmination, at the time of the first Russian Revolution, when he recognized as necessary the seizure of power by the Russian Social-Democracy, and attempted to inoculate the German working class with his theoretical conclusions from the experience of the general strike in Russia. The collapse of the first Russian Revolution at once broke off Kautsky's evolution along the path of radicalism. The more plainly was the question of mass action in Germany itself put forward by the course of events, the more evasive became Kautsky's attitude. He marked time, retreated, lost his confidence; and the pedantic and scholastic features of his thought more and more became apparent. The imperialist war, which killed every form of vagueness and brought mankind face to face with the most fundamental questions, exposed all the political bankruptcy of Kautsky.

He immediately became confused beyond all hope of extrication, in the most simple question of voting the War Credits. All his writings after that period represent variations of one and the same theme: "I and my muddle." The Russian Revolution finally slew Kautsky. By all his previous development he was placed in a hostile attitude towards the November victory of the proletariat. This unavoidably threw him into the camp of the counter-revolution. He lost the last traces of historical instinct. His further writings have become more and more like the yellow literature of the bourgeois market.

Kautsky's book, examined by us, bears in its external characteristics all the attributes of a so-called objective scientific study. To examine the extent of the Red Terror, Kautsky acts with all the circumstantial method peculiar to him. He begins with the study of the social conditions which prepared the great French Revolution, and also the physiological and social conditions which assisted the development of cruelty and humanity throughout the history of the human race. In a book devoted to Bolshevism, in which the whole question is examined in 234 pages, Kautsky describes in detail on what our most remote human ancestor fed, and hazards the guess that, while living mainly on vegetable products, he devoured also insects and possibly a few birds. (See page 122.) In a word, there was nothing to lead us to expect that from such an entirely respectable ancestor—one obviously inclined to vegetarianism—there should spring such descendants as the Bolsheviks. That is the solid scientific basis on which Kautsky builds the question!...

But, as is not infrequent with productions of this nature, there is hidden behind the academic and scholastic cloak a malignant political pamphlet. This book is one of the most lying and conscienceless of its kind. Is it not incredible, at first glance, that Kautsky should gather up the most contemptible stories about the Bolsheviks from the rich table of Havas, Reuter and Wolff, thereby displaying from under his learned night-cap the ears of the sycophant? Yet these disreputable details are only mosaic decorations on the fundamental background of solid, scientific lying about the Soviet Republic and its guiding party.

Kautsky depicts in the most sinister colors our savagery

towards the bourgeoisie, which "displayed no tendency to resist."

Kautsky attacks our ruthlessness in connection with the Socialist Revolutionaries and the Mensheviks, who represent "shades" of Socialism.

KAUTSKY DEPICTS THE SOVIET ECONOMY AS THE CHAOS OF COLLAPSE

Kautsky represents the Soviet workers, and the Russian working class as a whole, as a conglomeration of egoists, loafers, and cowards.

He does not say one word about the conduct of the Russian bourgeoisie, unprecedented in history for the magnitude of its scoundrelism; about its national treachery; about the surrender of Riga to the Germans, with "educational" aims; about the preparations for a similar surrender of Petrograd; about its appeals to foreign armies—Czecho-Slovakian, German, Roumanian, British, Japanese, French, Arab and Negro—against the Russian workers and peasants; about its conspiracies and assassinations, paid for by Entente money; about its utilization of the blockade, not only to starve our children to death, but systematically, tirelessly, persistently to spread over the whole world an unheard-of web of lies and slander.

He does not say one word about the most disgraceful misrepresentations of and violance to our party on the part of the government of the S.R.s and Mensheviks before the November Revolution; about the criminal persecution of several thousand responsible workers of the party on the charge of espionage in favor of Hohenzollern Germany; about the participation of the Mensheviks and S.R.s in all the plots of the bourgeoisie; about their collaboration with the imperial generals and admirals, Kolchak, Denikin and Yudenich; about the terrorist acts carried out by the S.R.s at the order of the Entente; about the risings organized by the S.R.s with the money of the foreign missions in our army, which was pouring out its blood in the struggle against the monarchical bands of imperialism.

Kautsky does not say one word about the fact that we

not only repeated more than once, but proved in reality our readiness to give peace to the country, even at the cost of sacrifices and concessions, and that, in spite of this, we were obliged to carry on an intensive struggle on all fronts to defend the very existence of our country, and to prevent its transformation into a colony of Anglo-French imperialism.

Kautsky does not say one word about the fact that in this heroic struggle, in which we are defending the future of world Socialism, the Russian proletariat is obliged to expend its principal energies, its best and most valuable forces, taking them away from economic and cultural reconstruction.

In all his book, Kautsky does not even mention the fact that first of all German militarism, with the help of its Scheidemanns and the apathy of its Kautskies, and then the militarism of the Entente countries with the help of its Renaudels and the apathy of its Longuets, surrounded us with an iron blockade; seized all our ports; cut us off from the whole of the world; occupied, with the help of hired White bands, enormous territories, rich in raw materials; and separated us for a long period from the Baku oil, the Donetz coal, the Don and Siberian corn, the Turkestan cotton.

Kautsky does not say one word about the fact that in these conditions, unprecedented for their difficulty, the Russian working class for nearly three years has been carrying on a heroic struggle against its enemies on a front of 8,000 versts; that the Russian working class learned how to exchange its hammer for the sword, and created a mighty army; that for this army it mobilized its exhausted industry and, in spite of the ruin of the country, which the executioners of the whole world had condemned to blockade and civil war, for three years with its own forces and resources it has been clothing, feeding, arming, transporting an army of millions—an army which has learned how to conquer.

About all these conditions Kautsky is silent, in a book devoted to Russian Communism. And his silence is the fundamental, capital, principal lie—true, a passive lie, but more criminal and more repulsive than the active lie of all the scoundrels of the international bourgeois Press taken together.

Slandering the policy of the Communist Party, Kautsky

says nowhere what he himself wants and what he proposes. The Bolsheviks were not alone in the arena of the Russian Revolution. We saw and see in it—now in power, now in opposition—S.R.s (not less than five groups and tendencies), Mensheviks (not less than three tendencies), Plekhanovists, Maximalists, Anarchists.... Absolutely all the "shades of Socialism" (to speak in Kautsky's language) tried their hand, and showed what they would and what they could. There are so many of these "shades" that it is difficult now to pass the blade of a knife between them. The very origin of these "shades" is not accidental: they represent, so to speak, different degrees in the adaptation of the pre-revolutionary Socialist parties and groups to the conditions of the greater revolutionary epoch. It would seem that Kautsky had a sufficiently complete political keyboard before him to be able to strike the note which would give a true Marxian key to the Russian Revolution.. But Kautsky is silent. He repudiates the Bolshevik melody that is unpleasant to his ear, but does not seek another. The solution is simple: *the old musician refuses altogether to play on the instrument of the revolution.*

In Place of an Epilogue

THIS book appears at the moment of the Second Congress of the Communist International. The revolutionary movement of the proletariat has made, during the months that have passed since the First Congress, a great step forward. The positions of the official, open social-patriots have everywhere been undermined. The ideas of Communism acquire an ever wider extension. Official dogmatized Kautskianism has been gradually compromised. Kautsky himself, within that "Independent" Party which he created, represents to-day a not very authoritative and a fairly ridiculous figure.

None the less, the intellectual struggle in the ranks of the international working class is only now blazing up as it should. If, as we just said, dogmatized Kautskianism is breathing its last days, and the leaders of the intermediate Socialist parties are hastening to renounce it, still Kautskianism as a bourgeois attitude, as a tradition of passivity, as political cowardice, still plays an enormous part in the upper ranks of the working-class organizations of the world, in no way excluding parties tending to the Third International, and even formally adhering to it.

The Independent Party in Germany, which has written on its banner the watchword of the dictatorship of the proletariat, tolerates in its ranks the Kautsky group, all the efforts of which are devoted theoretically to compromise and misrepresent the dictatorship of the proletariat in the shape of its living expression—the Soviet regime. In conditions of civil war, such a form of co-habitation is conceivable only and to such an extent as far and as long as the dictatorship of the proletariat represents for the leaders of the "Independent" Social Democracy a noble aspiration, a vague protest against the open and disgraceful treachery of Noske, Ebert,

188

Scheidemann and others, and—last but not least—a weapon of electoral and parliamentary demagogy.

The vitality of vague Kautskianism is most clearly seen in the example of the French Longuetists. Jean Longuet himself has most sincerely convinced himself, and has for long been attempting to convince others, that he is marching in step with us, and that only Clemenceau's censorship and the calumnies of our French friends Loriot, Monatte, Rosmer, and others hinder our comradship in arms. Yet is it sufficient to make oneself acquainted with any parliamentary speech of Longuet's to realize that the gulf separating him from us at the present moment is possibly still wider than at the first period of the imperialist war? The revolutionary problems now arising before the international proletariat have become more serious, more immediate, more gigantic, more direct, more definite, than five or six years ago; and the politically reactionary character of the Longuetists, the parliamentary representatives of eternal passivity, has become more impressive than ever before, in spite of the fact that formally they have returned to the fold of parliamentary opposition.

The Italian Party, which is within the Third International, is not at all free from Kautskianism. As far as the leaders are concerned, a very considerable part of them bear their internationalist honors only as a duty and as an imposition from below. In 1914-1915, the Italian Socialist Party found it infinitely more easy than did the other European parties to maintain an attitude of opposition to the war, both because Italy entered the war nine months later than other countries, and particularly because the international position of Italy created in it even a powerful bourgeois group (Giolittians in the widest sense of the word) which remained to the very last moment hostile to Italian intervention in the war.

These conditions allowed the Italian Socialist Party, without the fear of a very profound internal crisis to refuse war credits to the Government, and generally to remain outside the interventionist block. But by this very fact the process of internal cleansing of the party proved to be unquestionably delayed. Although an integral part of the Third International, the Italian Socialist Party to this very day can put up with Turati and his supporters in its ranks. This very powerful group—unfortunately we find it difficult to define to any extent of accuracy its numerical significance in the parliamentary group, in the press, in the party, and in the trade union organizations—represents a less pedantic, not so demagogic, more declamatory and lyrical, but none the less malignant opportunism—a form of romantic Kautskianism.

A passive attitude to the Kautskian, Longuetist, Turatist groups is usually cloaked by the argument that the time for revolutionary activity in the respective countries has not yet arrived. But such a formulation of the question is absolutely false. Nobody demands from Socialists striving for Communism that they should appoint a revolutionary outbreak for a definite week or month in the near future. What the Third International demands of its supporters is a recognition, not in words but in deeds, that civilized humanity has entered a revolutionary epoch; that all the capitalist countries are speeding towards colossal disturbances and an open class war; and that the task of the revolutionary representatives of the proletariat is to prepare for that inevitable and approaching war the necessary spiritual armory and buttress of organization. The internationalists who consider it possible at the present time to collaborate with Kautsky, Longuet and Turati, to appear side by side with them before the working masses, by that very act renounce in practice the work of preparing in ideas and organization for the revolutionary rising of the proletariat, independently of whether it comes a month or a year sooner or later. In order that the open rising of the proletarian masses should not fritter itself away in belated searches for paths and leadership, we must see to it to-day that wide circles of the proletariat should even now learn to grasp all the immensity of the tasks before them, and of their irreconcilability with all variations of Kautskianism and opportunism.

A truly revolutionary, *i.e.*, a Communist wing, must set itself up in opposition, in face of the masses, to all the indecisive, half-hearted groups of doctrinaires, advocates, and panegyrists of passivity, strengthening its positions first of all spiritually and then in the sphere of organization—open, half-open, and purely conspirative. The moment of formal split with the open and disguised Kautskians, or the moment of their expulsion from the ranks of the working-class party, is, of course, to be determined by considerations of usefulness from the point of view of circumstances; but all the policy of real Communists must turn in that direction.

That is why it seems to me that this book is still not out of date—to my great regret, if not as an author, at any rate as a Communist.

June 17, 1920.

Selected Readings

Historical

Bunyan, James, and H. H. Fisher. The Bolshevik Revolution, 1917–1918, Documents and Materials. Hoover War Library Publications No. 3. Stanford, 1934.

Carr, Edward Hallett. The Bolshevik Revolution, 1917–1923. New York, 1950, Vol. I; 1951, Vol. II.

Chamberlin, William Henry. The Russian Revolution, 1917–1921. New York, 1935. Vols. I & II.

Trotsky, Leon. The History of the Russian Revolution. Ann Arbor, 1958.

Polemical

Hillquit, Morris. From Marx to Lenin. New York, 1921.

Kautsky, Karl. Democracy or Dictatorship. Berlin, 1919.

Kautsky, Karl. Terrorismus und Kommunismus. Berlin, 1919.

Lenin, V. I. The Proletarian Revolution and Renegade Kautsky. New York, 1934.

ANN ARBOR PAPERBACKS FOR THE STUDY OF COMMUNISM AND MARXISM

For a complete list of Ann Arbor Paperback titles write:
THE UNIVERSITY OF MICHIGAN PRESS ANN ARBOR